BRIAN HATTON
A biography of the artist (1887-1916)

Also by Celia Davies—

Clean Clothes on Sunday
Far To Go

BRIAN HATTON

A biography of the artist (1887-1916)

by

CELIA DAVIES

Foreword by Wilfred Blunt

TERENCE DALTON LIMITED
LAVENHAM . SUFFOLK
1978

Published by
TERENCE DALTON LIMITED
ISBN 0 900963 84 0

Printed in Great Britain at
THE LAVENHAM PRESS LIMITED
LAVENHAM SUFFOLK

Contents

For Marjorie

Acknowledgements

I wish to express my thanks to Wilfred Blunt for writing the foreword to this book and for his valuable and constructive comments on the text; to Marjorie Hatton, without whose inspiration and unceasing hard work it would not have been written. Never has there been a more helpful collaborator.

My thanks also go to those owners of Brian Hatton pictures who have granted me permission to reproduce them here and to Derek Foster who has photographed them so beautifully, and lastly to Mrs Newland who typed the manuscript.

Celia Davies
Therfield.
November 1977.

Index of Illustrations

Many of the sketches within this book are reproduced from Brian Hatton's letters and are not recorded in the following index. The originals are owned by Miss Marjorie Hatton and the publishers wish to record their thanks for the use of these.

Foreword

IT IS good that Celia Davies has been able to produce this biography of Brian Hatton, and especially that she has provided the reader with a rich selection of those juvenile letters so wittily illustrated by himself.

Brian was born in 1887 and gave early sign of his very considerable talent as a draughtsman. A drawing of three birds, made when he was little more than two, survives, and his childhood sketches are delightful. But precocity is less uncommon than is sometimes imagined, nor does it always herald a great future. One is reminded of the French artist, Gaston Latouche, who at the age of two and a half was invited by a visitor to the house to "draw a horse". "What kind of a horse?" asked the infant — "a cart horse, a race horse, or a carriage horse?" — and immediately proceeded to draw all three. But who remembers Latouche now? And yet, look at Brian's "Horse Fair", drawn when he was thirteen and hung in the Paris Salon in 1900; surely this shows him to have been more than just immensely talented?

Brian had the great advantage of sympathetic, understanding parents and a happy home life. But against this must be offset a dangerously highly-strung nature which was no doubt in part responsible for his stutter, his tendency suddenly to faint or be sick, his hay fever, and what might perhaps today be diagnosed as dyslexia. He was in some ways as retarded as in others he was precocious, and it is the resultant mixture of the naive and the mature that makes his early letters so vivid and endearing. As one reads them one *knows* the boy completely, and likes him enormously — just as one warms to Daisy Ashford as one reads *The Young Visiters.*

A drawing of Brian's, sent in 1898 to an exhibition of the Royal Drawing Society (for young artists), won the Society's gold medal and led to his meeting G. F. Watts and his adoring second wife, Mary. The octogenarian Academician was later to predict that Brian would one day surpass him; but happily the boy was always far too sensible to be affected by any unwise adulation that came his way.

In 1904, when he was sixteen, his work was submitted to a group of artists at St Ives, and a level-headed friend of his mother's reported to her what they had said:

> The artists that Brian met on Monday were the men that will be his judges in the future, the present A.R.A.s or R.A.s, and one felt down there that there was calm, dispassionate judgement. They were kindness itself to him and said he was full of promise; but it was the old story, only education and work will give him

> his future success . . . Promise, even at sixteen, did not always mean fulfilment. They all admire Watts of course, but they say also that he is old and apt to be carried away by an enthusiasm . . .

The story of Brian's tragically short life, and of his death in Egypt in action in 1916, is faithfully related by Celia Davies; it remains for us to consider what he might have achieved had he lived. It was the opinion of the art critic Walter Shaw Sparrow that Brian possessed "the rarest of all things — true genius". The watercolour painter Adrian Bury was prepared to make even greater claims for him — "a genius unique in the history of British art". Exaggerated praise inevitably came the way of many promising young artists and poets who died in the war, and one is forced to the conclusion that Adrian Bury, at all events, has overstated Brian's potentialities. Brian was, undeniably, enormously talented. The pencil portraits and figure drawings of 1912, such as "Young woman combing her hair" and the studies of Beatrice Stewart, fall short of no one other than Augustus John, and then only by an occasional insensitive contour; which is to say that Brian here shows himself second only to the greatest English draughtsman of his day. His portrait of R. W. Raper (1913-1914), slight though it is, is brilliant; his "Mrs. 'Awkins" (1914) is worthy of Orpen, and one may well doubt whether either Lucy Kemp-Welch or Munnings at the age of twenty-six was painting horses better than those in Brian's three equestrian oils of the Morris family (1913).

In short, Brian — as I see it — would have become a very distinguished portraitist, animal painter and illustrator. He would have had a highly successful career in, I think, the orbit of the Royal Academy. But would he ever have shown that *originality* which is the hall-mark of true genius? I must leave this to others better qualified than myself to decide.

It has been suggested that Brian's work has not been properly appreciated because so little of it has passed through the salerooms; yet much of it has been shown at various times in London exhibitions, and now largely through the initiative and help of his sister Marjorie, the Brian Hatton Gallery has been built in Hereford, where all may see a cross-section of his *oeuvre*. He certainly deserves to be thus honoured and remembered, and those who make the pilgrimage to that little gallery will find that his sister's devoted labours have not been in vain.

Wilfred Blunt
The Watts Gallery,
Compton.

Postscript

MY FRIEND John Davies has most kindly asked me for a few words as a postscript to this book. My only real claim is that its subject, Brian Hatton, painted a magnificent full length picture of my grandfather Charles Fitzwilliams of Cilgwyn, Cardiganshire, in 1910. The artist was then but twenty-three and endeared himself to my family during his stay there. Unfortunately I (who was then eight) never saw him, but his sister Marjorie Hatton has been a good friend of my wife and myself since the day in 1955 when I first met her at an Exhibition of her brother's works at Leighton House. It was through her that we have known John and Celia Davies, his wife: she was killed tragically, but suddenly, in a road accident on the 14th December 1977.

Those who would know more of her have but to read her two previous books: *Clean Clothes on Sunday* (1974) and *Far to Go* (1976). She was also the author of articles on Essex and Suffolk history, notably with reference to her own family, whose ancestry is traceable for the last four centuries in Essex.

"Be careful to perform your allotted task while it is yet day", says the old ritual. Can it have been prophetic that she completed this book in due time? She was not one to put her hand to the plough and to look back.

A. H. Hastie

Bury St Edmunds
February 1978

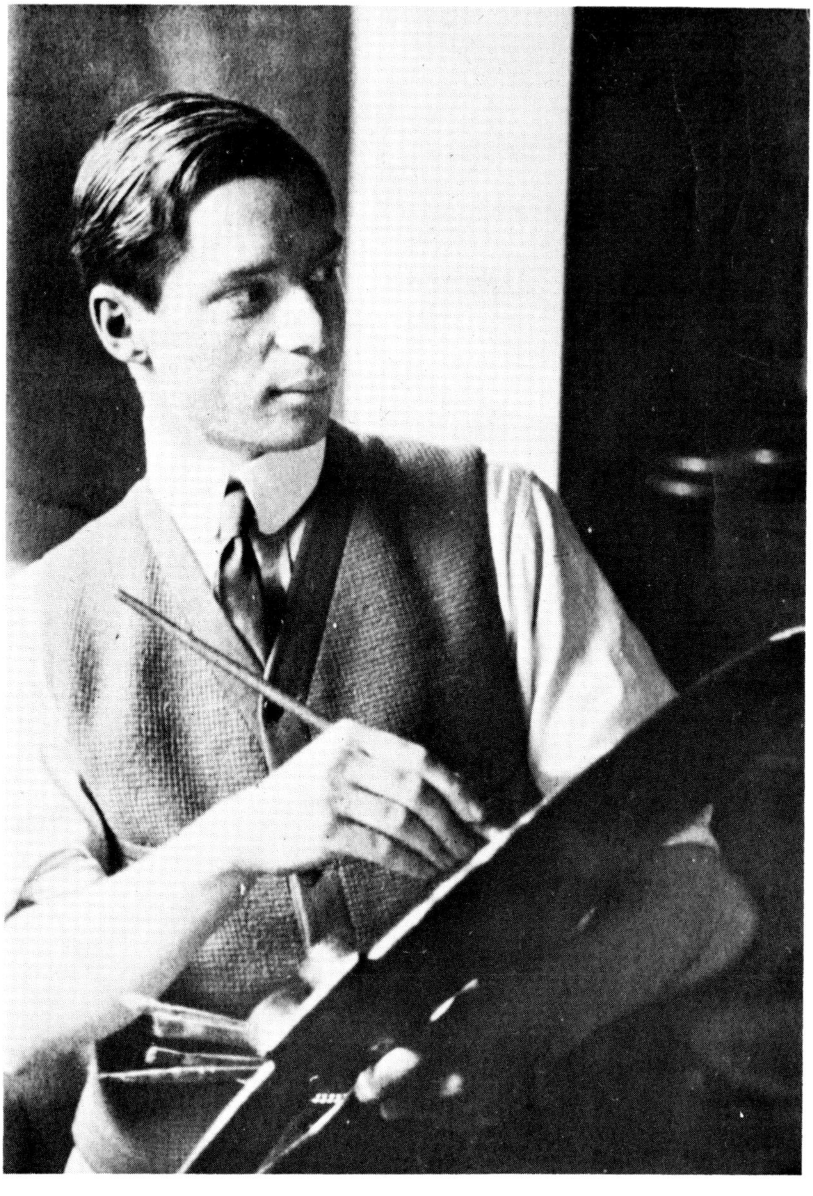

Brian Hatton, 1910.

CHAPTER ONE

Early Years

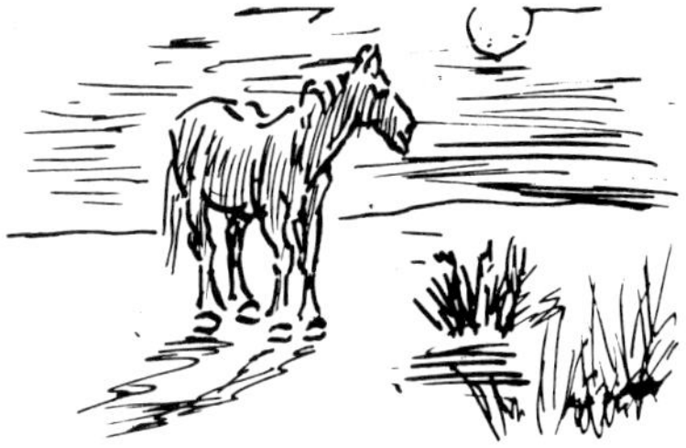

IT IS not easy to enumerate the qualities and characteristics which are required for the making of an artist, for they are many and varied. An artist must surely be possessed of great sensitivity and an emotional response to his environment. Driven on by his creative urge, his life might well be described as a perpetual love affair with the visual world. He may show signs of his calling at an early age, as did Brian Hatton, who was drawing from life with clarity, at the age of two years and two months!

Brian was the only son of Alfred and Amelia Hatton and he was born in Hereford, at Carlton Villas, Whitecross Road, on 12th August 1887. This was the year of Queen Victoria's Golden Jubilee and it might well be said that Brian's childhood coincided with the heyday of the British Empire when pride of country was the heritage of every Englishman. Brian had two younger sisters, Ailsa Marr, who was born in 1893, and Marjorie in 1895. From both his parents he inherited a rich endowment of talent and a deep appreciation of nature and the arts.

According to records, the first member of the Hatton family to settle in England came over with his sons, with William the Conqueror, from Hatton, a small township, twelve miles from Beauvais. William gave them land in Cheshire where the British branch of the family established itself, later to spread through the United Kingdom and overseas. A distinguished member of the family was Sir Christopher Hatton, Lord High Chancellor, a favourite of Queen Elizabeth who loaded him with lands and high offices. He was skilled in the tilting pageants, a "lover of learned men" and a friend and patron of Drake, promoting the voyage of the *Golden Hind*. One of his rings was said to have been passed down to a branch of the family.

The Hereford Hattons settled in the City in about 1800. Brian's great-grandfather, John Hatton, was a glover and the Seal of Hereford Glovers' Company is still preserved in the family. His grandfather, Charles Hatton, was a tanner; when he died in 1877 he was described as a man of generous instincts and unostentatious bearing with "a keen zest for our national sports". His four sons were made in the same mould. They all excelled in fishing and shooting, except Alfred, the youngest, Brian's father, who disliked killing anything. However, he was a keen sportsman who played tennis, cricket and golf and was one of the founders of the Herefordshire Golf Club. As a young man he raced on a Penny-farthing bicycle.

The Hatton brothers were all connected with the leather business and in their factory in St Peter Street, the "Wye Boot", was created and achieved not a little fame. Some members of the family thought that the boot should also have brought them fortune, but the business acumen was lacking. The brothers exerted great interest in their gardens and their hobbies. They had considerable talent in music and painting, they read widely and they were collectors.

Brian's maternal grandparents, Robert Keay, J.P. and Amelia Milne Keay (born Marr) also lived in Hereford, but both came from Troon in Ayrshire. Robert Keay was connected with tailoring. A man of advanced liberal views, he was a much respected citizen and a member of the Town Council. He was noted for his independence; "an honourable and just man, devoted to duty, he thought strongly and acted strenuously". He was also admired for his artistic and literary attainments. His beautiful wife was a woman of creative talents. No doubt she had inherited some rare qualities from her Milne (or Mylne) ancestors who from the early sixteenth century had been Master Masons to the Crown of Scotland and Master Builders of Holyrood House. Another prominent member of the family was Robert Mylne (1733-1811) who attained distinction in England and Scotland as an architect-engineer. Among his achievements were the first Blackfriars Bridge, the Avon Bridge at Warwick Castle and the screen and buildings at Inverary with innovations at the Castle. He was among the first to originate the smaller country house and as surveyor of St Paul's Cathedral, he arranged all public functions held there, including Lord Nelson's funeral.

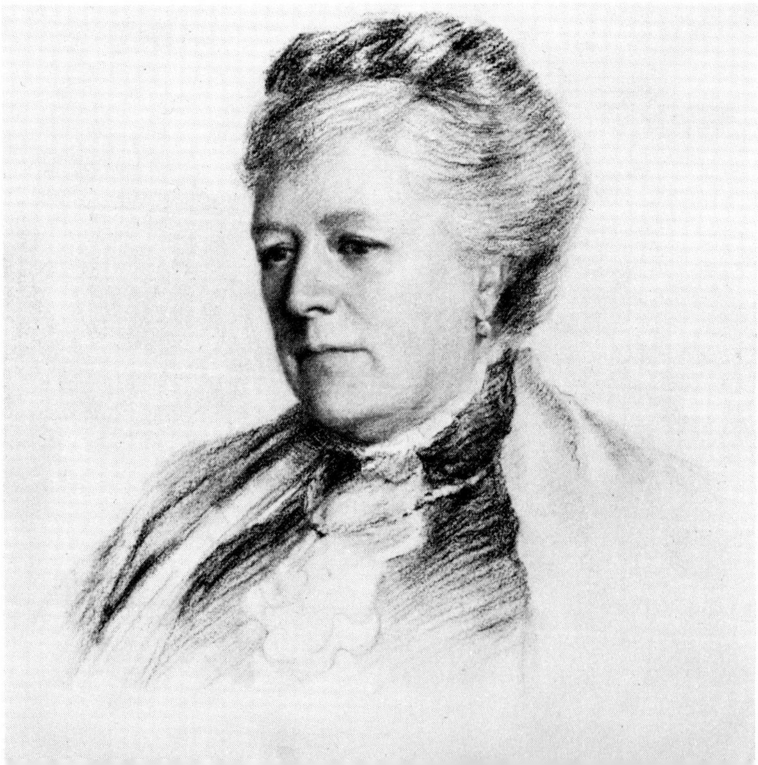

Mrs Robert Keay (née Amelia Kerr Milne Marr): maternal grandmother. Pastel, 1910

Mrs Anne Wilson

The Robert Keays had a family of six daughters and one son who were brought up in an atmosphere of music, painting and books. Music came naturally to them all and Grace Darling, the youngest daughter, was an excellent pianist. It was Amelia, the eldest daughter, who married Alfred Hatton in 1884, when she was twenty; an exceptionally cultured young woman with a gentle, sensitive nature. Alfred was twenty-eight. They were married in the Lady Chapel of Hereford Cathedral and spent the first eleven years of their married life at Carlton Villas.

In 1895, Alfred and Amelia and their three children moved to a larger house. They went to live at "Mount Craig", Broomy Hill, a stone-fronted mid-Victorian house, with stables and coach house and a big walled garden which provided vegetables, fruit and flowers for every season.

The Keay grandparents lived next door at 1, The Highlands. Another daughter, Ada Vevers, the wife of a prominent Hereford surgeon, lived not far off at Highmore House, Westfields.

The three households on Broomy Hill* formed a close community where relatives and friends would forgather for music, amateur theatricals, billiards and tennis, or just to compare notes on one another's gardens. From time to time the Scottish clan would swoop down from the north, to be distributed among the houses. They would revel in the gardens, gay with roses and herbaceous borders, and take tea on the lawn. There would be boating picnics on the River Wye, with its flowered banks and shady willow trees, and in the evening the families would entertain one another with music. An unfailing interest during these visits would be the young Brian who was showing such remarkable artistic talent. They would ponder over his sketch books and portfolios and wonder what the future held for him.

There was always a very close affinity between Brian and his mother and she soon recognised the seeds of genius in her son, just as did the mother of Wilfred Owen, the poet. She carefully preserved that first drawing he made — of three birds — when just over two years old, and all the others that followed afterwards. This remarkable child did not ask for toys but rather for pencil and paper, and he would sit in his pram making drawings. His childhood was indeed a happy one. He and his sisters were early tutored at home, with special attention to music and languages. There were plenty of books in the house for them to read, and the garden offered opportunities for rounders, hide-and-seek and later for croquet, badminton and putting. There were daily tramps through the fields and woods and long riverside walks, and Brian always carried a sketch book with him. There were the nextdoor cousins to play with and together they would make up charades, recite and act or row on the river. Sometimes one of them would be called upon by Brian, to pose as a model.

*The third house was the residence of another daughter, Helen, who was married to Arthur Croom-Johnson.

Brian never ceased sketching, both indoors and out. He was fascinated by all that he saw going on around him, by people, animals, shapes and movement; all had to be recorded. He made constant visits to the market, when twice a week cattle and sheep would be driven through the town. The May Fair, horse fairs, a meet of the hounds or a race meeting were all sources of inspiration. He loved to visit the farms and sketch the animals and men and women at work, as well as the cottages and the landscape. When coal or a load of manure for the garden was delivered to the house, he would rush out and make a drawing of the horse and cart, and he loved to sketch the gypsies when they came selling lace and pegs at the door.

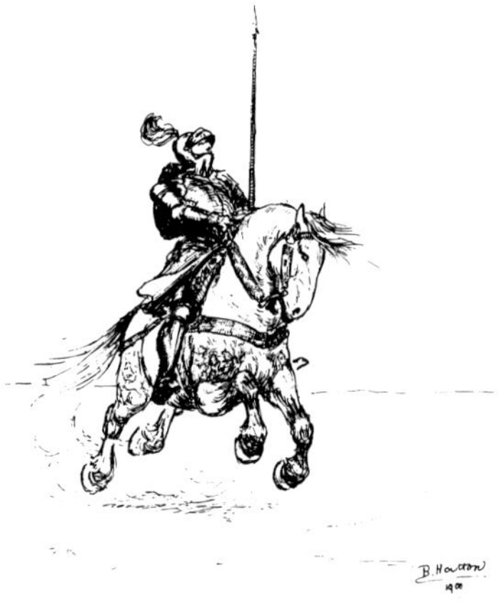

Knight in Armour.
Pen and ink, 1910

Brian had a strong romantic streak in his make-up and his imagination was fired by stories of King Arthur and his Knights, of Don Quixote and the works of Walter Scott and Byron, the Norse Tales and by the medieval and classic poets. In pencil and water colour, sepia, and pen and ink, he covered sheet after sheet with lively scenes. Incidents involving horses, especially when taking part in tournaments and jousting, were among his favourite subjects and one is reminded of his ancestor, Christopher Hatton, with his love of tilting and pageants.

It was in the early years at Carlton Villas that Brian started to ride, his first mount being a donkey. After the move to Mount Craig, when he was eight, he was promoted to a pony, Jenny by name, and riding became his favourite sport. It may have been from his great-uncle, John Hatton, who was an inveterate horseman and one of the founders of the Hereford race course, that Brian inherited his overwhelming passion for horses. His love and understanding of them and the relationship between man and horse runs like a thread through his work. Whether they were ponies, hunters, army mounts or hard-working cart horses, he had a special understanding of them all. When later he was commissioned to paint an equestrian portrait, he would give as much character and individuality to the horse as to its rider.

Both his parents were anxious that Brian should have every opportunity to develop his talent, but he needed no encouragement. At the age of eight and a half, he exhibited work at the Royal Drawing Society and gained a bronze medal and that same year he also won a prize offered by the Arts Schools Association.

It would be wrong to describe Brian as a delicate child, but at an early age he showed signs of asthma. It was thought that sea air would be beneficial to him and when he was nearly ten years old, on the recommendation of the family doctor, Mr Edgar Morris, a surgeon of Hereford, he was sent to live in Swansea. Mr Morris' son, Elton, was a close friend of Brian's and at this time, also for reasons of health, he was living at Winchester House, Swansea, with Dr and Mrs Lancaster. Dr Le Cromier Lancaster was a well known surgeon and his wife was Elton's aunt. This kind couple agreed that Brian should live with them during term-time, and this was a highly satisfactory arrangement which lasted for the next six years. Both Dr and Mrs Lancaster watched over Brian's welfare, his health, studies, art and recreation, with unerring commonsense and understanding and a close and lasting friendship was forged between them. Brian's health improved, the asthma left him, although hay fever persisted and he always had a tendency to stutter, especially when tired. He became a pupil at Swansea Grammar School from the summer term of 1899 till Easter, 1902, when he returned to Hereford.

Border Raid: Picts and Scots.
Water colour, 1903. 20¼″ × 29½″ *Brian Hatton Gallery, Hereford*

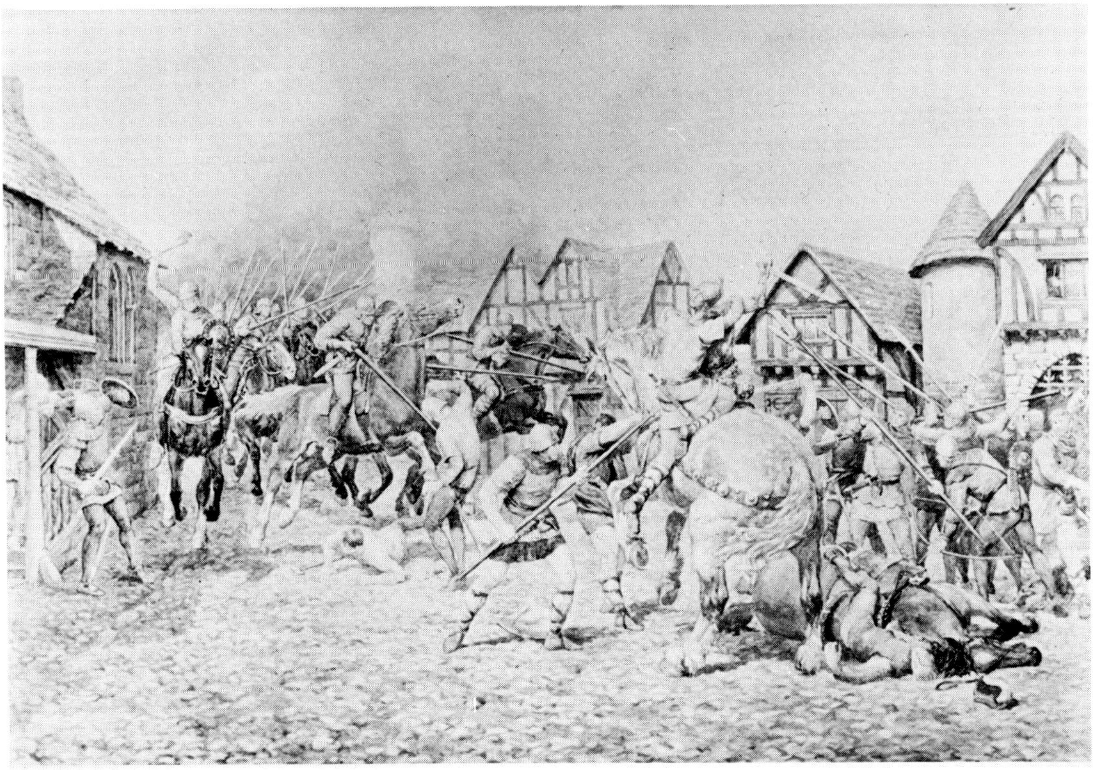

CHAPTER TWO

The Diamond Jubilee

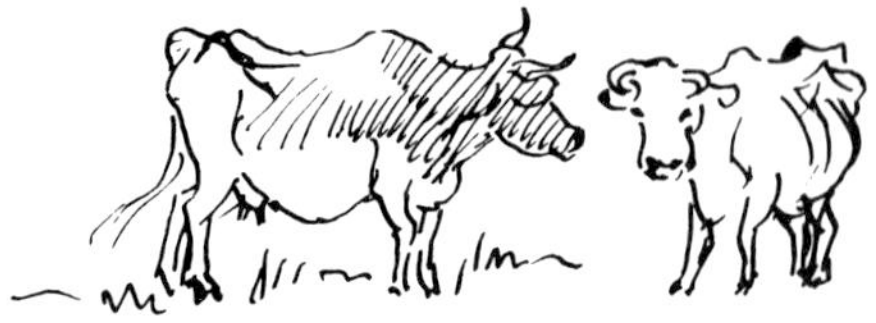

AFTER being surrounded by such a close-knit family, the departure to Swansea might well have had an adverse effect on a sensitive boy such as Brian, but this was certainly not the case. Much credit must go to Dr and Mrs Lancaster and of course the company of young Elton would have been a reassuring factor. However, I think that the real reason for Brian's happy acceptance of the situation was due to his ability to express himself in the letters he wrote to his mother. The correspondence which flowed between the two of them during the next five years forged a secure link with home and he never felt cut off from his family.

It is not surprising that Mrs Hatton preserved all her son's letters with such care. They are liberally illustrated and both the written word and the drawings display his rare powers of observation. His difficulty with spelling in the early years in no way inhibits his powers of expression and through all the letters runs a delightful vein of humour. It is curious that Brian, who had such a perceptive eye for detail, had no visual memory for the construction of words. Although the substance of his letters was unusually mature, the spelling was well below the average for a boy of ten.

1897 was the year of Queen Victoria's Diamond Jubilee, and Brian's first letter from Swansea describes the preparations for this national event.

> My dear Mother
> I could not writ be for becaus Mirs Lancaster said we must go out evey day . . . I liked your letter very much. I whis I could writ such nice letters . . . We are geting sand from the sea, Elton in his bucket, but I had a good load, my chool-bag full. We brugth it for the Juble-candls to stand in. Mrs. Lancaster is going to have a union Jack haging out of the widow and hundreds of candls in the widows. I dont know what iles to say. With tons of love & kiss to all
> from your loving
> Son
> Brian.

The next letter describes the events of the great day itself. Brian tells us that, "Swansea market was opened in the morning by the Mayor. I was there at the time". He also saw "a great many soldiers marching". The afternoon was spent at the fête in Victoria Park, where he saw tight-rope walking;

> The men had refreshments in the middle of the rope. I went on the roundabouts and enjoyed it very much. I also went to the dog show and saw the biggest dog in the world . . . So you see I enjoyed myself very much on Jubile Day.

On 9th June Brian writes his first letter to "My dear old Dad" and sympathizes with him for his lack of success on the golf course.

> I liked your letter very much but I am sorrey to here you have been playing badle. But I speted youle soon get all right again.

He goes on to give some good advice about Frisky, the dog. "What sort of muzzle has Friskey got. I thinks the wier ones are the best, its like a cage you know." He ends by saying, "You writ much planer than Mother".

With his observant eye, it is not surprising that Brian was fascinated by boats. He loved them for their beauty and was interested in the smallest details. He writes;

> Mrs Lancaster took us to [the] docks and there was a lot of shooners there with their sails up, drying so I had a splendid time of it.

Another day he describes how he went on board a lugger;

> The man shoed us round the deck and then he ask us if we would like to go downstairs (as I may call it), so we went down a little lader into a place with sits all round it and a lot of little door all round the wall, and some of these little doors were there bunks and how they sqesed in I can not thing. And the other little doors were they keeped there grube, and then we saw the hold, the man said theye had a rough passage and the sand had washed into the hold, and of course there was a lot of sand there when we look in.

Having had his interest roused over boats, it is understandable that Brian wanted to make one for himself.

> I have made a new raceing yat that will never uptup and even if she does, she will tupup the right way again. I call her the Caroline, her mast will come down and her bowspright comes out besides the sails coming up down and alltering just like a real one.

There is no mention of Brian doing any lessons during that summer, or indeed until the following year, but we must remember that he went to live with the Lancasters on account of his health. He says, "Mr Lancaster says we must go out every day", and there are constant references of visits to the beach and the pier and long walks on the sands. He often went to the baths where he soon learned to swim and the following letter shows how happily he settled down in his new home.

> My dear Mother
> I am very happy. I went to the sands yesterday and bought a bucket big enough to put Miss Holt in, she was afraid of tumbling in it. I went up the hill which they are making the electric tramway and got caught in a storm, but I am none the worse for it. It was wet this morning but I have been to town to get a hat and got a jolly one . . . I am going on the sands this afternoon.

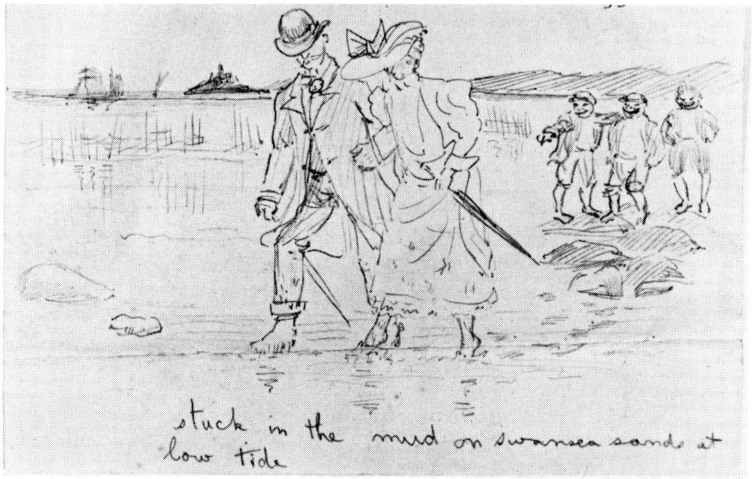

Miss Holt may have been some sort of mother's help, a useful addition to the household for it was unlikely that Mrs Lancaster would have had the time to accompany Brian on all his outings. At first there seemed to be some antagonism between Brian and Miss Holt. In an earlier letter, when describing a ride in a tramcar he says;

> I stood on the platform of the car you know behined. It was lovele I can tell you. And whats more lovely still [is] that weve got no Miss Holt.

It would seem that they made friends later when they joked about the big bucket Brian bought for the beach.

Brian's creative urge was not entirely confined to drawing for he was constantly making models. In one letter he says "I have made a bell bouy", and in another,

> I have made a little enguin sort of thing that heats watter and makes steam come out of it but we are not often alwod to do it.

A week or two later he says,

> I am riging up an old little flat bottomed boat as a Brigentine a little beauty I call her a model she's so perfect. I have been chiseling out some ancors of lead for my boats, I've got 9 boats all together.

Although he is doing no lessons, Brian is anxious to reassure his mother that he is not wasting his time.

> It is not all play I do a great deal of work I draw evre day for and hour and I have to do a little book of drawings for Mrs. Lancasters Cristmas present . . .
> I love my cold dips as you call them. That yat I was talking bout in my letter to Dad, went across Brynhill pond stoped in the midel spurting about at her own free will for about half an hour so of course the dinner got cold. . . I want to know wether you can afford to give me rides prity ofton or only now and then at one bob an hour. Mr. Lancaster says that I shant want leggings yet.

It is obvious that Brian understood quite clearly that he was an artist with a definite mission in life, just as Keats and Wilfred Owen realised their destiny in childhood. Boats and model making might be an absorbing recreation, but drawing was "work". His enthusiasm for horses never waned, but instead of taking his riding for granted, as would most boys of his age, he asks if his parents can afford "to give me rides pretty often". Even rocking horses had a special reality for him. He asks, "what is the name of the new rocking horse", and in another letter,

> We went out to Duglas Jones to tea on Friday, he is a little friend of Eltons, he has a spendid rocking horse. We pent most of our time on it. Duglas's tung was going the hoal time.

Mrs Lancaster, who had no children of her own, was a wise and loving foster mother and she wrote constantly to Mrs Hatton, giving her accounts of Brian's health and general progress. At the end of July she said, "he is perfectly satisfactory in every way" but went on to say;

> I think it is a mistake to let him get the idea that he can only draw when he feels inclined; his talent is very great but as I tell him he will have to work at it if it is ever to be of real use to him.

There must have been times when she found it difficult to handle such a sensitive, highly strung child and she says;

> I find in every way that the less attention he has drawn to himself the better. I quite think he has the supposed artistic temperament, he is both nervous and excitable and I can see that it takes very little to upset him.

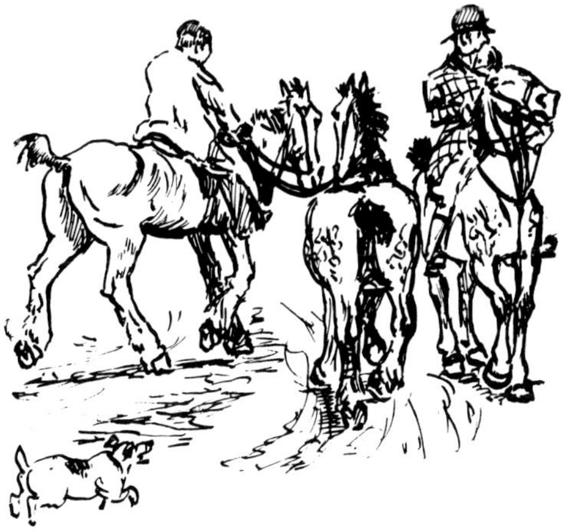

On 25th September Mrs Lancaster has important news to impart to Mrs Hatton.

> You will be pleased to hear that I think I have given Brian a start as regards his drawing. I went to see the head master at the School of Art and took his drawings with me; he was amazed at them, he described them as the work of 'marvellous genius' and told me that although he had been teaching for 40 years, had never seen anything like it before in a young child. But what pleased me most was that he appeared to understand the way Brian should be treated; he said you could not *teach* him, all that could be done was to guide him and show him his faults. . . . Unless you have any objection, I have arranged for Brian to go to the School of Art for two hours in the morning twice a week.

For reasons of health, Brian stayed on with the Lancasters over Christmas, but he does not complain about his separation from his family. His Christmas letter is a cheerful one.

> My dear Mother
> I went on the pier a few days ago and the east wind nearly blew me away, so I had to keep Elton to the windward of me for fear he should [be] blown away, while we were down thier a steamer raced from the Mumbles to Swansea docks in about ten minutes.
> Mrs. Lancaster says that she is very sorry that she can't send you the drawings but hasen't got time enough to breeth scarsly but she says she might have time to send them to-morrow. We are going to the pantomime on Monday it is going to be Robinson Cruso. We have got a new little kitten we got it yesterday its a real spitfire we found it hoping over our beds this morning, when [we] woke up. I cant think of anything more to say so goodby with tons of love and kisses to all and many wishes for a happy Xmas.
>
> from your loving son
> Brian.
>
> P.S. [in another hand] Brian's drawing is a present to his Father and Mother.

After Christmas Brian wrote his mother a detailed description of the Christmas festivities, and the incident of the Christmas pudding gives us a revealing glimpse of his generous nature.

> We had dinner in the evening at six o'clock, but we put down the gas when the pudding came in. The table was all decorated with flags, and we drank absent friends and pulled crackers and I got the sixpence out of the pud, and everybody [else] had nothing, so Elton and me divided it between us and [in] the evening we had snapdragon and Fanny got it.
> Thanks orfully for that lovely little train you and Dad gave me I can never thank you enough XXXXX it goes splendidly . . . The pantomime was very good. Of course there was a good and bad fairy and there was [a] little chap which did it

splendidly he was the best of all. I did not thing much of Robinson but Friday was very good. I am making a signal box and it is a very good one . . . give my love to Ailsa and give her a lot of thanks for the little tug, it is the very thing I wanted . . . And give Babs a lot of love and kisses too, for the little cannon, I am sure it will shoot down the enemy 20 at a time I should think.

The last letter written in 1897 was to Brian's father and it gives us another example of his descriptive ability.

My dear Dad,
I was very pleased to get your letter. I should [think] Mum, (as you call her) does keep me up with letters. Mother's little engnein goes capittille exceped that the elasttick keeps on braken . . . A funny little incedent hapend this morning it was like this, as we wear coming out the baths we got into a tram to come home (for it was raining cats & dogs) while we wear wating a boy came along with his gamp open in front of him and could not see so what does he do but runs strait into the horses, the one being figete [fidgety?] sprang up and fell down, up again and all over the sop [shop], the man came up and pretended to be very angry and [at] last the kid began to blub and then to bluber worse and the tears fell as thick as the rian drops.

With love and tons of kisses from you loving son

Brian.

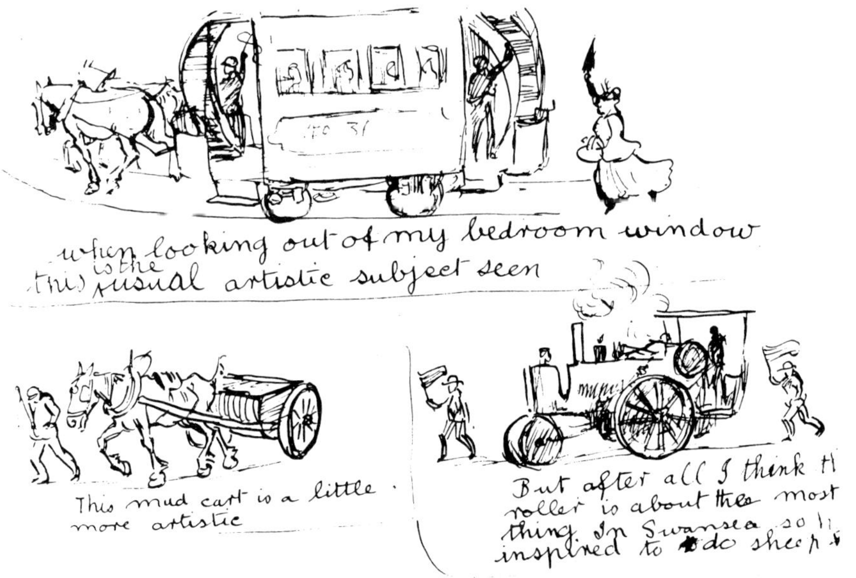

CHAPTER THREE

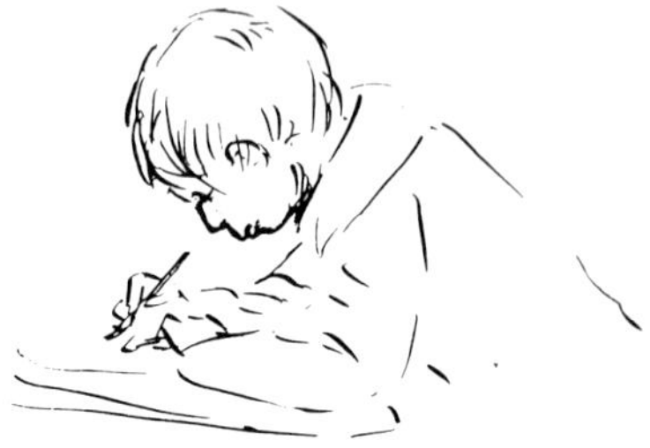

The Gold Star

THE NEW Year did not start too well for Brian. He says;

> I have lessons now, a Miss Russell teaches us. I have a nasty cold in my head and rather a croupy cough but all the same for that I went out this morning a thing you would faint at the bear sujustion. I have not been to the school of art lately the weather has been too bad.

In the following letter he has more to say about his lessons.

> I dont enjoy the lessons at all I simply haet them, and if you are the setest bit naughty she (I mean Miss Russell) looks as much as to say you vulger little boy . . . but she isnt too bad in other ways.

Brian soon seemed to get over the difficulty of settling down to lessons after his long holiday and has a lot to say about his new drawing master.

> My new master is such a jolly little chap and he teaches me such jolly stuff . . . When the weather gets a bit warmer he's going to take me out and teach me how to draw the things I see, but the principle thing he's teaching me is to draw with as few lines as possible and to get things in a curve and not to much rubber . . . I do drawing for an hour every day.

It is astonishing that a boy of ten should be so quick to grasp the technique of simplification and design . . . "to draw with as few lines as possible and to get things in a curve". He is so sophisticated in his understanding of art and at the same time, just a little boy.

> I have been drawing all the morning and have been cleaning my teeth every morning 'well' with that stuff Dad sent me . . . Every mealtime the Dr. and I have a staring compertichion but he always stars me out.

Golf is now one of Brian's interests. He tells us that;

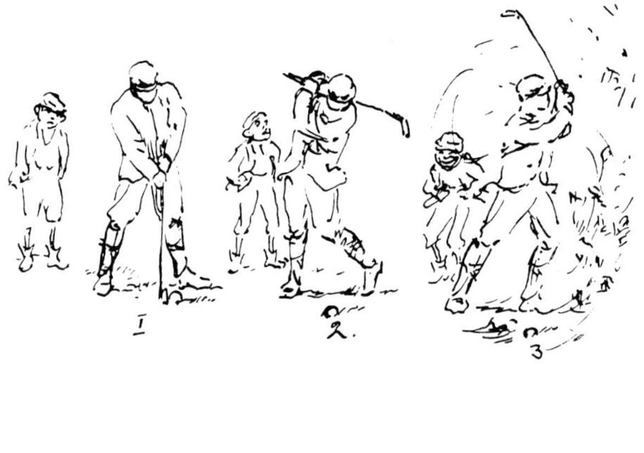

> I and Elton often caddy for Mrs. Lancaster and the Dr. . . . I have been playing golf this afternoon. I splite one ball and nicked a piece out of another one, there rotten things (you can tell Dad so) so Mrs. Lancaster had to give me one of hers. I did my worsed hole in 38 and my best in 16. I walked up to brim mill this morning. Elton took his curry and me another as the wind was pretty high there was quit nice little waves and boats rocked as if they were at sea. I am going to go in for the same drawing compitichon that I got my medal for and at least [hope] to get a silver medal this time . . . We have sent in lots of things . . . 5 sheets altogether with about two or three drawings on each.

Of course Brian was referring to the Royal Drawing Society and his success this year, 1898, was to be an important landmark in his artistic career. He won the Gold Star which was presented annually by Princess Louise, the president of the Society, to the best exhibitor, as well as a number of other prizes. The competition was open to the whole of Great Britain, the age limit being twenty. Brian, not yet eleven years old, took his success very calmly and on 16th May, he wrote;

> We got back the drawings from the Exhibition. Mrs. Lancaster's* drawings got the three big prizes with Briton Riviere's name on it and some more and 'with very great promise indeed' something Watts on it.

It turned out that it was G. F. Watts who had written "with very great promise indeed". Both he and Briton Riviere were aware that they were looking at the work of an infant prodigy and they became deeply interested in the boy and became his lifelong friends. Watts wrote;

> Of course for his age Brian Hatton's work is quite unsurpassed, the hand† is delicately felt and the drawing of the team in the reaper is quite astonishing.

Princess Louise, Queen Victoria's fourth daughter, was an artist herself — a sculptress of no mean ability and she took an active interest in the R.D.S. When she saw Brian's work her interest was immediately aroused and in the fullness of time Brian received a letter written by her equerry, Colonel Collins.‡

> 21st Nov. 1898 Kensington Palace
> Dear Brian Hatton
> By desire of H.R.H. the Princess Louise, Marchioness of Lorne, I am sending you by registered post today the gold star§, presented by the Princess to you for your very clever drawing, which won you the prize among all the other Royal Drawing Society pupils in the last Competition. I am sorry there has been so much delay in the matter but the star sent by the Drawing Society the Princess thought badly executed and of poor design. The one now sent H.R.H. designed herself and has been specially made, which I am sure will add to its value in your eyes. The Princess is a very capable artist herself and is in consequence all the more able to appreciate the decided talent and promise shown in your drawings
> Believe me, Yours sincerely
> Arthur Collins (Colonel)

*Presumably these were drawings which Brian had given to Mrs Lancaster.

†Brian had made a pencil study of his mother's hand.

‡Lt. Colonel Arthur Collins (who retired from the Army in 1885 at the age of forty) was attached to the Court, as Comptroller and Equerry to the Princess Louise, Duchess of Argyll, from 1880 to 1900. Subsequently he was Gentleman Usher to Queen Victoria, Edward VII and George V.

§The gold star designed by Princess Louise for Brian was subsequently adopted as the special prize.

This was an exciting letter for a little boy to receive and of course Brian wrote and thanked the Princess. When Christmas came he sent her one of his drawings and Colonel Collins wrote again, conveying the Princess's thanks and saying that she thought the drawing was "so well and carefully done". Colonel Collins added a wistful p.s. to the letter.

> If ever you have time to do me quite a small drawing, I should be so pleased to have it as a remembrance of our acquaintance 'by letter'.

Brian was only too pleased to oblige the Colonel. Making a drawing was no trouble at all, but he did get annoyed with having to answer so many letters. He envied the Princess who apparently never set pen to paper and wished that he too had someone to deal with his correspondence. Colonel Collins was delighted with the drawing, saying that it was "charming — extremely clever and beautifully done". He went on to say that he was having it framed and he hoped that Brian would come and see it "whenever you come to town". He said that, "The Princess says too I am to bring you out to see her". As a final bait he added "If you are fond of horses I will give you an order to see the Royal Mews when you come up to town". He had certainly guessed the way to Brian's heart.

Brian's success with the R.D.S. must have been a great stimulant to his work, and he now gives an account of his progress with Mr Littlejohn. It is refreshing to note that he never suffers from a sense of self-importance, and still identifies himself with the events in the nursery at home.

> Mr. Littlejohn and me went out sketching on Wednesday we'r making studies of backgrounds and tress for those are things I cant do and you must be able to do everything to be an all round man which I want to be . . . I have been painting some sheep under a tree in water colours, the tree being from nature and the sheep out of my head but the mixing of the colours is beyond me espeshly the greene . . . Thank dear little Ailsa for the nice letter she sent me. I'm sure it must be very dull up in the nursry on a wet day, but I expect the tea things will put it all right, tell her I'm quite well and I'm glad [to] hear she's ditto. Give baby tomboy, Dad and Mab* a nice big kiss each and tell Dad to give you one too.

About this time Elton returned to his home in Hereford and Brian was now on his own with the Lancasters. On 12th June he writes;

> Mrs. Lancaster telled me to tell you that I am a spoilt boy now, I dont get to bed till nearly nine and do pretty all what I like now that Eltons gone . . . I thought the animals at the Agricultural Show wouldn't be very nice to draw great fat straight becked, perfectly proportioned thick thrasted [breasted?] beasts.

In his next letter he has more to say about the prize cattle.

> Those cows of min you were talking about in your last letter are not at all good they are what I said in my letter about the prize bulls . . . The two sheep with the thick legs are quite right it is only the wool grown down them . . . I expect I shall

*Mab was a cousin who lived with the Hattons.

> be able to ride the pony by myself when [I] come home. Dad does not appear to be very forward in selling it . . . When we were going to the Grumble on Saturday . . . there was another boat waiting at the pier so there was an amusing sight to see the people runing down the hill to catch it most of the men being drunk . . . what was funnyer still was to see a cark of beer rolling down with all the beer sperting's out the poor ladies were frantic.

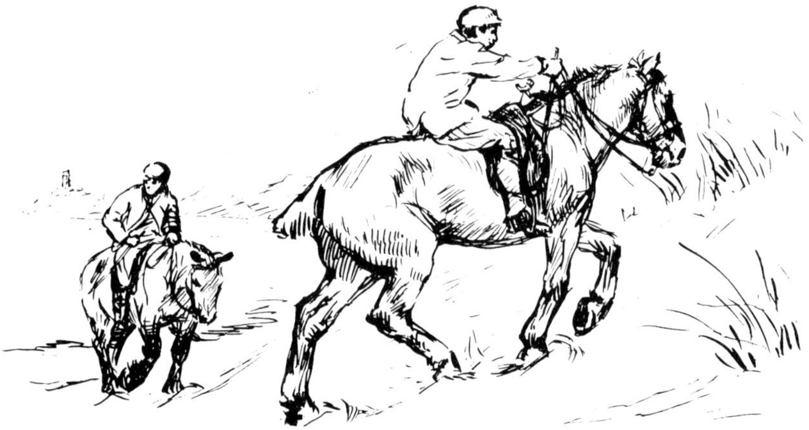

It is an exciting day when Brian receives some of his prizes from the Royal Drawing Society.

> Three of my prizes have come, the princesses will follow. Two of them are books one on art the other a fairy tale both splendidly illustrated the third a lovely little pictuer called 'The brook by the way'. Only one of the prints of the prize drawings have come the others will follow . . . I am sticking at the painting and not finding it so difficult. I take the Artist now and like it very much.

Brian has very little to say about his lessons at this time, but he tells his mother a lot about his other activities. He has had some coaching from the golf pro and he did a hole in 8 and another in 11, "so I dont think I play so badly as I might". He is often out riding or at the swimming baths or the gymnasium.

> Sargeant Bird teaches me a little single stick drill, so when I go home I shall be able to fence Dad . . . Last Saturday the girls drilled along with the boys at the Gim and were such a pack of fools, they geegled and funked the bar, couldent jump, and always asking favours of Mr. Bird. I think we are going to the tournament on Monday.

Brian did indeed go to see the tournament but with disastrous results. Always an imaginative child, with his mind steeped in the stories of King Arthur, pageantry held a special appeal for him; indeed, jousting knights are the subject of many of his earlier drawings. It is therefore not surprising that the scene before him took on a terrifying reality. To his mother he writes;

> I am a bit ashamed to tell you about the tournament as I fainted at the fencing and was laid on my back on the pavement with a crowed rowened me. You see I ceped [kept] thinking it over in my mind untill I thought it was a real one and when the one man sprained his foot I began to feel queer. Then when Mrs. Lancaster tried to walk me home I was just like as if I was drunk and couldn's see a bit . . . I dont think I have anything els to say so goodby.

Brian's teacher, Mr Littlejohn, appreciated the boy's interest in animals and as it was not easy to get live models for him to draw, he would order a sheep's head from the butcher. Brian describes some of the difficulties involved.

> Last Saturday we could not have any animals to draw, because the old sheep's head stunk so we could not have it up and the butchers had not sent another one so we tried the kitten but she would not keep stile, so then we had some very old books and set them in an artistic form and Mr. Littlejohn showed me how to paint them . . . We are going to have a cow's head next time if we can get one.

Christmas is drawing near and Mrs Lancaster had been stirring the Christmas puddings. Brian decided he would rather stay in Swansea and go home later. "I would rather come to see you after Xmas and for the races, which is half the fun of the year."

In spite of his mature approach to art, Brian was still a child who delighted in toys.

> I am making a man of war and if I make her well, she will be a splendid one. Mrs. Lancasters Mother . . . gave us each sixpence 'to spend not to save', she said . . . I am spending my sixpence on a lovely little box of Prins Alberts own Hussars with moveable arms just the right size to match mine and pretty strong too. Thanks orfaly for the other artillery horses I have mended them all now. The Dr. is always nicking my pliers havent he got a cheek, it strikes me all the people in Swansea have and I am learning it off them too . . . I dont think I need a whip for Xmas as I prefer a swhichy stick and would rather have a box of soldgers or a little clockwork luggage train . . . What a lark to have been in the tub when the wheels came off. I wonder whether they rolled away down the street like a hoop.

Mr and Mrs Hatton had been giving a great deal of thought as to the best way to educate their son both artistically and in general subjects. The Director of the Royal Drawing Society, Mr T. R. Ablett, had already expressed his views in a letter to Mrs Hatton. He said that there was no necessity for Brian to have drawing lessons, although he thought he might be helped to a fuller knowledge of the structure of animals by looking at really good drawings, adding that a book on the anatomy of the horse and other animals would be useful. He added a warning p.s. to his letter.

> P.S. You will no doubt carefully guard your little son from injudicious praise. I I have known many clever young people brought to naught by such a mistake as an over estimate of their work.

When Watts awarded his prize to Brian and showed interest in the boy Mrs Hatton wrote to him and asked for his advice. In his reply (from Little Holland House, 17th June, 1898) Watts said:

> I think your little boy's work displays more than ordinary ability and power of observation. I should very strongly advise the present should be given to sound education fitting him for future competition in the world. It is not necessary that the study of Art should in early life take the place of everything else. Art does not require the same kind of dexterity necessary to the executant of music! Sir Edward Burne Jones, who may be said to take the highest place at the moment did not take to Art at all until after he had finished his career at Oxford. Your little boy should exercise his observation and hand which he is sure to do in hours of recreation and *no time will be lost* . . . If you should be in Town it will give me pleasure to see you and the little man.

Mrs Lancaster also had some suggestions to make about Brian's education. In March the following year she wrote and said she felt sure it would do him good to go to school. He was obviously bored with his solitary lessons and in spite of his quick intelligence, he was far behind boys of his age. What was more, he had little sense of responsibility and was very forgetful over small things, his excuse always being, "I forgot". She felt that school would alter all this. "Of course his health has been a drawback but I cannot see why it should continue to be . . . Exceptional bringings up are generally a failure."

The Hattons were loath to take Brian away from Swansea. Although he was still not a very robust child, his health had improved since he went to live with the Lancasters, it therefore seemed that the wisest course would be to send him to Swansea Grammar School. Mrs Lancaster consulted with Dr Turpin, nicknamed "Turpentine" by Brian, head of the middle school. He was a family friend and had always taken a great deal of interest in Brian. He said he would like to have the boy in the school. He would let him take up the subjects most likely to be beneficial to him, and he would give him extra time for drawing.

As it turned out, Brian's entry to the Grammar School was no easy matter. Before he was due to sit for the entrance examination, Mrs Lancaster managed to obtain some exam papers set for former years, for boys of nine and ten. When confronted with them, Brian was unable to answer a single question, "not so much because he did not know them but he had never written an exam and he did not understand the way they were put".

Mrs Lancaster informed Dr Turpin of the predicament. He kindly said that he would take Brian for half an hour and see if he could get some idea of how much he knew and decide whether he could admit him at the school without his taking the exam.

What happened during this interview is now told by Brian himself.

> Mrs. Lancaster took me up to the Grammar School yesterday for Dr. Turpentine to examing me, I went into his study, oh that little room of his was like an oven. I took my things off and settled down to the first sum, by the time I'd finished it the heat began to make me feel a bit queer so when Dr. Turps came to correct it I was vionluntly sick on my knickers (the stink) and dizzy in my head. Dr. Turps said 'I think you had better come out a minite' but bless you I couldn't walk. I went bumping into desks knocking down books and at last came a cropper against the door so Dr. Turps had to haul me along to the bath room where Mrs. T. had to wipe me.

Mrs Lancaster had her own ideas about the incident.

> . . . Brian thought it was because the room seemed hot but we think it was simply nervousness, just like he was that night I took him to the tournament . . . There is no doubt he possesses a very highly strung nervous organisation and I agree with you that . . . he will want watching and looking after. My husband says this mental condition of his must not be encouraged, that if possible he should be hardened mentally as well as physically, and he urges most strongly that he should try what school life will do.

In the end Dr Turpin said that he would let Brian off the entrance examination and that he could come to school for a few weeks as an experiment. He would start at the beginning of the summer term, in mid-April. This arrangement suited Mrs Hatton very well, for she was planning to take Brian for a long promised visit to London towards the end of May, for a meeting with Princess Louise and with Watts.

Brian stayed on in Swansea over the Easter holidays of 1899. He told his mother that "I made nearly everybody here an April fool", but added that he would be "*quite* in the *dumps* at missing the races". He went on to describe an incident which had made a deep impression on him.

> Yesterday I went out with Mrs. Lancaster in a hansom and we made Peter run behind but he's a very bad carriage dog, always barking at the horse so when we were on the Murbles road he snaped at the horses heels, the horse plunged and kicked out. We heard a yell then silence, the cabman pulled up and we looked round and there was Peter limping along in a river of blood (orful good colour). Mrs. Lan got out helped him in. I looked the other way. When Mrs. Lan got to were she was going to . . . make a call I had to look after this bleeding wretch till I got home but I didnt do a sleep this time.

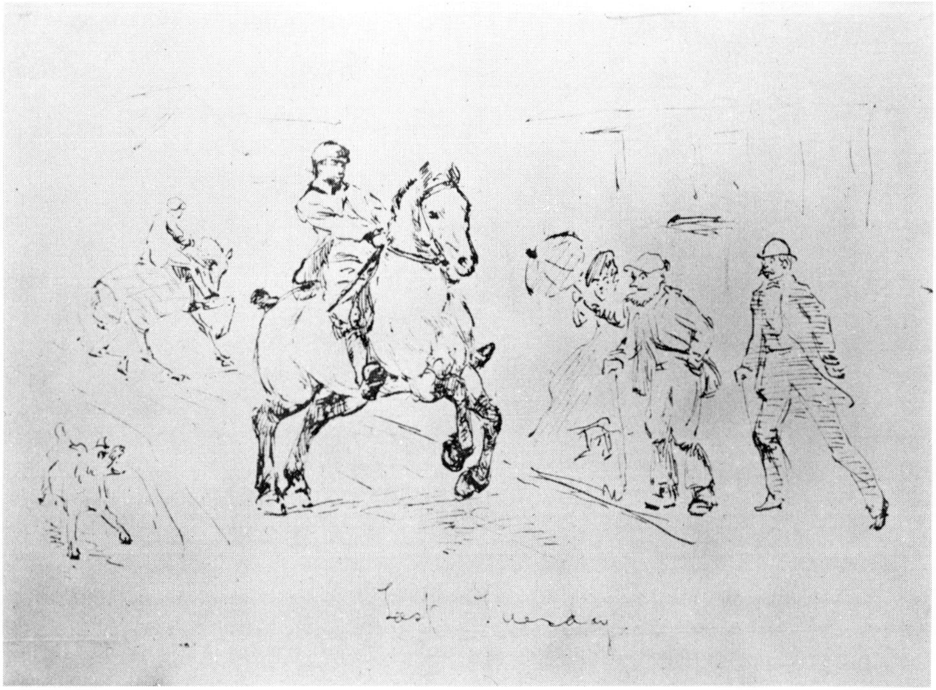

Riding being Brian's favourite pastime, many of his letters were illustrated with drawings of horses and he gives some nice descriptions of his equestrian adventures.

> I have just come from a pony ride with Elton, the man has got two ponys now, and the grass cutter and she slped twice and I had to pull her up pretty quick or els she would have been down [with] me and all. But she's a splendid troter for all that and outstripes Tommy in a minute.

> On Wednesday I had Blanch the little pony she seemed to be a bit fresh when I started and when I got into Walter rd she went faster than I wanted I just raised my hand to fix my cap a bit firmer when off she started as hard as she could go. I stuck fast and tride to pull her round but I couldn't, away goes my cap all the people starde (Gilpin No 2). I didnt know where I was going to, then I saw a side street I pulled her up it as though it was my last chance and just going round the corner she stoped. Coming back to look for my cap I meet old Bulin (where I got her from) he told me I was to get off and lead her back. I resented at first but had to give in. The next day pouring with rain and sea mist but I went for a ride on the same pony with Bullins nephew soak through, none the worse.

Later on he had a new mount and gives another graphic account of a ride.

> The pony is not at all like Jenny more like this very thick set and excepting her mouth which is very tender, clipped everywhere except her thick ugly legs. An ugly pony altogether, thats my verdicked. I went for a ride on her on Wednesday to fairwood common which is about 5 miles square. As soon as I was fairly in the middle of it (after having been nearly blown off the pony 3 times, never was in such a wind in my life) it came on to rain with such a force that it is a miracle I was not drowned. So I made the best of my way home 'up hill and down dale through bush and through briar' across the common by the time I got half way home my saddle was like a wash tup or a duck pond I dont know which praps you do, do you? But I'm safe and sound none the worse.

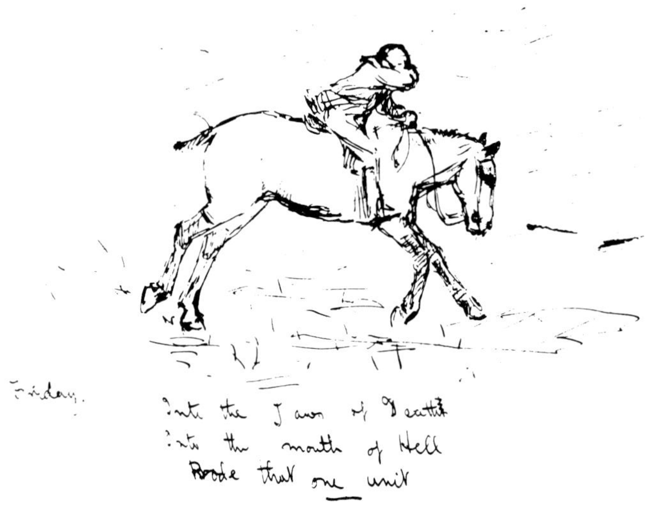

When the summer term started, Brian was eleven years old. His twelfth birthday would be in the following August. On entering the Grammar School, he evidently had to do some sort of test, but this time there were no ill effects.

> I got through the Exam all right without fainting or been sick and now I am in the baby school at the bottom of the bottom form but we cant all be at the top . . . the boys at the Grammar School call me Bonnet cause my name begins with B and the other with Hat, but I like the school all right . . . Dr. Turps gives us exam every week (offal fun) and the one that got most marks was top of the form for a week. I came out amongst the top for writing but I didn't make blots like this; I find lessons more fun in a class but just about as easy as by myself. I am doing Don Quixote in water colour charging the sheep.

Although Brian threw himself whole heartedly into all the activities of school, they never diverted him from the real purpose to which his life was dedicated. He was a compulsive artist and drawing came as naturally to him as breathing. Dr Turpin understood the boy and gave him every encouragement, not so his form master.

> The other day Jenkins (our form master) caught me drawing on my paper and gave me a 100 lines it toke up the whole of the evening. Yesterday Mrs. Lancaster and me went down to Orstermouth castle and I sketched it (might come in for a background for my knights). Dr. Turpintine saw it and said that the drawing was all right but the pencile work shading was not quite right . . . I have nearly finished old Don Quixote dont get much time now . . . I am doing some seapia knights and Dr. Lan has some rather good books on armour . . . Dr. Lancaster says that perhaps Col: Collins would get me an order to handle the armour in the tower because when you are takin over it they rush you along without giving you time to see anything.

Brian's interest in knights and jousting scenes made him anxious to study armour. However careless he might be about everyday affairs, he was never slipshod in his artistic work and was forever seeking detailed information about the subjects he wished to draw.

The Tournament.
Pen and ink, 1899. 8¾″ × 11¼″ *Brian Hatton Gallery, Hereford*

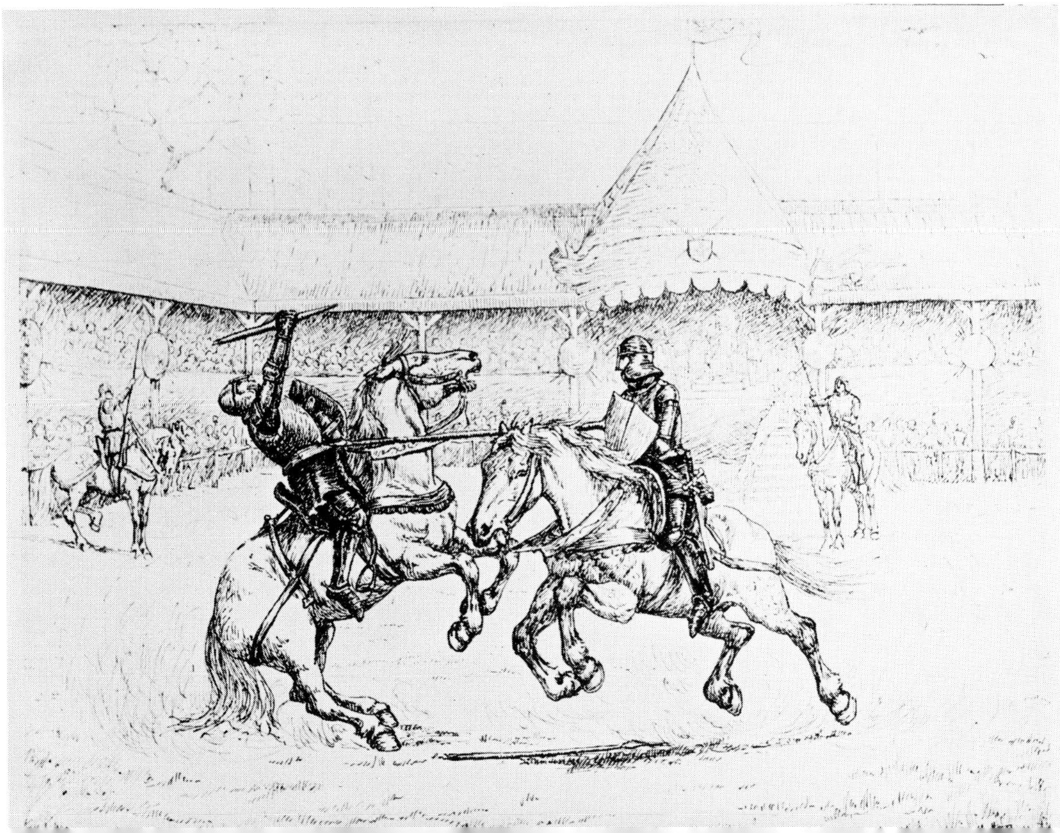

CHAPTER FOUR

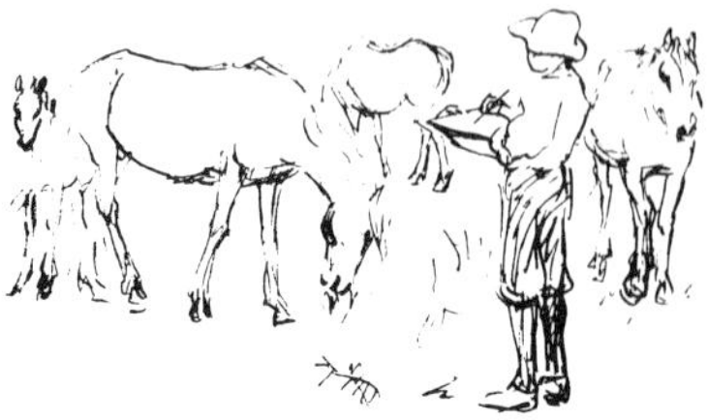

A Royal Occasion

BRIAN had only been at school for a month when it was time for him to go home and accompany his mother on the long promised trip to London to visit Princess Louise. He had taken quite happily to school life; the trial period had been successful, and Dr Turpin had decided that the boy should become a permanent pupil of the Grammar School.

Just before term started, Brian had heard the result of the 1899 Royal Drawing Society Competition. Once again he had carried off a number of prizes including G. F. Watts' award. Mr Ablett (the Director of the Society), had written to Mrs Hatton, telling her that Brian's work was far in advance of all the other competitors. He said that Princess Louise would have liked to have given Brian the gold star again but she thought it desirable that it should not be won twice by the same competitor.

When Mrs Lancaster heard the news of Brian's success she said she was so excited that she could eat no breakfast. She wrote to Mrs Hatton saying;

> There is no doubt the child has true genius, and like all those who possess the real thing, he has not the slightest conceit over it . . . I read him the report . . . the remark that really pleased him was *The Times* saying of his team of horses 'it would be difficult to find a fault'.

After viewing the exhibition Colonel Collins wrote to Mrs Hatton saying that everyone was full of praise for Brian's talent . . . "perhaps it's as well he does not hear all that is said of it! We must keep him simple if he is to be really great". He went on to say that there were notices in many newspapers, and sent her a copy of the *Daily Graphic*.

Among the drawings sent in by Brian was a self-portrait, entitled "Myself in the Looking Glass". There is so much subtlety and feeling in this charming little study that it would be difficult to contemplate it without an emotional response. It depicts the deep concentration of a child in love with his task. Brian had promised to give this drawing to Colonel Collins, who told Mrs Hatton how very pleased and proud he would be to have it. He ended his letter by saying,

> Give him my love and tell him to write to me. His letters are as delightful as his drawings.

Brian had very different thoughts about his correspondence with Colonel Collins and he complained bitterly.

> . . . when am I to write to Colonel Collins. Would next Sunday do? . . . Its cronick having to write to the Colonel. I thourt I should get out of it this week. He says he has been very sick in the Bay of Biscay on returning from Spain. I should like to see him sick.

Mrs Lancaster agreed with Mrs Hatton that Colonel Collins was a very valuable friend for Brian, but said that it was impossible to make the little monkey see it. She added that it was perhaps unwise to teach him to make friends purely for reasons of self-interest. She triumphed over Brian in the end, saying;

> After endless grumbling and wishing Col. Collins at the bottom of the sea, I have got him to write at last . . . he flatly refuses to write to you as well . . . I think it is far better for him to write naturally to Col. Collins, spelling and all. I am sure he will like it better.

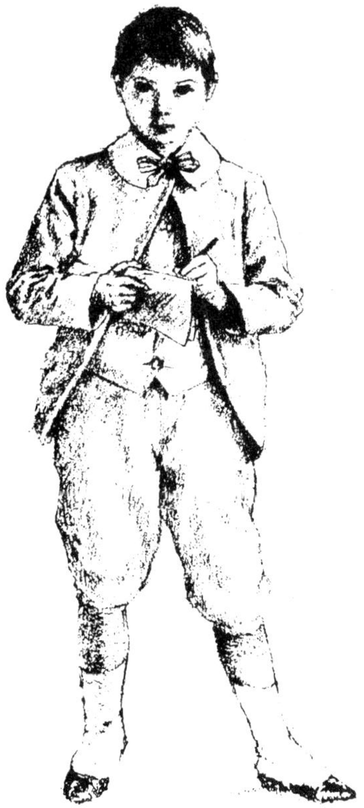

Myself in the Looking Glass.
Pencil, 1898
Brian Hatton Gallery, Hereford

On 18th May Brian and his mother set off on their long awaited visit to London. When they arrived at Paddington they took a cab to the Howard Hotel in Norfolk Street, just off the Strand. The following morning Colonel Collins came to call on them. He proposed that he should return in the afternoon and that they should take a hansom cab to the Tate Gallery, where Brian could see a small collection of the best known pictures, which included some of Watts'. Afterwards they would return to Colonel Collins' chambers at 24 St James Street for tea.

Princess Louise was out of town for a few days, but Colonel Collins was kindness itself, escorting Brian and Mrs Hatton to picture galleries and to St Paul's Cathedral and arranging visits to the Royal Mews and the Tower of London. A real and lasting friendship grew up between Brian and the Colonel whom he nicknamed "Curly".

The Royal Command came eventually and it was a nice sunny day when Brian and his mother set out for Kensington Palace to meet the Princess. Mrs Hatton must have been apprehensive about the visit, knowing how Brian could be affected by nervousness. Mrs Lancaster had predicted that he was sure to be sick, and bearing this in mind Mrs Hatton decided that they should walk quietly through Hyde Park and Kensington Gardens, keeping Brian's mind on all that he saw around him until they reached the Palace.

Brian enjoyed the walk and arrived in good spirits. Colonel Collins who was waiting to receive them, took them to the Princess's room. They were all admiring some of the pictures on the walls when Princess Louise entered, carrying a little dog under her arm. She received them in the most genial manner and after looking at some of Brian's drawings she moved over to the tea table. There were no servants present, but the blue spirit flame was flickering under the big silver kettle, and the Princess proceeded to make the tea herself. She chatted all the time while she poured out and handed round the bread and butter. She talked to Mrs Hatton about her own early training as an artist and stressed the point that it was better to have no teaching at all unless one could be sure of the best. "Do take care of Brian's eyes," she said. "My own suffered through working at night."

And then, perhaps because she was struck by something fey in Brian's character, she advised his mother to try and make him strong . . . "not too many fairy tales and sugar plums". She was very impressed by his drawings of animals and suggested that he should go to Windsor and sketch the deer in the park. When she offered them some tickets for the Military Tournament, Mrs Hatton thought it wiser to refuse. She remembered how Brian had reacted when watching a tournament at Swansea and decided that it would be too great an embarrassment if he were to faint or be sick in the Royal Box. After tea the Princess took them into various rooms hung with pictures, both modern and old and she drew back the curtains to give a better light. She showed Brian bronze models of horses, the best of these being a very fine prize horse executed by Edgar Bohem. There was armour in the hall and Brian was given a knight's lance to handle.

The highlight of the afternoon came when the Princess ordered her pony to be brought round from the stables for Brian to see. It was rather fresh but Brian mounted it and rode it bareback up and down the courtyard. His cup of happiness was full.

The London interlude ended with a memorable visit to Mr and Mrs Watts, at Compton, near Guildford. Arthur Collins was a friend of "old Mr Watts" and together they had often discussed Brian's talent. Collins informed Watts that Brian and his mother were in London and this resulted in an invitation for the Hattons to visit him.

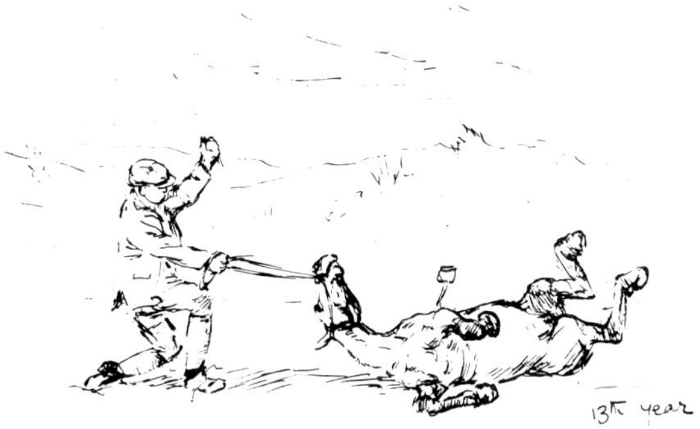

Mrs Hatton had already been in touch with Mary Watts who took upon herself much of her husband's correspondence. This rather formidable lady identified herself very closely with her husband whom she referred to as "Signor". She took great care of his health, guarding him from fatigue and unwanted disturbances, and generally protecting him, as if she were the custodian of a national institution. When Brian won Watts' award for the second time, his wife wrote to Mrs Hatton saying that she wished to tell her what "very *great* pleasure it gave my husband to be able to promise his prize to your little son". She ended rather pompously, saying "I need not say that we look forward to seeing your little son distinguish himself in the kingdom of art".

Mr Hatton and Mrs Hatton's sister, Mrs Vevers, came up from Hereford to join Brian and his mother towards the end of their visit and on 31st May they all travelled down to Compton to lunch with Mr and Mrs Watts at their house, Limmerslease. Mary Watts had written to say that she regretted she was unable to arrange for them to be met at the station as their pony cart and brougham were both too small, but that there would be plenty of "flies" at the station.

The visit was a great success and they received a warm welcome from both Mr and Mrs Watts. Watts took them into his studio and showed them a large canvas on which he was working. The unfinished picture was "The Court of Death" and Watts talked about it in detail. Mrs Watts showed them her studio and pottery works where she taught the villagers to mould the clay, making "beautiful shapes for ornament and usefulness", as Mrs Hatton noted.

Some of Brian's sketches had been brought for Watts to see and he expressed great interest and pleasure in them. Again he emphasised that Brian should be given a conventional education for the next few years, without any special training in art.

The Hattons returned to Hereford and a few days later Mrs Hatton received a letter from Mrs Watts in which she said:

> Your visit was *a great pleasure* to us. We so greatly sympathise with you in all your hopes and desires for your dear little son, whom nature has so remarkably endowed! . . . it is a great joy to find him so unspoilt, just the natural unself-conscious boy! Great men differ very widely but . . . they are *all* of them of childlike simplicity.

It must have been difficult for Brian to return to school life again after such an exciting interlude. His first letter is full of nostalgia for his beloved Hereford.

> My dear Mother
> The first night I came I did not like it much it was so dusty and dirty and miserable after bright little hereford. The sea air makes me awfully sleepy, I never seem to get enough of it . . . I was quite 'comfy' as you call it in the carriage another man came in at Pontypool-rd he was allmost [as] fat as Lizzie* and the clergyman looked me up at Cardiff, were I met Lizzie. Mrs. Lan and I went out to Puddicome the milkman's dairy to sketch some cows in water-colour yesterday . . . We got half way when we saw some cows in a field so we thourght we'd sketch those but it wasn't the will of Heaven . . . for when I'd just begun we were turnedout so we . . . went to work to find the other dairy . . . After wandering about for over an hour we found ourselves in Mumbles Road where we waited for the steam tram. When we were coming back we saw a lot of cows grassing on the golf links as if to mock our stupidity . . . My back aches now from carrying that bag. O dear how different from Hereford, dear little Hereford.

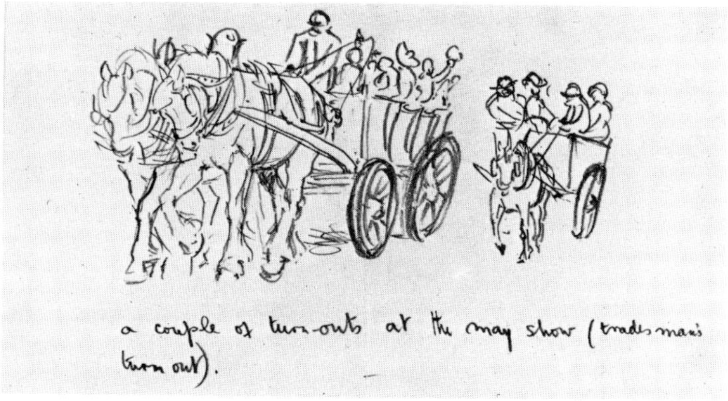

On 29th June he was ill again.

> Excuse my writing in pencill because I am in bed with what Mrs. Lan calls a stumach out of order and Dr. Lan a little influenza but I think its a bit of both, but I dont care a sou cause I dont go to school this is the third day I've been in bed, but Mrs. Lan bought me a book to read, nice old thing . . . I am in the middle of doing some watercolour knights and Mrs. Lan is reading Ivanhoe to me.

Ten days later Brian says "I am going to school tomorrow, boo-hoo-o-o". He was touchingly concerned to hear that his mother had also been ill and wrote sympathetically, saying, "You must buck up and get well quickly and dont try to do too great things just when your nearly well".

*Lizzie was Mrs Lancaster's cook.

When term ended Mrs Hatton was still unwell and Brian's return to Hereford was delayed, much to his annoyance.

> I want to come home quick! Sharp! Jack! Robinson! . . . I hope you are much better mind you get well soon because I dont want to spend half of my holidays in this hole of a place heat or no heat . . . You must get Dad to see about a pony for me . . . Mrs Lan and I have finished Ivanhoe this morning . . . My shirts are more holy than rightous.

When Brian returned to Swansea at the end of the summer holidays, Mr and Mrs Hatton and the two little girls went to visit their relations in Ayrshire, and Brian follows their activities with great interest.

> O let me see, its Ailsa's birthday today, little six year old, wish her many happy returns of the day if its not too late when this little scratch reaches you. Actually *you and kids* going through the docks on a *steam launch* and the [wind] blowing you nearly off your feet, well I'm surprised at your pluck. I wonder where old Dad is now somewhere up the west coast I bet (but still think thats rather vague).

Later he says, "Fancy poor Dad had to retire to his bunk for *two* days . . . How did grandfather weather it then I wonder".

When term started Brian seemed to settle down quite happily. He was now twelve years old, and no longer a new boy and he found plenty to interest him.

> School's all right at present but the hard work begins on Monday. Our new class rooms are awfully nice there are three very good engravings, one called Shakspear is a little naked baby and two women kneeling almost naked and some very good trees in the background. Another is a man boossing in a stable with an ox and an ass but I forget what the other is like . . . There are lots of new boys at school now there's one called 'Tissen' and when 'Ol' Ambe' asked him his name he began to blubber so 'Ol' Ambe' says 'Tissen-t nice to cry', all the boys roared . . . The other day at school in middle lessons Dr. Turps walked in with a little boy behind him dressed very rum, Dr. T. said he was German and did not know English except 'yes' and 'no', and the masters that dont know German have to talke by signs but he can do Algebra and Gym A.1. Toping and as soon as he knows some more English he will put all the other boys into darkness.

Brian had few prejudices and was very ready to praise other people's ability, but he was still modest about his own work, in spite of the interest taken by Watts and Colonel Collins.

> Fancy curly going to show that little scratch I did to Mr. Watts. Am I to write to Curly again next Sunday or will this little Scrapy note do? . . . I am so glad you liked that little daub . . . I began it one evening after tea . . . and when the gas was lighted I sketched in Don Quixote and Rozonande . . . I'm not sure whether Don Quixote's armour is good though.

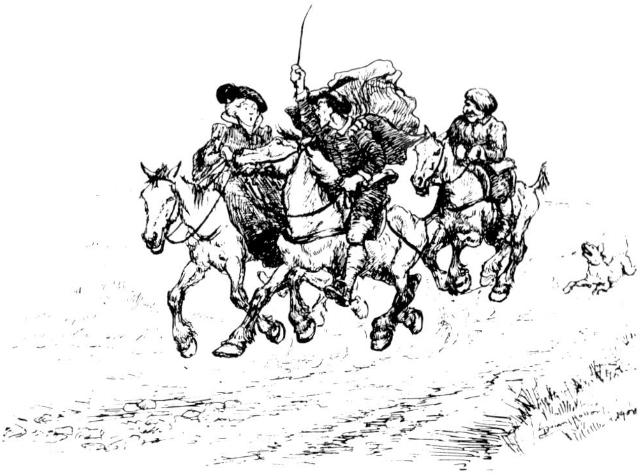

Illustration. (Horsemen)
Pen and ink, 1900. 6¼″ × 8¾″

Brian Hatton Gallery, Hereford

Whether Brian's letters to Colonel Collins were carefully written or were just "scrappy little notes", they were always deeply appreciated and Collins remarked that "there is even talent in the way he spells wrongly at times".

Mrs Lancaster was delighted with the way Brian had settled down at school. Writing to Mrs Hatton, she said:

> I have not heard a single grumble this term . . . He is getting on famously with his work . . . He really is a sterling little chap . . . I never met a child so full of character. My husband has the greatest liking and respect for him, as for me, well he is half like my own . . . I had an old gentleman here last week (an architect) who knows many artists, and has some knowledge of art himself, he is simply amazed and charmed with the pencil drawings . . . He could not sleep that night for thinking about the child and his work. His opinion was that his pencil work was so good that he should stick at that and not trouble about the colouring. But . . . to become one of the greatest artists he is bound to be a painter and . . . with his gifts he ought never to be content to be less than a Landseer, Rosa Bonheur, Turner.

Brian went home for Christmas and revelled in the large family gathering and festivities which included amateur theatricals performed by the younger generation. He sent Christmas cards of his own design to Princess Louise, Mr and Mrs Watts and of course one to "Curly". Arthur Collins sent him a paint box. It came "from the man the Princess always gets her paints at, and I know he is the best in London!". He was delighted with Brian's Christmas card and showed it to his friend Lord Battersea, who thereupon decided to lend Brian a volume of autotypes of the Rembrandt and Vandyke drawings at Windsor Castle. Colonel Collins said:

> You can keep the book till the summer, for he thinks it must help you very much to see these wonderful studies . . . I hope you are having a merry time with your cousins; next time you write you must draw in the letter to show me what some of you looked like in the play.

CHAPTER FIVE

"Life Is One Great Fight"

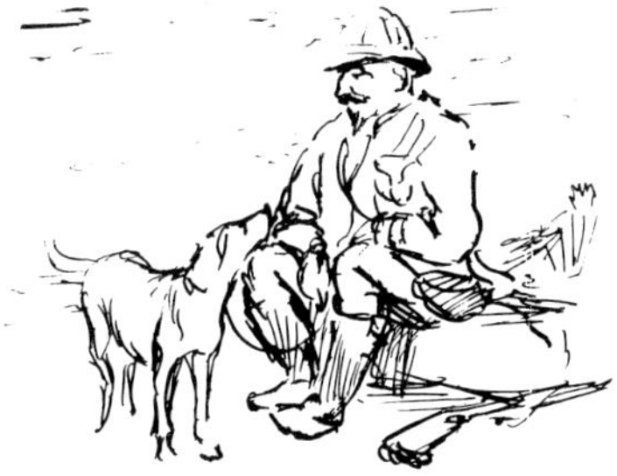

BRIAN Hatton was no pacifist and when the Boer War broke out he expressed his views about it very clearly.

> Sargeant Bird the gym master at the school (the same that used to teach us before) has joined his old redgment and gone to South Africa. And now we have an awfully stupid fellow who teaches us all kinds of silly exercises, I think he's gone dotty . . . I hope Dad has given up the *Daily Chronical*, its views on the war are rotten.

On 28th January, 1900 he writes:

> Things have been going badly latly Spions Kop recaptured by the boers!!!!!!!!
> If I'd got Old Kruger in my clutches I'd first do this

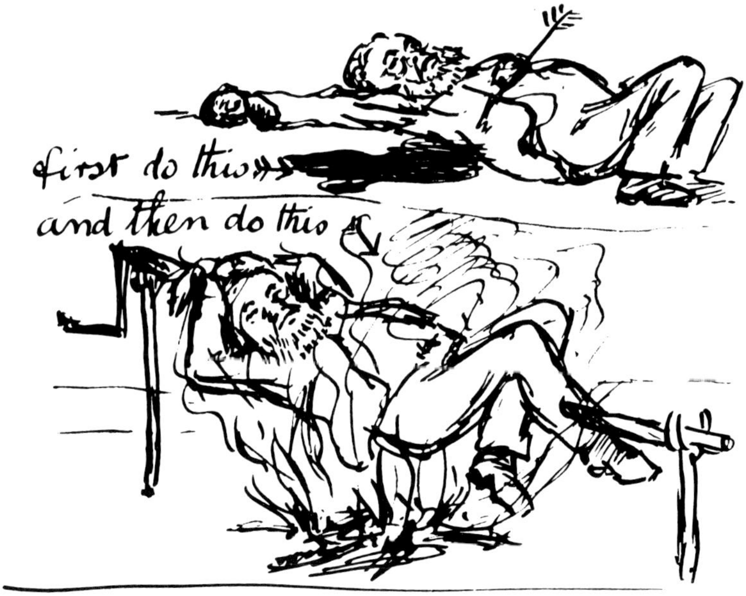

> and then send his skull as a present to his generals. And then I would most likely end up by fainting.

Like his father, Brian could never stand the sight of blood!

> March 4th
> We were all very busy at our studies (I mean the 2nd form including me) Ambi was taking impositions, when all of a sudden we heard a trimendus row going on down by the docks it sounded as if all the hooters were going off at once (and so they were). 'Hello' say'd Ambi 'What's up, hooters 20 to 11. There's something in that boys'. The whole form yelled out 'Relife of Lady-y-Smith! I expect Lady Smith is relieved Sir', 'Hush silence boys' says ol' Ambi 'dont let yourselves be deceived boys, lets make sure first of all' etc. etc. Well after a bit we heard the newspaper boys calling out but couldn't exactly hear what they said but presently we heard one with a voice like an hippomottimus call out 'R-nOelife o-o-of La-a-dy-Smith' then there was ructions. Ambi danced up and down like aminionette (or whatever you call them) with one hand in his trouser pocket the other clutching a ruller and keeping time with it on one of the boys heads (who by the way sqealed in an unrich unmelodious voice) shouting out 'Three cheers for the Queen' etc. etc., but his voice was drowned in one long continuous shout that filled the whole school. One by one the other classes took it up and you might have heard it down at the Mumbles. Then the bell rang and we yelled and trouped out or rather flew out some of the fellows got knocked down and were run over. Once out of school, we kicked up a duce of a row forming into bands of 20 or 30 and rushing down the streets shouting and knocking over everything that came in our way Bobies included. One enterprising paper boy mounted himself on a donkey with two flags stuck in its head he sold all his papers before he had gone 50 yards. Little Gower Griffiths of the 1st form who is the size of a brickbat collected a little under 6£s in pop bottls. People were so delighted that they litterally jumped along the streets. Of course bells were ringing and hooters going the whole time. I saw in the *Daily Post* afterwards that the hooters consumed enough steam to last the s.s. 'Oliver' a 12 month . . . On Thursday afternoon I went for a ride and met two khaki Yomenry so I rode along with [them] down Oxford St. Everyone said there goes General Buller and his troops. I chaffed them a good bit and told them that they would never get to South Africa at that rate on horse back and that they'd better take a moter-car etc etc.

A few days later Brian wrote an indignant letter saying that they had only had *two hours* holiday for the relief of Ladysmith! It happened to be on St David's Day, which was a half-day holiday anyway, so he reckoned that the only bonus they had was from 11 to 1 o'clock. The following day the boys worked themselves up into a state of indignation and wrote a petition "signed by about a hundred and 30 boys (including me) but when all was ready we found that the Dr. had gone away till Saturday!!!!!!!!!

> Mrs. L. had a letter from her brother who has been shut up in Kimberley. he's going to send a full account of the seige by the next post. He says 'as 'ow 'e's lost 16 pound 'o flesh in fewer months. P.S. I am taking in 'With the flag to Pretoria'. it's a fine book I can tell you I'm going to get all the nos and have 'em bound.

This wasn't quite the end of the Ladysmith affair.

March 18th
On Saturday morning I had to write an essay on anything connected with the war so I chose Ladysmith day in Swansea. I wrote it much as I did for 'The Highlander'* only I put in much more rot about Ambi, anyhow next lesson 'Botofeet' . . . on looking over the papers saw mine and (so the fellows say) burst out laughing and was so pleased with it that he read [it] out to the First who went of in hesterics but I expect I shall get into rather a row because I put some awful rot about Ambi.

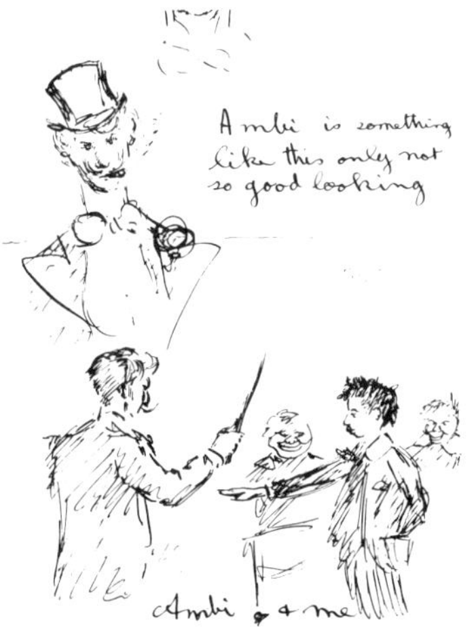

Brian could never resist "taking the mickey" out of his masters and the "awful rot" that Brian wrote about Ol' Ambi did not improve his relationship with his form master. Recently they had been on very good terms and Brian said "Ol' Ambi calls me 'his dear Brian' and says that when I've mastered the art of the french language then he'll privately teach me Italian, so as to be able to speak when I go there". A week or two later Brian wrote (in what he termed "double Hebrew"),

Ambie an' I haven't bin on very gude terms o' late 'as bin an' given me bout a hundred strips 'cross me 'and but thots nothink new, no, no for sure.

It may have been that "war fever", stirred up by the South African campaign, roused Brian's fighting instinct, for it was about this time that he became involved in several fights at school. The first of these occurred in February, after a heavy fall of snow. One afternoon Brian and a friend placed themselves in a strategic position on a hill overlooking the entrance to the school and pelted the people down below.

All went well until I hit a beastly pugilistic fellow on the neck . . . He simple flew up those steps (the other fellow ran away but there was no time for me to) and came and asked me if I threw the snow down his neck. I replied in the affirmative then he smacked me in the face and swore like old Bogey, then seeing my beautiful store of snow he picked it up and rubbed it all over my head and knocked that same valuable member against the wall and said 'God 'elp you if oi iver cops yer agin oop to thot job'. I felt too greviously insulted to answer, but as soon as he had gone, I got some more ammunition. I recontinued my snowy work, one old fellow said 'It stroikes me you be 'aving a d--d foin time of it opp

*"The Highlander" was an illustrated family magazine, edited by Aunt Grace.

thir'. . . . Oh! I forgot to tell you that I nearly killed one fifth form boy with snow-balls and he in turn nearly killed [me] with fist'cuffs . . . There was a grand snow [fight] in recess, lower school against upper school, good old lower school won . . . The snow was thick enough . . . for me to make old Kruger about 4′ high.

A few days later Brian got mixed up in another spectacular skirmish.

Feb 17th
I had rather an eventful day on either last Monday or Tuesday . . . It happened like this:— Kiddie freedman and Brum, two kids in the school had been abusing one another, which ended in a fight after morning school in a little lane a short way from the school. Most of the school went up to see it myself amongst them. After Brum had nearly been punched into a jelly fish with bloody mouth he gave up, howling like a baby. Then some Blooming Ladies came along and began their insane talk about poor little dear! What a shame of that other naughty boy to have hit him about so! There! There? Don't cry dear! etc etc. Then some men (*they'd* call *themselves* gentlemen) came along and one of these started saying things about the school how troublesome we were in the streets, and how could we see two fighting [under] our very noses without attempting to stop it. How ignorant we were, at which I (who was standing close to him but with my back to him) remarked to a 6th form boy standing by me that half of us couldn't speak Welsh so we must be ignorant. This caused a general laugh but my mirth was suddenly stopped by finding my head hit violently first on one side and then on the other, and my ears nearly pulled out by pieces. On looking round I found it to be Eddershaw as I was afterwards told his name was, who had just been abusing the school. He seized me by the collar and demanded my name so as to be able to report to Dr. Turpin. I told I wasn't going to give my name up in the street to anybody who demanded it, and the boy who I had spoken to before chimed in and asked him if he was a police constable. This [made] him awfully angry and he said, drawing himself up to his full hight and expanding his chest 'I'm police constable enough to take you both up to Dr. Turpin', which he did. He went in to interview Dr. Turps leaving us both outside in the porch. By and by Dr. Turpin came out with Eddershaw. Dr. said that he'd see us again in the afternoon. When Afternoon assembly came the Dr. gave the school a little lecture on impertinance and being a nusiance to others. he said that the punishment for myself and the other fellow was to go to Eddershaw and apoligise while a boy from the sixth form was to apolagise to Eddershaw for the school. Just before we went I told Dr. Turpin that Eddershaw hit me about and the Dr. [told] me to mention the fact to Eddershaw and then he might have to apoligise to me instead. And so he did and when he said he hoped I would accept his apology I said 'Oh yes pleasure'. I thought I scored splendidly . . . Love to all and Dad and 'The *nice* little sisters'.

Your loving son
Brian
not Brain as Ailsa put

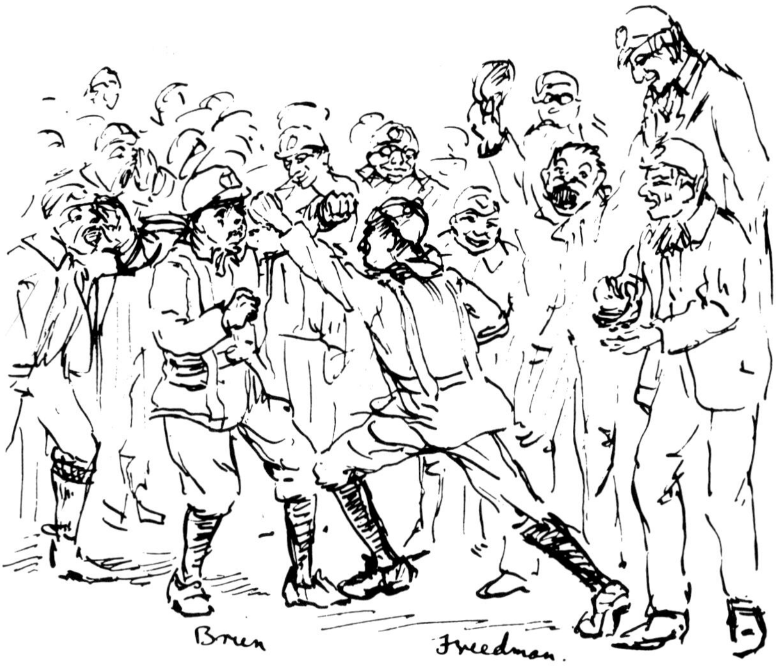

the fight

Mrs Hatton evidently did not entirely approve of Brian's fighting instincts and wrote a reproving letter which Brian replied to in his usual forthright manner.

Feb 24th
My Dear Mother
I cant agree to what you said about the fight episode nor can the Dr. nor Mrs. L. for even Ruskin says that fighting is essential; every nation who cannot fight goes to the bad and produces no really great men or great things, take Switzerland for example and Portugal, and nothing does boys and men more good than a few minutes fair fighting occasionally not for a big man to come slyly up behind a small chaps back and to start clouting him unawares like Eddershaw did. Why, we are taught boxing down Gym. And when you said that Masters ought always to be with the boys that simply means that every [boy] must be escort home to dinner by a Master. Fudge!! And as to no fighting at good schools why at Harrow the little boys are bullied and put upon and fighting most dreadfully. Mrs. L. has been told so by a friend who was nursing an epidemic there once. *Life is one great fight* . . .

Your loving son
Brian

P.S. Dont think that I mean to be impertinant in what I have said. I only meant to give another side of the question.

There is something very touching about the P.S. to this letter. Although devoted to his mother and in very close sympathy with her, Brian refused to bow to her influence when it came to a matter of principle. He reserved the right to his own opinion, at the same time he didn't want to hurt her feelings. A month later he was involved in yet another fight and he had no compunction of telling his mother about it.

> My dear Mother
> I havent got much to say . . . excepting that I had a fight with a much bigger boy than myself and I got a 'good hiding' as the boys call it, but I tapped his claret for hime just by the side of his eye, but he gave me a dickins of a lot of bruises on forehad jaw etc that havent gone away yet . . . But it was hardly a fair fight because this cockney had much longer arms and was a much bigger and heavier boy so that I couldnt get a reach on him. But he was a terribly bad fighter no guard no anything except weight. And I was just going to give a lovely 'knock out' bit at his great jaw when one of the 4th modern fellows came and seperated us and wouldn't let us go on, so it ended. But I'm going to have another smack at the blooming cockney crow.

A week later Brian had more to say about this fight.

> As to your question I'm afraid it was my fault you see we were playing at wrestling (up allmost under the Dr.'s study window) when he suddenly tripped me up and kneeled on my chest and at last by an allmost super-human effort flung him off and got up and went for him but I soon had to stop, cause the Dr. was in his study so we ran down to the fives courts were he couldn't see us and then had it out with this result allready known. So you see I have no love for him. All I can say is that I didn't fight a boy smaller than myself or my own size a thing that I am very glad to say and what the 'cockney crow' cant . . . I have persuaded Miss Hall to let me learn the Gypsie Ronddo.

This last remark refers to Brian's music lessons. Knowing him to be musical, like the rest of the family, Mrs Hatton was anxious that he should learn to play the piano. Brian had no objection to the music lessons but he flatly refused to practise regularly, much to the annoyance of his teacher. Mrs Lancaster was inclined to side with Brian over this matter, saying, "I really cannot worry him over the blessed music . . . what other boy spends his time with his brush and pencil that he does?"

Mrs Lancaster never ceased to watch over Brian the artist, and she felt that all his other activities were secondary. She took great care of his health and had no compunction in keeping him away from school when he developed one of his frequent colds. Brian openly enjoyed these interludes and turned them to good account.

> I have a little cold or something or other anyway I was kept in bed Wednesday and have been in my room ever since. I have had a sheep's head up and have

done a watercolour of it as large as I could get it on my block . . . nearly life size . . . I have been reading a little bit of Lionardo's life and find that he was *left handed*!!!!!!

A fortnight later he again stayed away from school.

I have had a little cold . . . Next day in bed all day (very happy) Next day up in time to draw a model who came at 11 am. He had come round begging on previous evening 'cause he was out of work. The tin plate works where he went being shut for want of orders, Mrs. Lancaster engaged him to stand for me striped to the waist for a shilling an hour. I made a very middling sketch of him on Saturday . . . but I made him a chicken chest when he really had a very fine one . . . So when he came again today I had him the same pose unfortunately I drew it a little too large for the paper and couldn't get the whole of the lower hand in but on the whole the second one was a great improvement on the first I am doing them in red chalk on creamy papers and looks awfully well. If I don't go to school on Monday and he comes again I shall get the Dr. to break it to him to pose in the nude full figure or perhaps with bathing draws or something. The poor chap finds it awfully cold standing even in front of a gas fire with a screen half-way round him. He stays 2 hours and stands perfectly still for ¾ of an hour at a stretch (tell Dad that). He's a very quiet chap and never troubles me with talking . . . I have just finished reading David Copperfield, Esq. Junior. I must say it's a very fine book though not so nice as Don Quixote or Legends of King Arthur or anything of that kind.

Brian wasn't able to do much riding that cold winter, but he wrote to his father, begging him not to sell the family pony, saying that he would never get a better one even if he were to try for a year and a day. He evidently won his point for a little later on he said, "I'm so glad the pony is not sold, pip pip". In March he was riding again and enjoying himself.

I'm getting quite a horse breaker when I took the pony (that I'm riding on now) first in hand she'd hardly face motor cars now she passes them as if she was one herself all through my powers.

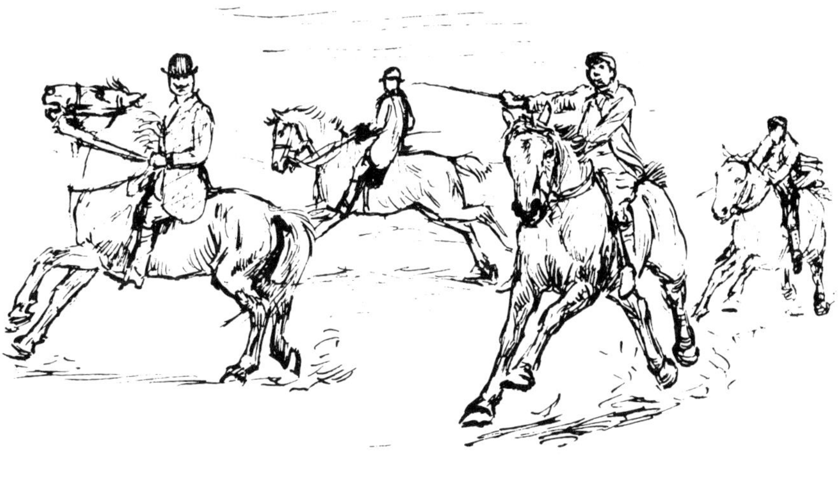

CHAPTER SIX

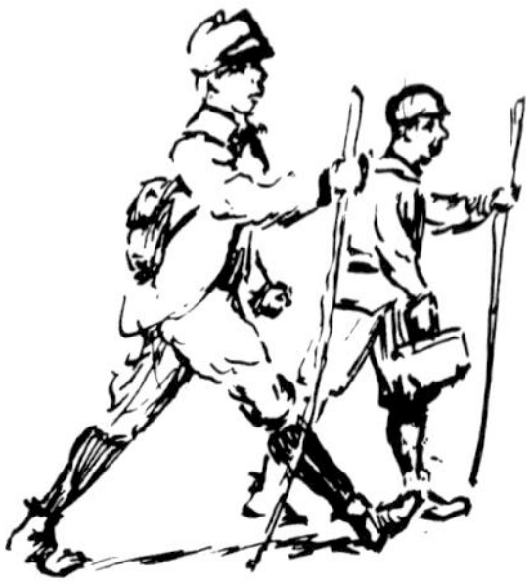

Unwillingly To School

THE SUMMER term started pleasantly for Brian in spite of the fact that he and his form master were not on very good terms. "Ambi and me have been having ructions already although nothing serious." Brian was delighted to hear from his mother that Aunt Ada Vevers was staying at nearby Langland Bay, together with her surgeon husband and their son, Geoffrey. Saturday being a half-holiday, he went to visit them.

> They were all very pleased to see me and I the same . . . I think they are quite enchanted with the peace, indeed the whole place smells like peach skins from the double gorse and plants of heather 6 ft. high, ssmtch! lovely! allmost as nice as home.

A week later Brian was back at Langland Bay for the week-end.

May 20th 1900

Langland Bay Hotel
Nr. Swansea.

My dear Mother
You see I am down here today. The school had a whole holiday yesterday and tomorrow in honour of Mafeking. So I came down to stay the week-end. When I heard the hooters at ¼ to X I was in bed just sinking into my fust sleep, up I jumped and hollowed out for all I was worth. I asked Mrs. L if I might go and she answered in the affirmative. So in two shakes of a gnat's b--m I dressed and ready to start. So off I went and a jolly crush it was. My feet are all skined in some places from being stepped on. I was never in a more muddling place than a hustling, jostling, feet-treading, stomach-bumping, shouting, singing, yelling, flag-flying, squib-letting, noisy, patriotic, drunken crowd at night. I sang 'God save the Queen' ½ a 12 times and 'Soldiers of the Queen', 'Dublin fusiliers', 'He's a jolly good fellow', 'Rule Britania' twice as many times. At last I got in at ¼ past 11 and wasn't in bed until ¼ past 12.
Aunty Ada sends her love she's too lazy to write and says . . . they haven't had a wet day since they came here, lovely weather . . .

Your loving son
Brian

Brian's descriptive powers were always good, whether he was describing events of national importance, such as Mafeking night, or simple domestic scenes as in his next letter.

I have actually been to church this morning all by myself too. And there was a boy ther that, iether fainted or went to sleep, anyway he fell wolop splosh bang off his seat in the middle of the Litany and had to be hauled out.
I have just finished copying one of Michel Angelo's sketches of a stark naked man it's awfully awkward to do when you not used to it, but I've done it as well as I can and it is said to be all right.

A few days later Brian reports that he is still copying the Old Masters.

I have done another figure of Raphael's and a half of another one it is very slow and tiresome work as well as being a bit dull, and I am sure I am not doing what Mr. Watts said viz: 'Just as you feel inclined'. But I suppose I must worry away at it though Mrs. L. too is very doubtful as to wether I ought to be copying or not and as to wether it's doing me any good . . . I went to Swansea art gallery on Friday and a very well chosen little set of pictures and engravings they are too.
3 water colour portraits of old fashioned boys attracted my attention greatly they were so clean and bold and yet all the detail that was wanted, fine things all round.

Half term brought a welcome break and Brian said:

I am off to Pullche Dee Bay or whatever you call it tomorrow if it's fine being half-term holiday you see. We (that is a school chum of mine besides myself) are going to start by the quarter to 10 tram to Oystermouth *and* then walk from there to pullch-Dee and neighbourhood along the road a distance of 3 to 4 miles or so and take our lunch in our pockets . . . Mrs. L. says that there is a Pub and refreshment house all in one where we can get some stone ginger (if we can make them believe we're bona fide travellers, if not we must put up with water).

The outing was a success for the following week Brian says:

The little affair down to Pwll-du (you see I know how to spell it now) went off. William took me to a great smugglers cave known as Bacon hole which is round the far away point of Pwll-du bay . . . The cash'm immediately in front is very deep, the cave is ¾ way up the cliff. The cave cannot be seen from the sea.
We walked down through the wood which was *very* pretty but not any more so than lots of places about Hereford.

In July Mrs Hatton took the little girls to Scotland to visit her relatives. Brian wrote that he wished that he was going too, saying, "I shold think they've got over the last [time] I paid them a visit, shouldn't you?" Unfortunately Mrs Hatton was taken ill while away and Brian was very upset when he did not hear from her. The correspondence between himself and his mother was like a life-line linking him with his family and he became agitated when the flow of letters ceased.

July 8th 1900
My dear Mother
How is it you haven't written to me this week. You must either be ill or somebody else very ill so that you haven't time or else you must be *very* dilitory . . .
On Tuesday, when I went to Mrs. Dennis's I over ate myself consiquently next morning in school during 2nd lesson I had to be a little sick in the lavatory, after which I felt quite well . . .

In Memoriam Ode to Oom Paul Kruger

There was an old man in Pretoria
Who was growing gloria and gloria
Until there came a big shell
Which sent him to Hell
And put in his place Victoria!

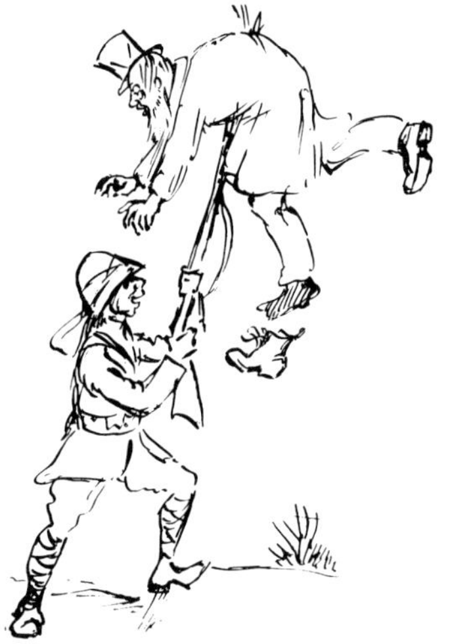

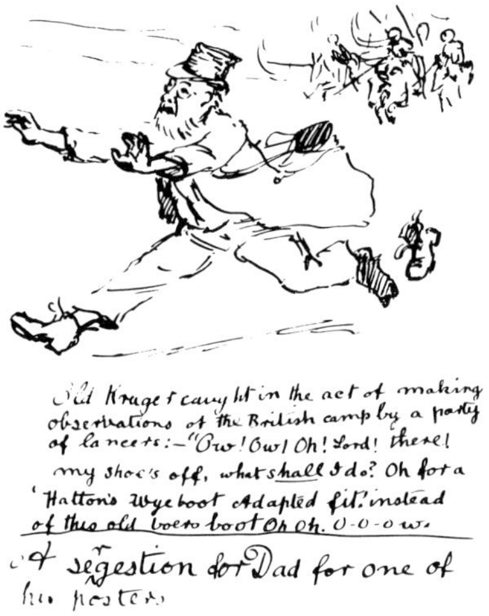

. . . give my love to everyone.
Your loving son
Brian

To his father, Brian says;

> You must excuse a short letter today as I have to write to Mum as well. What a nusance it is that she's not well. I had a postcard from her the other day, the first bit of writing from her for over a fortnight.

By the end of July Brian was feeling thoroughly neglected and to his mother he wrote;

> How is it that you haven't written to me again this week I should think you must be very bad indeed. I wrote to Dad last week but haven't received an answer yet not even from Mable so I'm not going to write this week I don't see why I should write to everybody and nobody write to me t'aint fair, no, not half.

Mrs Hatton was convalescing in Scotland when Brian returned home for the holidays. However, his father and Mabel were at Mount Craig to greet him, and there was a new puppy called Jess on which to lavish his affections. On 12th August he received a letter from his faithful friend Colonel Collins, who wrote to say that he had not forgotten his "little grouse's birthday". Curly was staying at Shrivenham at the time, but said that when he was back in London, he would choose a present for Brian, unless there was anything in particular he wanted. The Colonel had retired from the service of Princess Louise, but he was to become Gentleman Usher to Queen Victoria, and later to Edward VII and George V.

When Brian returned to Swansea in the autumn, Mrs Lancaster was recovering from what must have been a severe illness. It was therefore arranged that Brian should spend the month of October with a Mrs Elsworth, who lived nearby. He settled down quite happily and paid many visits to the Lancasters and the Doctor kept an eye on his health. In his first letter he describes his new living quarters:

> I have a very nice bedroom about 17 ft. long and 10 broad, with a large bookcase of 166 good bad and indifferent books . . . From my window . . . I can see the Pier, Docks, sea and Mumbles over the tops of the houses . . . I received a letter from Lord Battersea yesterday which I forward. I dont think it needs answering do you?

> Oct. 21st
> My dear Mother
> The New Portfolio is not a nice one as the others have been its mostly rough sketches of buildings etc in pen and ink by the best men from the French, German and Italian schools, but there are some very fine things by Albert Durer . . . I went for a ride last Wednesday and took a stick for the first time, the pony went splendidly and when I took her on the sands there were some more horses exercising and no sooner did she hear their feet echoing along the sands, when she fetches her feet under her belly gave one or two springs in the air and *flew*, without any exadgeration, she simply *flew*. There was no bumping up and down at each stride (like in an ordinary gallop) But she put down feet and picked them up again so quickly that you didn't know she was moving them at all, [all] you felt was a sensation of being pressed back over the crupper by the force of the air against your chest and stomach. However I didnt lose my seat or head [or] anything else and after about a mile and a half of this sort of thing I was able to stop her and for punishment rode her back as fast as she could go but nothing compared with the few seconds . . .
> For goodness sake give me an Idea of what to say to Lord Battersea. My love to all so buck up
> Your loving son
> Brian.

What an illuminating piece of writing is Brian's vivid account of his ride on the sands. One senses his complete "oneness" with his pony and the ecstatic joy which enveloped them both as they pounded along. Even Browning's poem, "How they Brought the Good News from Ghent to Aix", with its rhythmical beat, does not give a better picture of a horse at full gallop.

Mrs Hatton evidently assisted Brian over the difficulty of writing to Lord Battersea, for he says "I wrote to Lord B on the day you telegraphed merely adding in my letter 'thanking you very much for the Portfolio'".

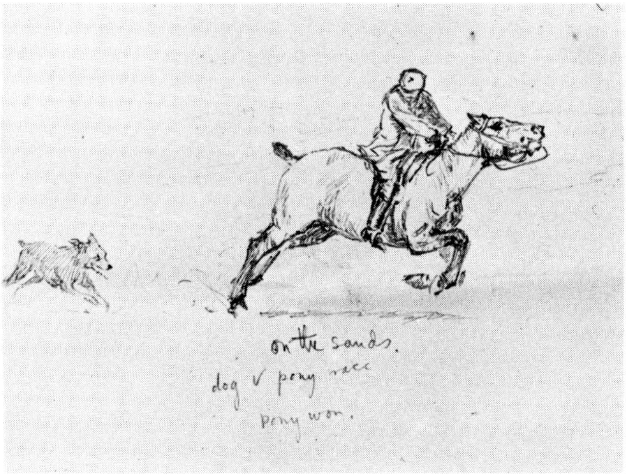

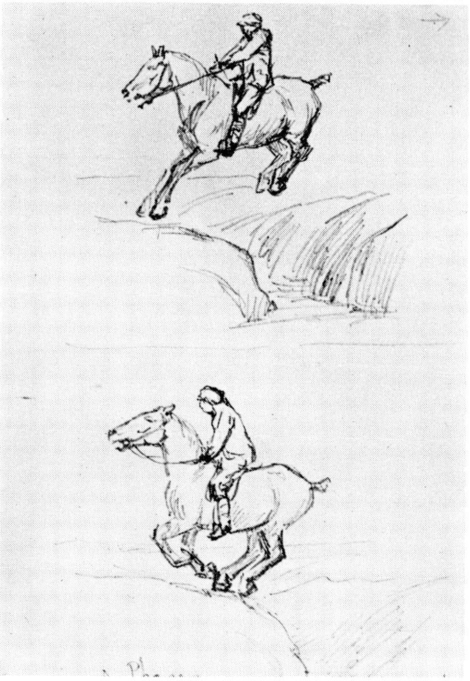

It may have been because Brian was missing the support of Dr and Mrs Lancaster that he got into so much trouble at school at this time.

> Last week was awful. I had four marks in all. 1 conduct mark from Davies down Gym on Friday, which landed me in evening Punishment Drill. 1 ditto from Ambi on Monday morning which ditto. 1 ditto from Hockin on Monday morning which put me in P.O. on Tuesday. 1 Detention from Hockin for not having done my homework to please him. So the consequence was that I was landed in Wed. P.D. for having over 3 marks in a week. Luckily it was a sea mist so I didn't lose much by having a half holiday taken. But I am going to turn over a new leaf (cabbage I think or turnip, I haven't decided yet) this week . . . Mrs. L. is much better as far as I can tell, And up a little every day.

On 4th November Brian writes to say that he is back at Winchester House. Mrs Lancaster is still not very strong but comes down to the drawing room every afternoon where she lies on the sofa until 8.30 p.m. A week later Brian says;

> I don't know if you see the *Chronicle* or not but it was in it some weeks ago. 'It' means that Mrs. L's brother who was out at S. Africa and who was shut up in Kimberley and wrote home a long letter of over 24 pages has been killed. At present Mrs. L. knows nothing whatever about it . . . I suppose you know Dr. Tup has typhoid. Had it for some days.

> Nov. 25 1900
> My dear Mother
> I had another Wednesday afternoon last week too but I hope it will be the last this term . . .
> I have no school news to tell you except that Dr. Turps is better, and that a boy in the fourth form upset a waste paper basket and when the master asked who did it he wouldn't own up even [when] he told the boys that he wouldn't punish them, if they owned up. But he wouldn't say and the consequence was that after school there was a whole mob (myself being one) waiting to maul him but somehow or other he managed to slip away unperceived by anyone. After school in the evening the same thing happened, next day it was discovered that he slipped away and left his bik at the school and some dirty cad went and punctured his tires so the boys evidently thought that that was punishment enough and felt more inclined to maul the boy who had punctured the tires than the boy himself. Anyway there was no mob waiting for him after school that day nor since.

Brian evidently considered that it was fair enough to carry out justice by "mauling" a delinquent boy, but puncturing his bicycle tyres was a "cad's trick".

At Christmas Brian sent some of his drawings to Colonel Collins who wrote to say how pleased he was with Brian's progress and how delighted he was to have them.

> I'm going to send them to Sir E. Poynter to see, and will write and tell your mother what he says.

He went on to tell Brian that he had taken a house at Hayling Island "where there is golf and other nice things". The house would have to be done up before he moved in, but it had a lovely garden and he hoped that Brian would visit him there from time to time, adding "your last two pictures will be framed and hung there. I hope you won't stop putting little pictures in your letters".

Although it is obvious that Brian had a full and happy life at Swansea and that he was on the best of terms with the Lancasters, he remained as closely linked as ever with his family and "dear little Hereford". It is true that he never liked school much, although he enjoyed the fights and scoring off the masters, but all his spare time was happily occupied. Back at Swansea after the Christmas holidays, he was still dependent upon regular letters from his mother.

> 3rd Feb: 1901
> My dear Mother
> I thought you said you were going to write twice a week, but I have only had one letter this week. I hope you are not ill or anything. I went to the theatre on Thursday evening . . . The piece was 'The School for Scandal' by Scheryden . . . I have done you a few sketches. It was awfully good and I enjoyed it awfully . . .

Brian goes on to describe the way Swansea paid tribute to the aged Queen who died on 22nd January 1901. His personal verdict that it was "an awful sell"; he aptly described what was an unimaginative and inept piece of organisation.

> Yesterday was a general holiday of course the whole school (including myself) walked in a dreadfully long procession comprised of 1100 soldiers, Board of Guardians, Foresters, Friendly Societies, tramway men and officials, Postmen and telegraph boys, Mayor and Corporation, Sir John Llewelyn and several big wigs, Grammar School boys and masters (in mortar boards and gowns) Salvation army, Doctors and clergy and officials and societies without end. I should [think] it must have been at least two miles long . . . Now all this crowd tried to get within the parish church. But by the time the soldiers were in, there were only 600 seats left so that two thirds couldn't get in at all, Grammar School lot amongst them which was an awful sell after walking all round the town 3 miles at least in water and slush at a snails gallop.

A week later Brian writes more cheerfully. He has been to a performance of "La Poupee" which he says was much funnier than the "Geisha" and that he laughed until he cried. As always, he is much occupied with riding.

> I went for a ride on Saturday and had a rare old time powthering up and down the sands, jumping a sort of wooden palisade . . . I started the pony at the lowest part and gradually jumped it higher and higher up till . . . there wasn't anything higher to jump . . . the sensation of up and down is simply lovely.

Mrs Hatton was naturally afraid that Brian might take unnecessary risks and therefore told him not to ride mounts which he might not be able to handle. But he did and his open nature made it impossible for him to hide this from his mother.

> I have been extremely naughty and disobedient for on Friday afternoon I was going to have a ride when at the last minute Old Small wanted the pony and in spite of my telling him what you said, made me take a mare, not the one that I told you of before but another one he has bought since then. It was a nice quiet looking chesnut and ten times quieter than she looked, for she sailed along at one uniform trot and it was with the greatest difficulty I managed to make her canter and then she went along like an old market horse three half pence and two pence. I want to know if I may have this one again when I cant have the pony, for I like the pony better for she has more life and tricks . . . and the mare is so tender mouthed you can pull her up with your little finger while the pony takes some

little strength and shows off nicely so that there is more fun to be got out of the pony . . . Please dont row me when you write because I've been rowing myself a good bit.

Again Brian managed to score a point against "Ambi", and this time with the help of the understanding Dr. Turpin.

My dear Mother March 17th 1901
How is it you have not written twice this week, I hope you are only lazy and not ill . . . The other day Ambi gave us so much homework etc that Mrs. Lan went to the Dr. about it. The Dr [Turps] said, it was impossible for me to do so much and strongly advised me to go to Beauland's class for French. (The IIIa and IIIb are divided into two classes for French. Ambi takes the more advanced lot while Beany takes the others . . .) I used to be in Ambi's but in consequence of too much homework am now in Beany's . . . It strikes me very forcibly too that if Ambi doesnt stop some of the homework that he'll find all his boys gone to Beany's class and he'll be left in the lurch. Serve him right too if he is!"

Village Horse Fair.
Pencil, 1900

Brian Hatton Gallery, Hereford

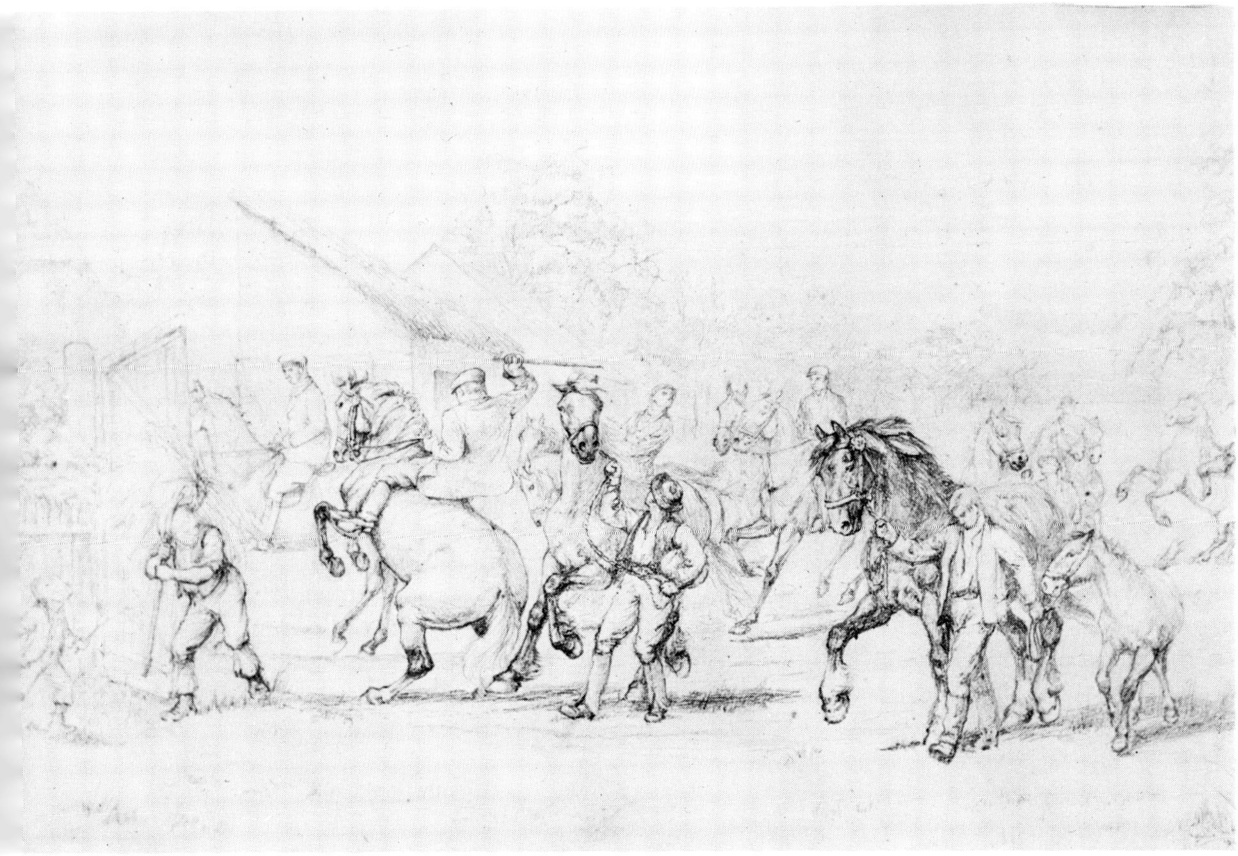

CHAPTER SEVEN

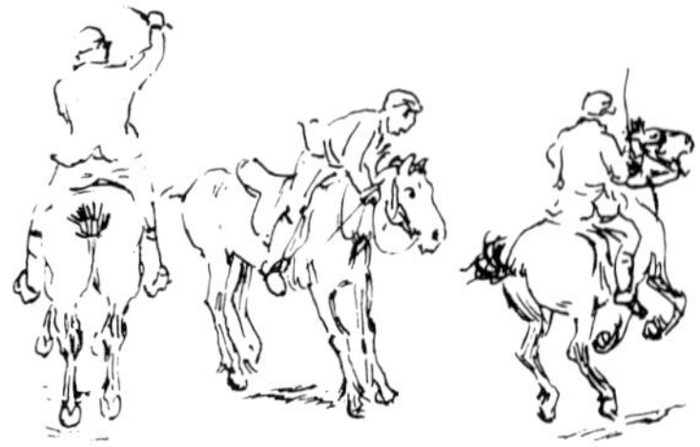

The Work Of A Prodigy

IN MARCH 1901 Brian sent his usual portfolio of work to the Royal Drawing Society. Again he scored a major triumph and this year there were to be strange repercussions. Brian was now 13½ years old and although his work was astonishingly mature, he still remained as modest and unassuming. He wrote home saying, "What do you think of the R.D.S. result this year? I never expected anything like it; for in my own mind I didn't think I had improved much".

Brian had won six prizes including the Silver Star offered by the Clothworkers Company, his chosen study from nature being a nearly life-size watercolour of a sheep's head. Two pen and ink drawings, "Mazeppa" (an illustration for Lord Byron's poem) and "Tam'o Shanter", won Lord Leighton's prize and the memory drawing from nature which was a water-colour called "Carting Sand", gained the G. F. Watts prize.

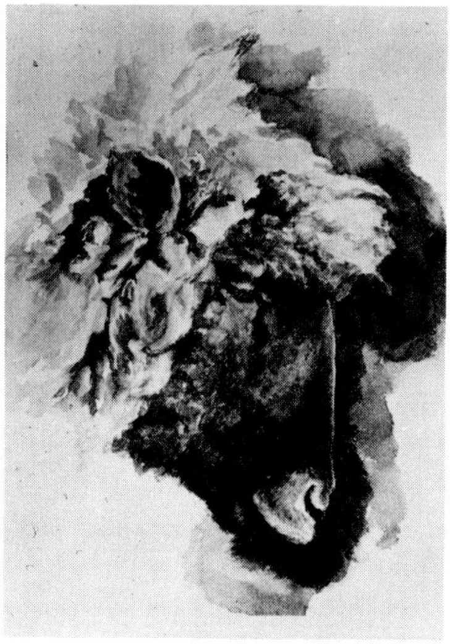

Sheep's Head.
Water colour, 1900. 11¼″ × 9¼″
Brian Hatton Gallery, Hereford

Mary Watts wrote to Mrs Hatton, saying,

> Now the portfolio has just been, and Brian's 'Carting Sand' has gained admiration and his (Watts's) prize. One other drawing ran it hard so he will also give a prize to young Bunbury's 'Stage Coach'. But between ourselves Brian is still unquestionably first and the poetic sentiment of 'Carting Sand' is a very interesting development of his work.
> I do hope he is pretty well and growing stronger. We watch his career with the greatest interest. Will you help me to get him the prize he would like?

It was the water-colour entitled "Carting Sand" and the drawing "Mazeppa" which caused such wide-spread interest and admiration and later — controversy. They are both remarkable works by any standard and it is indeed difficult to believe that they were executed by so young an artist. In "Carting Sand" one can sense the convincing movement of the two horses straining against their heavy load as they move up the beach, while the sea breeze lifts their manes from their necks. There is something quite terrifying about the vigour and movement of the wild horses in "Mazeppa". This work, together with other drawings and water-colours of Brian's, was chosen by Mr Ablett, the Director of the R.D.S., to be sent to the Paris Salon. They were first taken to Buckingham Palace and shown to King Edward and Queen Alexandra who expressed great interest. At the Paris Salon, Brian's work attracted the attention of President Loubet, and the International Congress of Drawing Teachers said it was "the work of a prodigy". An annual publication, "The Year's Art" made a whole page reproduction of "Mazeppa" and gave a short account of Brian among the list of outstanding works of the year.

It was in November that trouble began about the authenticity of Brian's memory drawings. Mr Hatton received a communication from Mr Ablett, enclosing a letter from The Hon. Lyulph Stanley, Vice-Chairman of the London School Board, which was at the same time both flattering and grossly insulting and must have caused Brian's parents considerable consternation.

> 17th Nov: 1901 — 18 Mansfield Street, Portland Place.
>
> Dear Mr. Ablett,
> I have to thank you for the copy of drawings from your twelfth annual exhibition. Many of them are remarkable and some extraordinary. I should like, however, to know the conditions under which Brian Hatton's 'Mazeppa' and 'Carting Sand' were produced; much that seems a power of original drawing may be combination of memory work from copied drawings. A boy fond of drawing animals may get a number of horses in various attitudes from the picture books and then combine these horses in a composition.
> In order to test his power of original drawings, I would like to have the candidate in an examination room and set him a subject in order to see his real form. I should like to tell him to draw the same sand cart going away at the same angle as it is shown advancing, so too I would turn round the figure of Mazeppa and let him draw it from the other side and the hind quarters, and a foreshortened view of the rearing horse in the foreground. This would test better his grasp of the animal form and bring out whether he was reproducing some drawing or really using his memory and observation of the real animal . . .
>
> Yours sincerely,
> E. Lyulph Stanley.

Mr Ablett took the attitude that it was "very flattering to have raised such doubts" and thought it might be a good idea to give conclusive proof of Brian's ability. He suggested that Brian might like to make a drawing in the presence of some responsible person who would certify to its authenticity.

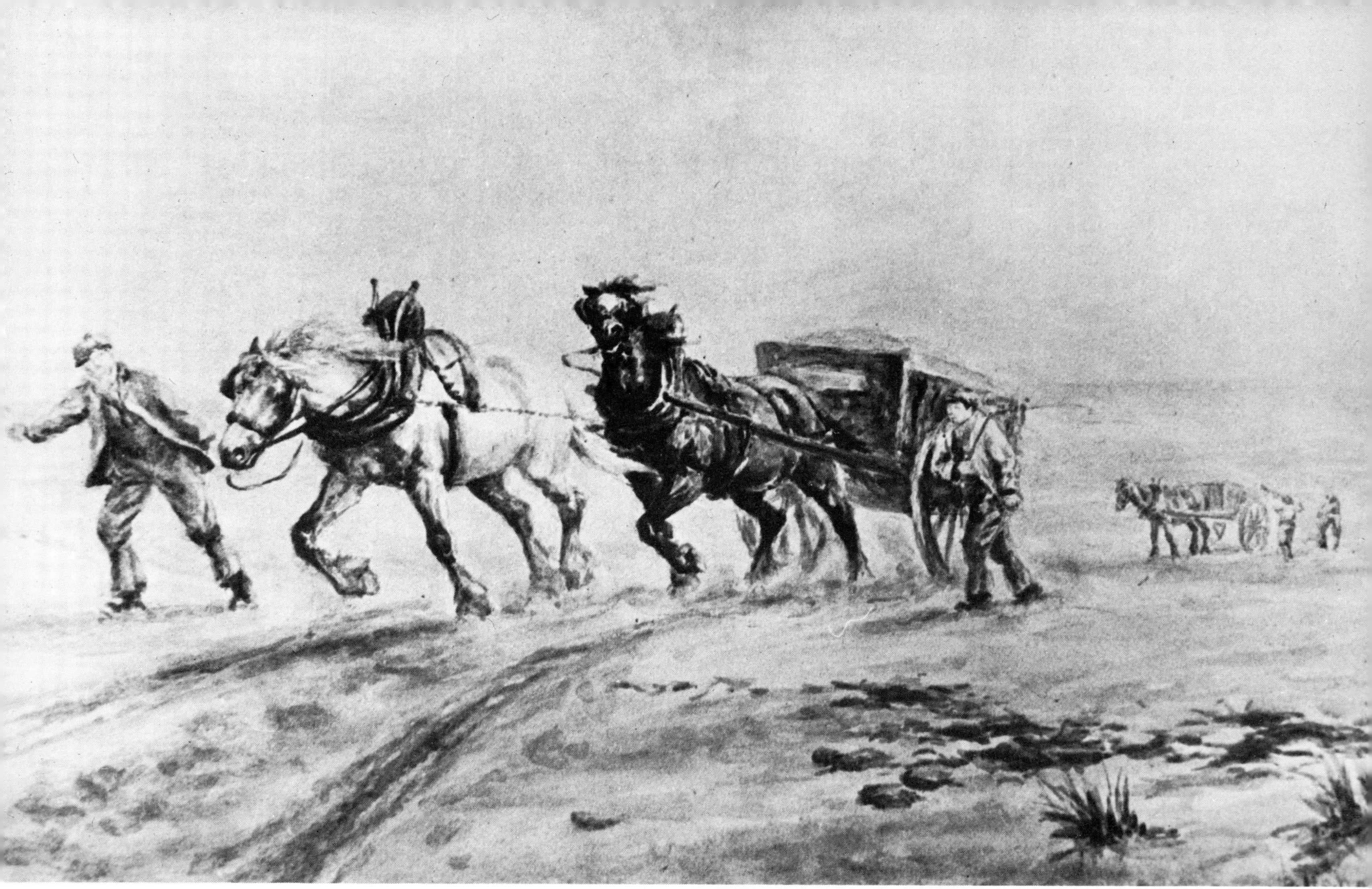

Carting Sand. Water colour, 1900. 9″ × 13½″

Brian's friends took a very different view of the matter and rallied to his defence, and Dr Lancaster went into action on his behalf and wrote the following letter to Lyulph Stanley:—

Dear Sir,

Your letter to Mr. Ablett re Brian Hatton's drawings.

On account of his health Brian Hatton lives for most of the year in my house at Swansea, virtually I am his guardian and have had the opportunity of watching him do much of the work that he has exhibited at the R.D.S.

You refer more especially in your letter to two pictures, 'Mazeppa' and 'Carting Sand', and you express some doubt as to the genuineness of the methods employed by Brian in his memory work. Mazeppa he drew at his home in Hereford, I can therefore only answer for Carting Sand, which was done in my house and was *solely* the work of Brian Hatton. He drew from his memory — the memory of a scene on the seashore some 1½ miles from this house which he had watched in varying phases during the autumn afternoons of 1900. There is no one here capable of helping him, he had neither copy or pictures, as I certified on his drawing to be a definite fact; viz the fact that he drew from memory and not from copy. I cannot speak as having any knowledge of art; but speaking as an anatomist may I say that your suggestion that the anatomical correctness of the particular attitudes of the two horses (the result of the correlated actions of numerous muscles) could be obtained from a combination of several positions selected from picture books is I think scarcely feasible.

He is at present doing a water-colour of Sanger's circus horses. The circus was here for two days in the summer; he went both evenings to watch the horses being watered; a few days later he began drawing the scene and has not yet finished colouring it. The only assistance of any kind that he uses being rough sketches that he himself has made from the living animal in field or stable, and all his memory work is done in this manner.

Brian Hatton is no ordinary child and is not (acting on the advice of G. F. Watts) being educated by the ordinary methods.

If you wish to have the most conclusive proof of the genuineness of his drawing, I should be extremely pleased to at any time give you the opportunity of seeing the boy at his work, and I must ask you to accept this in lieu of compelling the boy to draw under forced and artificial conditions; for him to do his best work he has to have absolute freedom to follow his own impulses. As a Physician I have no hesitation in saying that his mental powers are far nearer those of genius than of talent. He has great gifts, only those who know him well can realise how great; and it would not be conducive to his present or future interests to in any way falsify his work.

With apologies for the length of my letter, I am Sir,

Yours faithfully

E. C. Cronier Lancaster (B.A., M.B. Oxon etc)

"Brian is no ordinary child". That was the crux of the matter and Dr Lancaster was prepared to go to great lengths to convince the critics of this fact, and also to protect the boy from anything that might interfere with his artistic ability.

Poor Mrs Lancaster was quite overcome by the fact that anyone should cast doubts on the ability of her beloved Brian. She sent a copy of her husband's letter to Mrs Hatton saying that he thought it would be a good plan to send a copy to Mr Ablett,

> . . . if you think so, please copy it out and send it. I am just weary of writing and cannot trust myself to write to Mr. Ablett. All he says about the R.D.S. is all very fine, and I don't want to forget the advantages it has given Brian, but we cannot have the R.D.S. interfere with him.

Curly took the same line as Mrs Lancaster. He looked upon Brian as his especial protégé, an honour that he was only willing to share with G. F. Watts, and he had a fine contempt for the London School Board and anyone connected with it. He wrote a characteristic letter to Mrs Hatton.

> 28 Nov: 1901 — 24 St. James Street.
> Dear Mrs. Hatton,
> I confess I side entirely with Dr Lancaster: Brian is not a board school boy and it is quite immaterial what Lyulph Stanley thinks about his work. The fact is Brian has been a mine of wealth to Ablett, and he has boomed him accordingly, and I dare say thinks the boy's talent comes direct from himself! If you take my advice you will tell Ablett you are quite satisfied the drawings were done according to the regulations, and you cannot have Brian's time taken up by these unnecessary tests — diverting him from his other studies. I think the whole thing rather impertinent after what Mr. Watts has written about his work, it is ridiculous these Board School people questioning it.
> Yours sincerely
> A. Collins

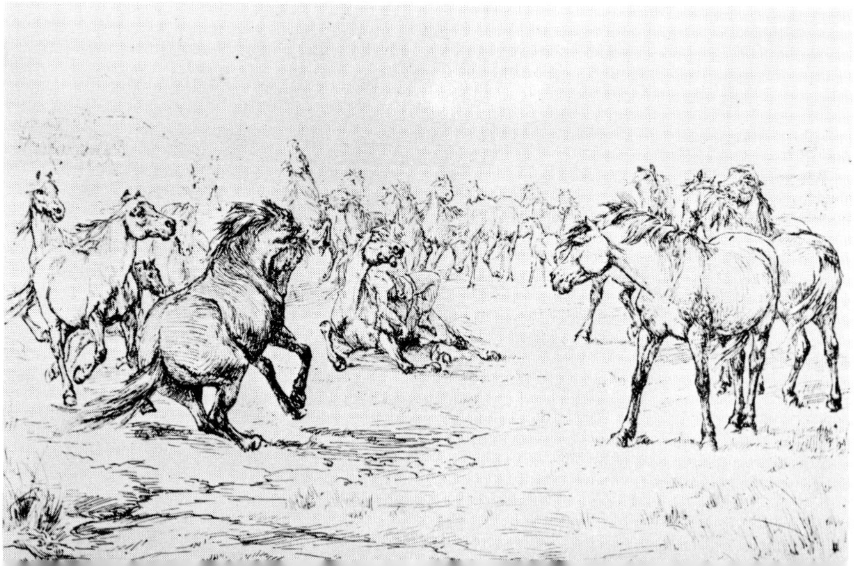

This unfortunate episode came to an end when Lyulph Stanley replied to Dr Lancaster's letter. He accepted that Brian was a boy of remarkable power and should be left free to carry out his own ideas and impressions, but he could not resist giving some schoolmasterly advice!

> I think that if there is a wish to test his power no harm would be done by an occasional exercise of a special character, e.g. to draw foreshortened the same subject which he had drawn from a different point of view.

It was in April this year that Brian got his first commission for a drawing. Curly wrote to his mother saying that his friend, Miss Chappell, had seen some of Brian's drawings and she wanted to know if he would make a sketch for the title page of a song to be published by Metyler & Co. The song, which was by Paul Rubens, was called "A Very Dark Knight". Curly sent the words of the song, saying:

> A knight will appeal to him . . . I think it would be an incentive — not that he needs any — to know that he can get a little money for his work.

Brian decided to make a pen and ink and sepia wash drawing of a knight on horseback. He said, "It would have to be a very dark affair altogether, so I *must* have a bit of the moon out to catch his armour and throw him up". Curly was delighted with the drawing, saying that it was "quite remarkable, he is a real genius if ever there was one, and the best of it is he isn't the least conscious of it". He expressed displeasure at the poor reproduction of the drawing and asked if he might keep the original. Brian was paid two guineas for his work. He said he would save up the "chink" until he got more and then "buy a bic or a saddle". The song was sold for 4/- and Brian used to play and sing it at the piano. It became one of his favourites, along with Scottish ballads, Lewis Carroll and Harry Lauder. He loved music and would suddenly break into song when at work on his drawings. He was a perfectionist about music and could not bear to hear anything badly rendered. He said:

> The other day I sang One Fish Ball to the Dr. & Mrs. L and now of course she's got it on the brain (all out of tune too). I am learning one of Beathoven's easy little sonatinas. Mrs. Lan's Dachshund has arrived . . . a most commical little piece of goods.

About this time Mary Watts wrote to Mrs Hatton to say that a friend and neighbour had asked if she could buy one of Brian's drawings. She had seen some of his work at Limmerslease which she admired, saying, "some day that boy will be a famous painter". Mary asked diffidently whether Mrs Hatton would be willing to part with one of her son's early works. Brian's output being so prolific it is more than probable that she was willing to do so.

Mazeppa.
Pen and ink, 1900. $9\frac{1}{4}'' \times 13\frac{1}{2}''$ *Brian Hatton Gallery, Hereford*

Brian was doing a lot of life drawing at this time. With the help of Dr Turpin he persuaded Sergeant Bird to come and pose for him. Brian described him as the best model in Swansea because "his muscles are so evenly developed all over". He made a drawing in red chalk and Dr Lancaster said it was the best thing he had done so far. "Next time he is going to bring his foils so that we can have some fencing attitudes." A week later Brian says;

> I did Bird in this attitude on Sunday: just preparing to fight, next time I do him in the engage, next time in the lunge and so on.

These fencing studies would be useful to Brian when he was depicting tournaments and jousting and the medieval scenes his romantic nature revered. He wrote to his mother, saying:

> I read Tennyson's Lady of Shalott the other day and I think I can see a picture in the description of Lancelot riding by and surrounding country, etc. You ought to read more Tennyson than you do I think his poems and descriptions are so nice; perhaps wanting a little in force and strength now and again but it's hard to be perfect. George Sangers Circus was here last Friday-Sat.

One would have thought that Brian had such a full life that there would be no spare time for fresh hobbies, but this was not so. On 30th June he wrote:

> I have become an entomologist or in plain English a bug hunter, I only collect Moths, Butterflys and Beetles and preserve miscellaneous creatures in spirit. It gives me a much greater interest in taking walks etc . . . Cedric, Elton, Dr and myself went down to Jersea Marina this morning early and Cedric *and* I found a heap of insects and Dragon flies etc (also . . . some sticklebacks all of which I have bottled) while Elton and Dr found some shells.

A fortnight later Brian says:

> When Cedric was here I caught a lot of caterpillars of the Peacock butterfly they turned to chrisilis soon after I had them and today I found them turned into the most beautiful butterflies. I kept 8 and killed and set them, the majority I let fly away.

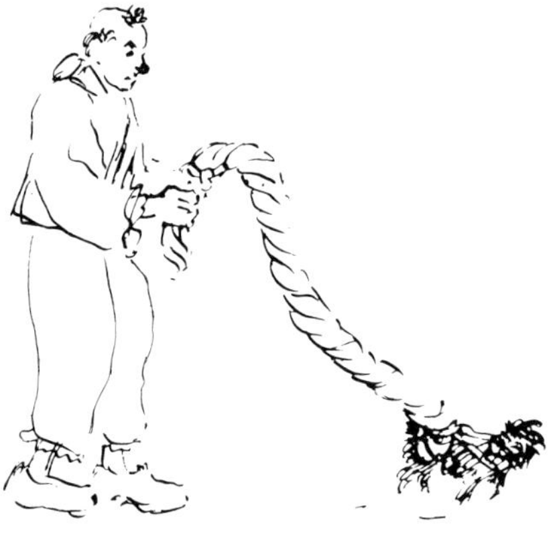

Elton had returned to live with the Lancasters that summer and had become a pupil at the Grammar School. At the beginning of term Brian remarked that "Elton likes school all right so far but I am afraid the tune will be changed in another fortnight". The old friendship continued and the two boys had a lot of fun together.

> Elton and I went to Chyne Valley this afternoon and had an awful lark climbing trees and hauling the dog up with us etc became Devilish thirsty and of course all the Pubs were shut not a drop to drink Abominably! . . . Elton has had some Plastacine sent him, it's rather decent stuff much easier to mould than the wax . . . I should like to model a knight on horseback *when* I have time.

It may have been Elton's "plastacine" which made Brian so keen on modelling about this time. In November Mrs Lancaster wrote to Mrs Hatton saying:

> I'm longing for you to see his 'model' work this term. We think they are just lovely, and I'm inclined to think will convince them more of his talent at the R.D.S. than anything he has yet done . . . You must send three or four of them, whatever the cost.

Both Curly and Mary Watts wrote to Brian for his fourteenth birthday. Mary had taken her ailing husband to Scotland — quite an achievement — but she had time to write Brian a long letter.

> August 7th 1901 — Dalcranbie
> by Achnabot
> Inverness.
>
> My dear Brian
> I have an idea that the 12th August is your birthday so . . . I hope this will reach you about that day and give you our love and may we hope you are going to have as many and more birthdays (and do as much work too) as Titian or Mr. Watts! We are hoping he may have as many as Titian — 99!
> We often think of you here and wish you could see the highland sheep, they are so pretty and climb about the hills and the rocks almost as well as goats . . . Mr. Watts is very well and has a nice little house for painting in, standing on the moors near our house . . .
> We saw some wild goats the other day and hope to see highland cattle soon . . .
> On your birthday, if it doesn't rain in torrents, we are going to picnic on the moors, with the shooters . . .
> We have such wonderful white water-lilies on a loch here. I am sure your mother and aunt would love them as I do. They are so pure with their golden hearts and lie so calmly on the water when the wind allows them, and yet riding so bravely over the rough waves. One does not wonder that they became a very sacred parable from east to west. Heaven above them, and its colours reflected all around them, and the splendid strong roots and stems holding the sap. We row amongst them sometimes, but I don't like to see the boat going over them.
> I do hope your mother is better. Will you give her my love.
>
> Your affectionate friend
> Mary S. Watts
>
> Do you read about Arthur and his knights? There is a nice book called Legends of King Arthur by James Knowles, I think you would like.

One wonders what impression Mary Watts' letters made on Brian. Already she had welcomed him into "The Kingdom of Art" and now her descriptions of the beauties of nature had a distinctly sanctimonious flavour. As we know, Brian was also a past master of the art of description, but sentiment never distorted his vision.

Brian continued to show a fine contempt for authority in the form of schoolmasters. At the opening day of the autumn term he was delighted when the new headmaster (understandably nervous, perhaps) came to grief in the Lord's Prayer, saying "give us this day our daily . . . trespasses". Of another new master he says:

> He's an awful idiot, keeps on saying 'Fold!' 'All Fold!!!' meaning to fold your arms, then Stand! Sit! Forward March! Out. In short he's the most dithering idiot under the sun!

Brian even managed to score a point against the sergeant when doing Punishment Drill.

> We had an awful lark. Old Sargeant made me lead (being an old hand) and he was too lazy to say wheel so we all went bumping into the wall, made him awfully ratty.

The boys were asked to vote as to whether the School should play Rugby Football or Soccer. Brian said, "Rugby did the trick, with a huge majority. I stood up for Rugger because it's most fun". Among his other activities he was now having dancing lessons, and he sends home some sketches of Miss Gaydin the dancing mistress, saying "she is very funny". She is certainly a very solid looking lady with an hourglass figure and she pulls up her skirts a few inches to show her feet in the fifth position. A week or two later Brian says, "I can now waltz".

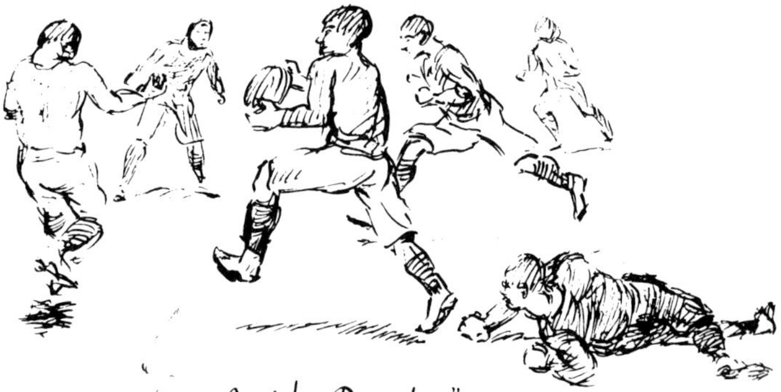

"An Irish Rush".

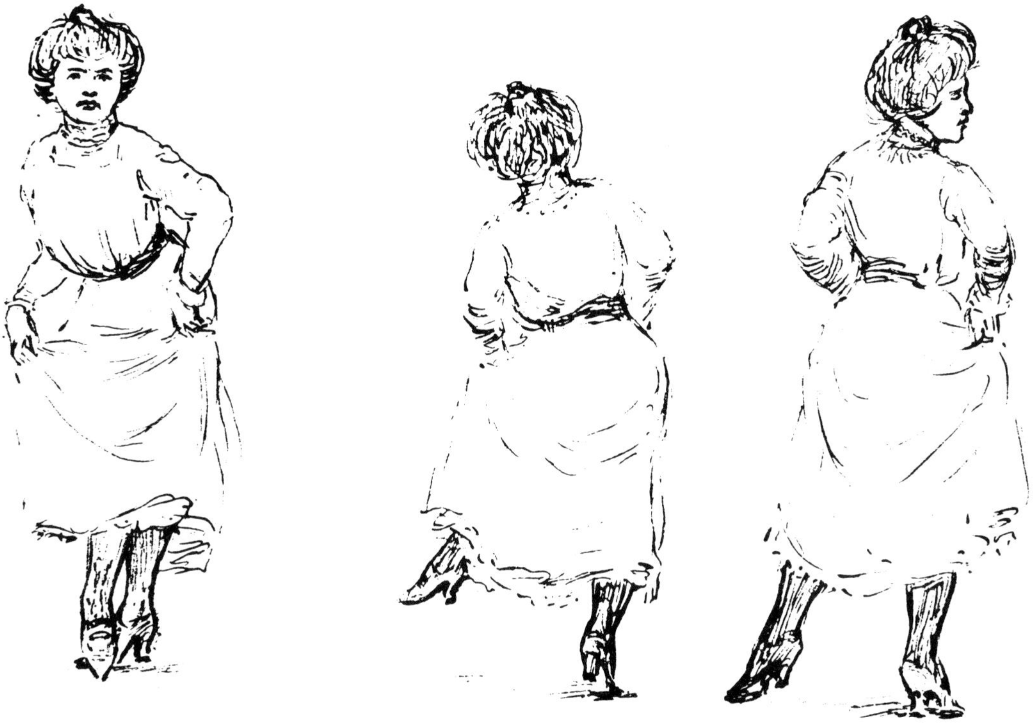

Mrs Hatton was busy organising some family theatricals to take place in the Christmas holidays, but Brian was doubtful about the part he had been allocated, and wrote:

> I am not quite sure about acting, will you kindly let me see the part and play 1st. I dont think my figure is adapted for the part, I think I'm too big.

A week later hc said;

> I was very glad to hear you could manage old Benjiman's part for me. I suppose it rather put you out having to make new arrangements . . . but still I really couldn't think of being Will, fancy me as an elf, you want a little critter about the bigness of a flea, à la Ion or Frank.* Imagine me falling down on my knees to Stella. Oh yes, very exceedingly, no no Mrs. H. that little gime wont work, oh no not a bit of it . . .
> P.S. Write more often there's an angle, no I mean an angel.

*Ion and Frank were cousins.

CHAPTER EIGHT

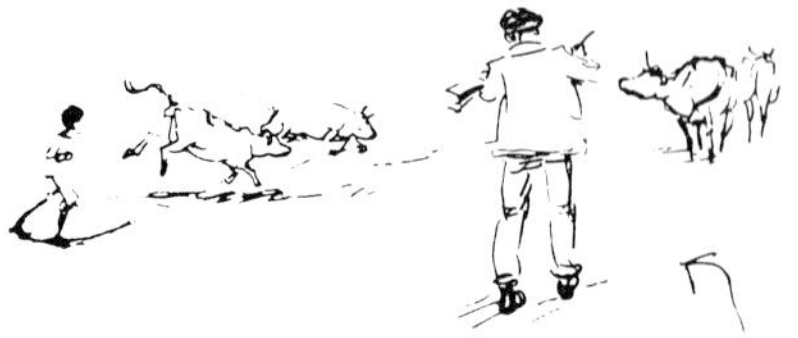

Paying Visits

IN JANUARY 1902 Brian returned to Swansea after "a very comfy journey". At school he was sorry to find that his form master had left and been replaced by, "an awful old fogy named Kirby, a most peculiar weak eyed individual. I will sketch him when I have more time to observe his peculiarities . . . I don't altogether what you might call enjoy my extra French Tu' in fact if I heard that Monsieur thin-a-me-bob had give up the Ghost I don't think I go into sackcloth and ashes".

At present there have been no punishment drills and Ambi is going to teach him Italian. There has been an outbreak of small-pox and Brian has been vaccinated but says, "I didn't kick my heels up (much to Eltons disappointment)".

Portrait painting now seems to be Brian's chief preoccupation. He started on a life-size water-colour of Elton, with disastrous results. There was a defect in the paper and water made it come out in spots, and "poor E. looks as if he had small-pox". Lizzie the cook was Brian's next subject but she was not a very satisfactory model. "You see she doesn't get much time off while the light is good and hates sitting." The next victim was Mrs Lancaster. Brian said that she had "Invested in a huge turbanish hat (see sketch) quite different from her usual little hats with half a bird in one side of them. She now looks like a giddy little actress". He went on to say that Mrs Lancaster was reading a play aloud to him, perhaps while she was sitting for her portrait. The play was "Ulysses".

> A play now going on in London, by Stephen Phillips, one of the coming poets the author of Herod, it is very interesting all about the Gods and Ulysses and Penelope his wife and suitors etc much as you read it in Homer. The poetry language is very beautiful. When we are up in London we might have a squint at it, what say you it will certainly Helevate my mind much more than San Toy etc. Mrs. L. is very keen on my going . . . So if we go you would do well to read it before hand, and if you cant get it at the library Mrs. L. has volunteered to lend you hers because it is only just out.

Mrs Hatton illustrated some of her letters to Brian with some animal drawings about this time, much to Brian's delight. He writes;

> The 'cat' which you drew in a letter about a fortnight ago is an elegant animal so full of life and go etc. Shows such observation such knowledge of the animal and all contained in a few but exquisitely delicate lines; but without joken Mrs. H. it only shows that you could draw very decently if you liked. Then I suppose, you say, 'Ah the spirit is willing but the flesh is weak'. Well there you are — I discreetly leave a blank.

It is hard to believe that this is a fourteen year old boy criticising and encouraging his mother's artistic efforts, rather than the other way round. A little later he says; "Your quack quack was splendid, pray restimulate yourself to further efforts".

When Mrs Hatton sent Brian a sketch of a new hair style she had adopted, he approved of both the drawing and the new coiffeur.

> According to your sketch (such a gloss depicted in so few flowing lines) your hair must be 'illigant'. Anything almost would be a relief after the other coffee-er or whatever you call it . . . I have started modelling a trotting (horse) in the red wax in fact it is quite ⅔ done, it has to have a support up the middle as the one leg isn't strong enough.
> Elton is and has been in bed for some days not at all well. Last night Mrs. L. had to sleep in my bed and I had to sleep with the Dr. in a FEATHER bed. Awful rot.

In March Brian was in serious trouble at school, and his mother wrote to him in some distress, asking for an explanation she said, "I think I know everything about you so do not be afraid to talk to me about it all tomorrow when you write to me". Brian replied in his usual candid fashion without endeavouring to cover up his misdeeds. He explained how he had failed to do a Latin exercise, so borrowed a crib from another boy . . . "instead of altering it a bit I like the silly fool that I was, copies it down word for word, so that I was found out".

Brian was reported to Mr Owen, the head master, who gave him "a jolly good lecture" and some Punishment Drills. It seemed that Brian was not taking the full school curriculum, but Mr Owen said that unless he improved his ways he would have to go back to the ordinary routine. Brian told Mrs Lancaster about his troubles and she went to interview Mr Owen . . . "She jaws and he jaws (for he's Welsh) and they both jaw . . . and they both decide that I shall go back to ordinary school." This arrangement would leave Brian less time for drawing, and he said, "it put me in a huff and I swore I wouldn't do a scrap of work (although I have done some)". Brian went on to say that he got into a "don't care way" and in Punishment Drill he became "what the sergeant calls 'insubordinate' and let my tongue wag". He had a great contempt for the sergeant who he said was often drunk, "topples about and turns up late". When the sergeant reported Brian and several other boys to Mr Owen, Brian said, "this riled us awfully and I openly derided his orders . . . besides calling him a sneak to his face". Brian was a born rebel for he admitted that he found this way of behaving "more entertaining and exciting than the ordinary way of acting while at school". However he said that he would try and mend his ways. He had another talk with Mrs Lancaster who said she would see Mr Owen again and see if Brian could go back to his old school schedule. In return Brian promised to reform and try not to get so many Punishment Drills. He ended his letter:

> Your very loving and to be a better Son
> Brian.

Term ended with no more trouble and Brian returned home for the Easter holidays. For a long time Colonel Collins had been trying to arrange that Brian should stay with him at his house on Hayling Island, and now the long awaited visit was planned for the latter part of April.

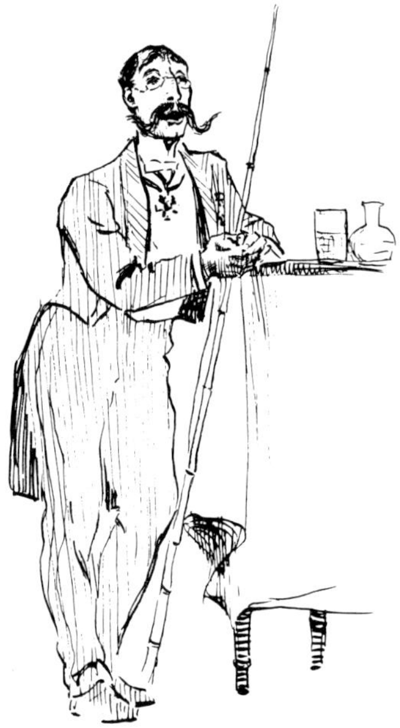

The Colonel was delighted with "Cow Leaze" which was a peaceful retreat from the pressures of Court life. The place was surrounded by great elm trees and the garden abounded with roses; nearby was a farm with fine barns which Curly felt sure would interest Brian. He wrote to Mrs Hatton saying:

> You may be sure my house-keeper and myself would take every care of him . . . Though I have seen little of him, his charming letters make me feel I know him very well and I am sure on his side he would feel at home with me.

As it turned out, the visit, which was the first of many, was the greatest success, although poor Curly had some anxious moments. He wrote to Brian's mother, saying:

> It was very nice having him and I think he enjoyed the visit. He looked dreadfully tired on arrival and frightened us all in church on Sunday by nearly fainting — a kind of seizure. However he was quite a different boy when he left me, having been out of doors all day.

Brian certainly did enjoy the visit. He went on to London to stay with Aunt Ada Vevers at Lancaster Gate and from there he wrote to his mother,

> I had a bee-oo-tiful time down with Curly. His brother's wife and niece were down there when I arrived but only stayed till Mon morning. He is Sir Robert Collins who was knighted not so very long ago . . . He is an awfully springy old chap, jumped a funny little low 5 barred gate on the way from Church, rather a jolly old boy though *of course* not as nice as Curly . . . Hayling is just by Isle of White between Portsmouth and Chichester, about 15 miles in circumference, not one hill, plenty of wind and singularly, plenty of trees . . . Didn't golf as it rained in morning when we intended to play and hadn't time afterwards (Thank Goodness) so did pen and ink of farm buildings and cart etc out of window . . .

Did small water colour of distant farm, meadow and trees. Col: delighted with it, he wanted me to do something of his garden but I didn't, too finicky. Met boy name Bob Mens, gave me some bugs etc . . . I went out birds nesting with Bob and Curly and newt fishing also bike rides. Curly rides a Tric as he cant bic . . . When we arrived at Victoria the King arrived and drove off amid much excitement, crowds of people to see nothing but a carriage and pair drive off like lightening, nothing visible of the king at all.

Brian spent a few happy days in London while awaiting his mother to join him before going to visit Mr and Mrs Watts, and he kept her informed of his activities.

April 24th 1902 — 64 Lancaster Gate,
London.

My dear Mother
I was only able to give you a very hasty scratch last night and I'm afraid you wont get much more today. Aunty A and Maud and myself went to the Wallace Collection this morning, it's simply A.1 topping as Mabel would say. Ever so many suits of armour men and horses I shall take a book and sketch next time I go, as you are allowed to, I did some scribbling in the fly-leaf of the catalogue this morning.
This afternoon I stayed in . . . and did a little pen and colourwork drawing, very effective without much work, while Aunty Ada sketched me, splendid likeness . . . For goodness sake make haste and come down. I [want] to show you lots of things and want you to come with us to Uylses . . .
Your very loving son
Brian.

Mrs Hatton duly arrived in London and on Saturday, 26th April, she and Brian travelled down to Guildford in order to spend a few days at Limmerslease with Mr and Mrs Watts. Brian was always at ease with artists, and the disparity of age between himself and "Signor" troubled him not at all. They all forgathered in the studio on Sunday morning and Watts discussed anatomy, technique and the basic structure required for picture making. A human skeleton was brought in and Watts explained the similarity of bone structure between horse and man. He said that Brian's drawings were very dexterous, but it was important for him to gain complete knowledge of structures. He therefore advised the boy to give up picture making for the present and devote himself to drawings of minute detail. On looking through some of the sketchbooks, Watts came across a profile drawing of a cart-horse's head, and to illustrate his point, he outlined the nostril in pencil. He wished to emphasise the eloquence of the nostril in a hard-working horse.

Watts told Brian not to worry if his drawings looked laboured, tight or niggled. Later on he could work as freely as he liked. Rembrandt, the greatest master of painting, had started in this way.

While Watts talked, Brian was making an anatomical study of a horse. After looking at it, Watts went across to Mrs Hatton and said, "He is a born artist, he must take a high place."

Mary Watts continued to keep in touch with Mrs Hatton and after this visit she wrote:

> It was so interesting to me that you say Brian felt that Signor had opened his eyes. It is exactly what I have always felt he does do. So different from any other teacher I have come across — they too often want you only to see how they would draw or paint. Signor makes you see for yourself.

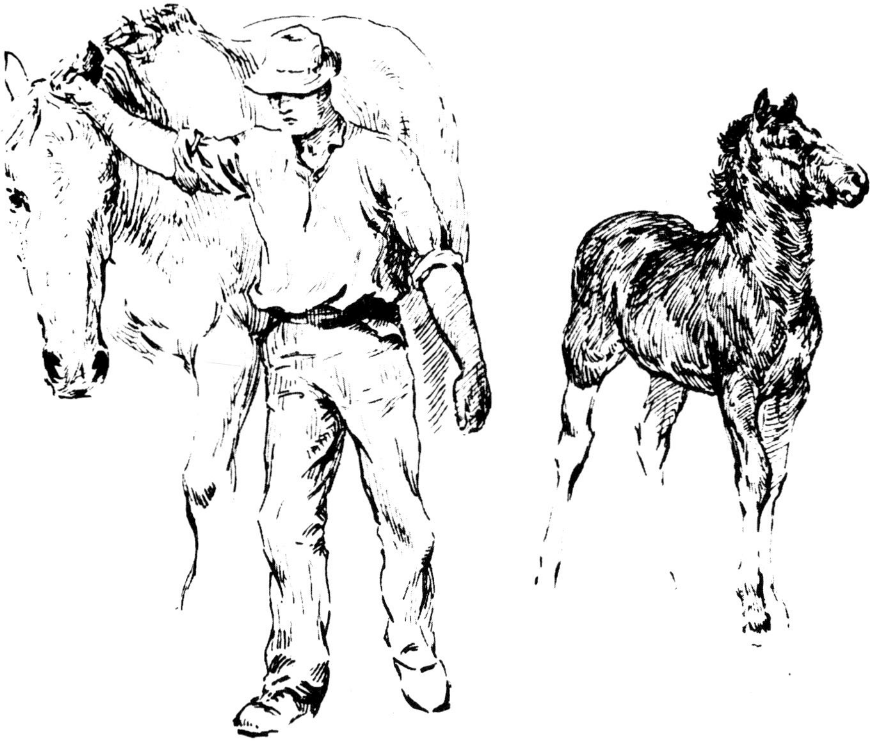

Man with Mare and Foal.
Pen and-ink, 1902.

Brian Hatton Gallery, Hereford

Mrs Hatton sent some of Brian's more recent drawings and these delighted Watts, and Mary wrote;

> Signor is *charmed* with the drawings . . . He can't resist *the foal*, also he tells me he thinks the *careful* drawing leads to the successful easily done and perhaps *better* result. Brian is quite right in his instinct to do both . . . He says you need have no anxiety though I feel sure that is impossible. When one possesses a fine Kohinoor *uncut* one wants every facet to be perfect!

In another letter Mary said that her husband would love to have one of Brian's drawings to keep, and of course Mrs Hatton gave him one. Mary wrote and said that the drawing was always in the studio and that Watts showed it "with *such* praise to anyone who can appreciate it".

It was probably this drawing that Anne Thackeray Ritchie refers to in her "Notes of Happy Things" in which she describes a visit to Watts's London home, Little Holland House. She writes;

> The most charming thing was his delight over the work of a boy of sixteen* — Brian Hatton, I think the name was. I have shown it to Riviere, he is perfectly astounded, says Watts, look at the instinct for beauty, look at the sheep lying in the grass, look at the child sitting in the twilight; it is like Sargent.

Brian returned to Swansea for the summer term, and spent the first weeks of August at Porthcawl with the Lancasters, before going home. None of his letters for the next twelve months have survived, but he was in close touch with Mr and Mrs Watts during this period. Curly wrote to him in August saying that he was tired out with his involvement in what he called "this tiresome coronation"; the false one in June, cancelled when the King developed acute appendicitis and the real one in August. He told Brian that he had purchased Cow Leaze and now that it was his own he liked it more than ever, and was planning to plant more rose trees. On 27th December he wrote, thanking Brian for yet another drawing, saying,

> You are our English Millet . . . I can't tell you how much I appreciate your work; 'Even Tide' my favourite of all.
> I am sending you a pencil case; it is of the best metal we are supposed to possess, but it might be of diamonds and then not be worthy of you and your art.

*Brian was fourteen when he made that drawing.

CHAPTER NINE

The Unique Little Man

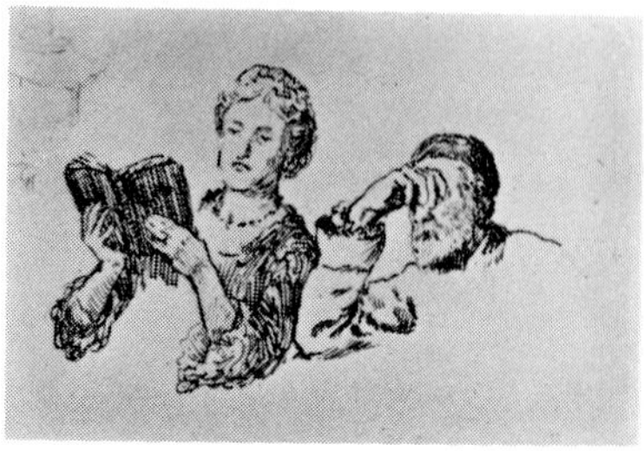

IN FEBRUARY 1903, when Brian was in his sixteenth year, Mrs Hatton received a request from Philip Gibbs asking for a photograph of Brian, together with one or two of his drawings. He also asked for particulars of his "career" up to the present time, as he wanted to write an article about him for a new publication called *Men and Women*. Mrs Hatton, with her usual caution, consulted Curly on the matter. He wrote advising her to "grant this man's request" provided he submitted a proof before publication, saying that the article would be of interest later on when Brian became famous.

In the spring, Mrs Hatton sent a parcel of Brian's drawings for Watts to criticise. He returned them with a long letter full of praise and suggestions as to the best way to plan for Brian's future.

> May 13th 1903 Limmerslease, Guildford.
>
> My dear Mrs. Hatton,
>
> All so absolutely right and so certain of success that I have nothing to say or advise . . . I think his schooling should be completed but he should not be kept over long at it; for the real schooling he must depend upon, he must get from his own observation and thought . . .
>
> I have shown Brian's drawings to several of the best judges and influential people; all agree with me that it is most undesirable to push him in his work, especially in the way of taking it up professionally and making money by it at all at present. Nature has endowed him in an extraordinary manner and he may — should! — become the greatest artist England has had. I should hesitate to say anything so strong but I think both you and he are too sensible to be injured by it. I want you to feel that nothing but serious accident bars his way to the highest place, there is nothing that anyone can teach him and nothing for him to do but observe and think . . .
>
> I should advise that the next few years be given up to healthful pursuits and enjoyment of life; his future is absolutely certain. I do not like his selling his drawings just now . . . I do not like to say do not sell anything at present, but I feel very strongly it would be a desecration of his great endowments to in any way identify them with the idea of money, until the time when he will work professionally . . . He should observe and draw and paint as he did when he was 3 years old, never thinking about the future (which is insured) at all . . . If he were my son I should like to see him idle, only laying in a store of health, enjoying all that youth and life can give him, so preparing for the great place intended for him.
>
> Very sincerely yours,
> G. F. Watts.

Mrs Hatton must have been profoundly moved when she received this letter from one of England's most revered artists. Watts had such unquestionable faith in Brian's genius and ultimate success; at the same time he seemed haunted by morbid fears that some dark fate might overtake him, before he achieved his goal. It is curious that he should disapprove of Brian selling his work when he sold his own drawings at the same age.

Brian and his mother paid a visit to London in July. They spent a great deal of time in the company of Watts and his wife, looking at the work taking place on the huge canvases in his studio and admiring his new statue, "Physical Energy", which stood in his garden.

There was a memorable day when they drove in a carriage and pair with Mr and Mrs Watts, visiting the Chapel of the Ascension, in Bayswater Road, which was decorated with paintings by Frederick Shields, and then on to various galleries to view works by Doré, George Harcourt and others. Brian did not think highly of Frederick Shield's work but was delighted with that of Harcourt and Doré. Mary Watts hinted that they should feel greatly honoured to be seen driving through the streets of London in the company of Signor. It seemed that he seldom made such expeditions; certainly wherever they went, great deference was paid to the unique little man in the black skull cap.

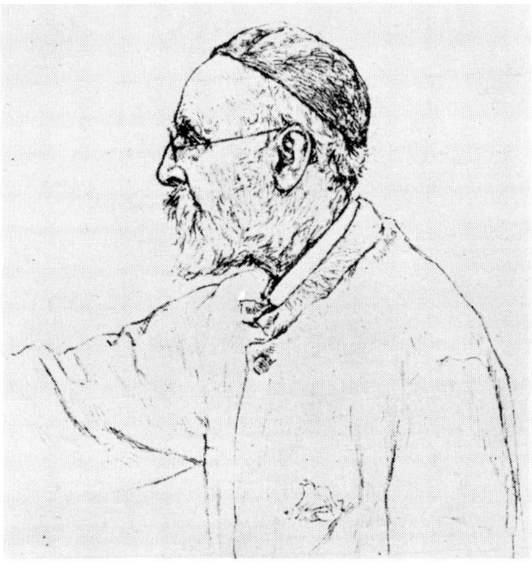

G. F. Watts, O.M., R.A.
Pencil, 1902. 8¼" × 5¾"
Brian Hatton Gallery, Hereford

Brian made a drawing of Watts and also a charming little pen and ink conversation piece of Mary reading aloud to her husband.

Mary was delighted with the pencil drawing, saying that it was a true likeness and every line well felt.

> Nature has equipped you with a fine pair of antennae and I know you will feel out the highest use for them.

"The highest use" apparently did not include payment for work done. About this time an acquaintance of Watts' was very anxious to acquire one of Brian's drawings. However, as Watts was so strongly opposed to the boy selling his work, Mrs Hatton suggested giving her the picture. Watts did not approve of this idea, saying that the woman was "the wife of a rich Brewer and always on the look out for a bargain!"

When they left London Mrs Hatton gave Watts some of Brian's most recent drawings for him to study at leisure. He returned them with the following letter.

> August 4th 1903 Limmerslease, Guildford.
> Dear Mrs. Hatton,
> I send back the drawings . . . I have shown them to several persons of importance and influence who still watch Brian's progress with great interest, all agree with me in my estimate of his very great natural endowments and my opinion that if he has health, fame and fortune await him and it would be well to delay as long as possible plunging him into feverish competition and the connection of money making with his fine powers, a connection which greatly injured Landseer and Millais, and destroyed Sir Thomas Lawrence all together. I feel a real anxiety on this point for I want Brian to take a greater position than any English artist can claim, for I know it has been given to him to raise the English school of art to a point it has not yet reached; of course he cannot fail whatever happens; but his place should be the very topmost. The great thing at present is that he should lay in a good stock of health and vigour and give all the time now to the enjoyment of his young life.
>
> Very sincerely yours,
> G. F. Watts.

Watts himself might appear to be a frail old man but he well knew what a great amount of vigour and physical staying power is required by an artist in the carrying out of his work.

Brian had found the London visit something of a strain. The weather had been very hot and he and his mother were glad to return to Hereford at the end of July. They arrived just in time for a large family wedding, after which they went off to stay at the Esplanade Hotel at Porthcawl. Brian didn't seem very well and was starting a cold, but presumably the sea air and a rest would soon put him right.

Brian celebrated his sixteenth birthday on 12th August at Porthcawl and the following day he suddenly became very ill. After five anxious days, Dr Lancaster came to the rescue. He pronounced that Brian's illness had been wrongly diagnosed and that he was suffering from typhoid fever and peritonitis.

It was decided that Brian should not be moved to a hospital. He stayed on in the hotel and Mrs Lancaster undertook the nursing with the help of Mrs Hatton. Mrs Lancaster was a qualified nurse and had great faith in her own ability, saying "I think it is the only thing in my own personality that I am really conceited over". Dr Lancaster remained in charge of the case.

There was, of course, tremendous consternation among Brian's friends and admirers when they heard of his illness. Was this to be the end for all their hopes and beliefs in the boy's brilliant future? It was not until the end of August that Mrs Hatton could bring herself to write and tell Mary Watts of Brian's illness.

Both Watts and his wife were deeply distressed by the news. Mary rushed out to send a pre-paid telegram asking for the latest bulletin, and on the way home she went into an empty church where she could sit quietly "communing with all that was spiritual and comforting". Not only did she and her husband send their sympathy and love to Mrs Hatton; they sent practical help in the form of a cheque for £20. Mary described this generous act as "a little thing we can do which will give us a great deal of selfish pleasure".

There followed many anxious weeks. Although Brian could not be described as a robust boy, his resilient nature came to his aid and with the help of the careful nursing he made a complete recovery. In October he left Porthcawl and went to the Lancasters where he stayed convalescing until Christmas. As soon as he arrived at Winchester House a barber was sent for and Brian wrote:

> My head looks quite rational again. We had to hire a waggon and 4 horses to cart away the clippings thereof.

Slowly Brian regained his health. He wrote home, saying, "I haven't been doing much painting as I am generally out most of the morning. I dont feel up to standing much in the afternoon". He started painting in oils but he did not take kindly to this new medium.

> On the whole I don't find oils as easy as water colour, I don't seem to be able to mix the colours so well to what I want . . . it's rather rot being beaten by a few dirty tubes of paint, but they are very unmanageable.

Brian spent a great deal of time out of doors, but of course he always carried his sketch book with him.

> Nov. 8th 1903
> . . . There is a very pretty little donkey and it's mother on the old links at Black Pill, it is hardly as big as one of Sammy's dogs, I was trying to sketch it the other day, while Garth was sniffing round it evidently under the impression that it was another dog. Suddenly the old mother charged and knocked Garth rolling over and over, trampling him under with her fore feet and if I hadn't come to the rescue he would certainly have been killed.
> I heard from the Dr. about his criticisms of my drawings and have been trying all day to explain to him what atmosphere in a picture means, he thinks its something to do with expression of faces.

> Dec. 8th
> We went to a lecture yesterday evening. The later Greek sculptures . . . It seems that the Greeks always exercised and played their games etc nude — both men and women . . . which of course gave the painters and sculptors a great pull over the modern one. The nearest approach we have is the swimming baths, seaside and river of course. Tomorrow night we are going to hear Dr. Dollinger on 'Are the Planets Inhabited?'

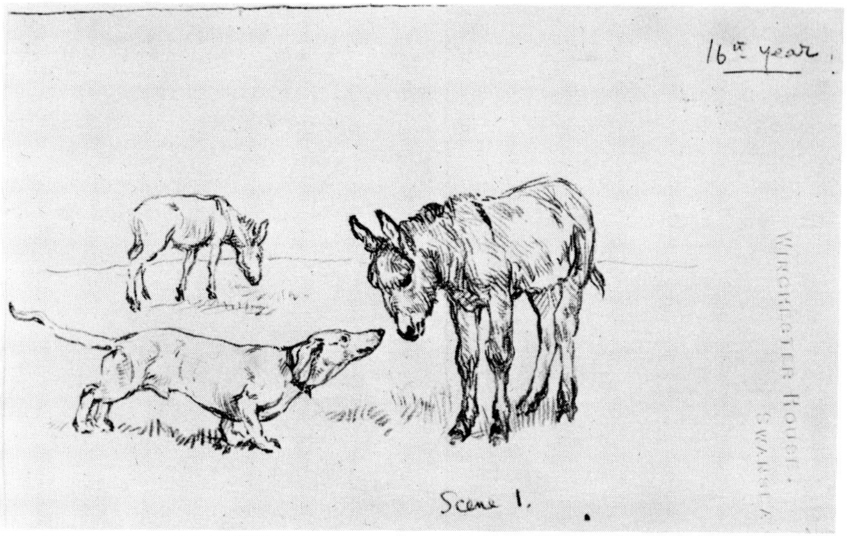

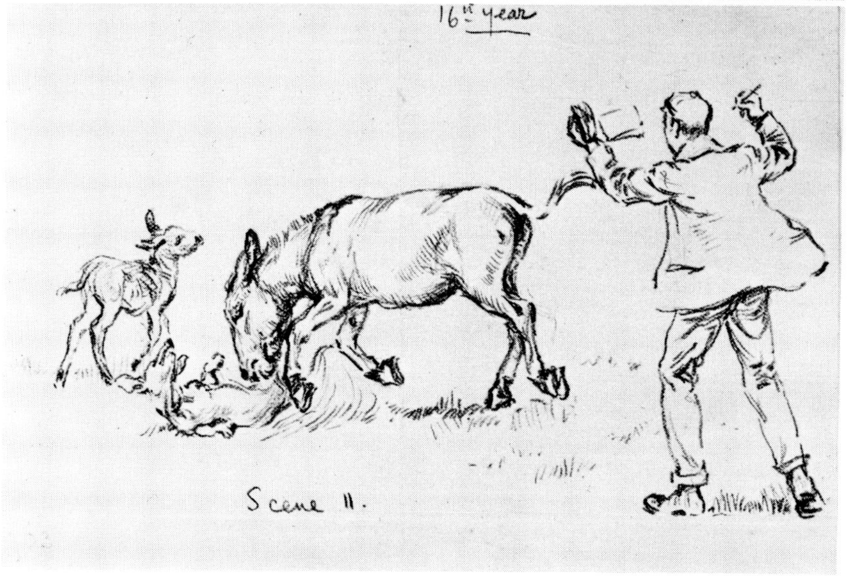

A few days later Brian wrote;

> Dollinger's lecture was very interesting. Mrs. L. and Dr. dined with him before the lecture. Mrs. L. was very careful what she said and marvellous to relate did not expose herself to ridicule . . . The other lecture at the School was even more interesting to me. The lecturer, Haskett Smith was more than huge, I have made some sketches of him. When he was at the Egyptian Museum at Alexandria (or Cairo) they were renewing the disinfectants of the Mummy of Rameses the Great and had removed the glass case. So when some of the officials weren't looking, Haskett Smith very gingerly shook hands with the great king.

Brian found a new diversion of which he sent his mother a full account.

Dec. 19th 1903

The Dr. and I have been amusing ourselves with Planchette the last one or two evenings. It is rather wierd if you believe it all. Yesterday we got a message from John Mentumen, a Russian artist who lived 123 years ago. Said he wrote the messages by means of a spirit flying in the air. Wouldn't show himself . . . (Of course all this was answered to repeated questioning and sometimes written in Russian and Polish so that we couldn't understand a word). There were at times 7 spirits in the room (!!!) among them Ada Lancaster (who Dr. said was very much alive when last heard of) and a William Jennings who murdered Mentumen for money. By the way Mentumen said he had two persons, one of which was in heaven doing better paintings than on earth and he knows Dr. Vevers he said, but although he gave Marjorie and Ailsa's ages said he did not know them. He also gave Dad's age and Mrs. L's (much to her disgust) and that the other person was the spirit 1 . . . He liked 'Carting Sand' best of my work so far. That I would fulfil Mr. Watts predictions but wouldn't be a great painter in oils, best in water-colours and pen and ink especially in water-colours . . . When asked if I would be a great artist, would only write 'men say so'. That I should go to Oxford, to Oriel (one of the oldest and finest colleges). That I should have 2 horses and a motor bike later on. My next horse ride would be in March. But would have it that I shouldn't go home before January 2nd. (which I don't like at all. We are doing our utmost to make it wrong, hope you will too.)
He said his spirit was going to remain in my room all night (which I dare say it did, he didn't disturb me, however, unless it was he who slammed the door and flapped the blind once or twice, but I put it down to the wind) . . . It wrote the result of the Test Match in Australia correctly long before we got the paper.
All this is what happened. The Dr. says he never moved the thing once (and he's not the sort to tell a lie . . .) and I never moved it once. Mrs. L. of course scoffs at the whole thing, consequently the instrument will often stop or run off the table, or scribble away like a baby and it generally turns out that it was angry — and being asked with whom, always wrote — Annie. We once asked why we should suffer because of her — it wrote — I don't know. Evidently spirits are just as fickle and inconsiderate as we are . . .
Dr. and Mrs. L. think of going down to Cornwall for a change after Xmas, St. Ives or somewhere down there, offered to take me, said yes for my part, next best thing to Japan, ey! . . .

Love etc.
Your loving son
Brian.

Brian's fame was beginning to spread abroad. A Mr Spielmann, who was a friend of Watts and the editor of a magazine called *Art*, asked to see some of Brian's work with a view to writing an article about him. When some drawings were sent to him, he admired them for the sincerity with which they were executed, saying, "What strikes me most about them is the earnest purpose and care and the complete absence of any attempt to be 'clever'".

Unfortunately Watts heard about the proposed article and wrote to Spielmann, asking him not to write about Brian, lest the article disturbed the quiet in which he wanted the boy to mature and develop. Mr and Mrs Hatton were understandably annoyed at this interference on the part of Watts, and Mrs Lancaster said she was extremely disappointed. She pointed out that Watts did not know Brian as they did and that he had not taken the slightest interest in the proposed article, one way or the other.

Although Brian was rapidly regaining his health, Dr Lancaster continued to watch over him with care. In order to avoid a set-back he thought it would be advisable to take the boy to Cornwall after Christmas.

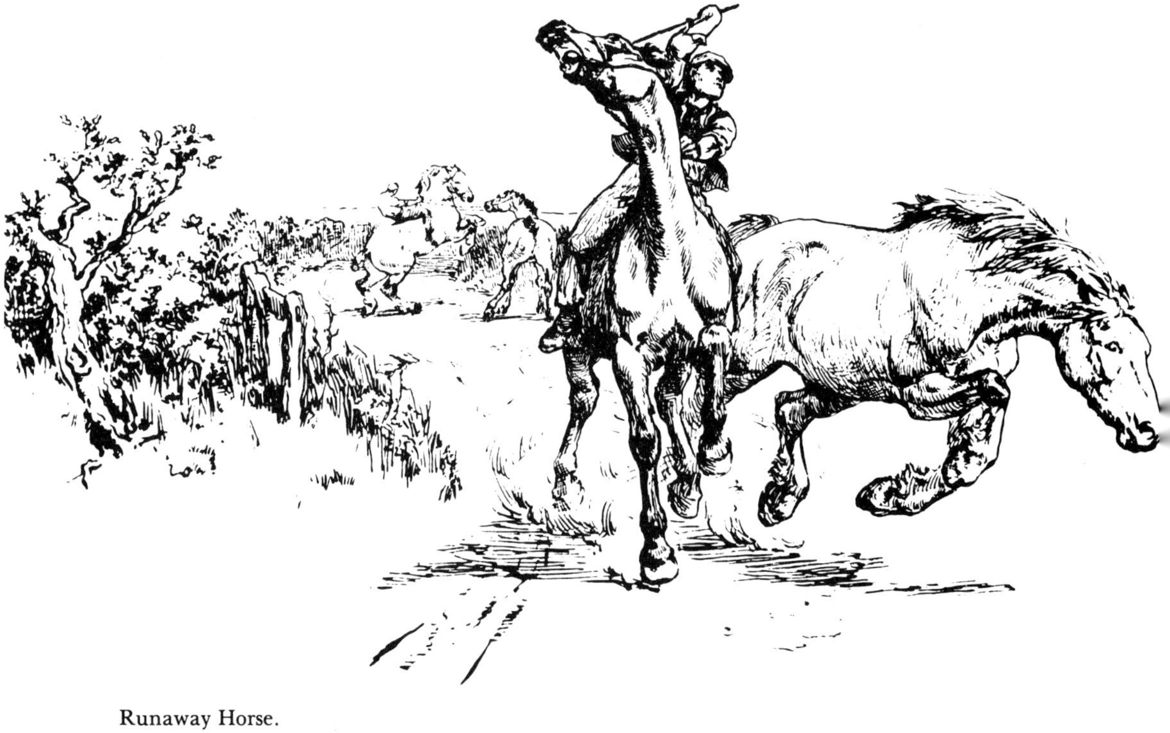

Runaway Horse.
Pen and ink, 1906. 10″ × 13″ *Brian Hatton Gallery, Hereford*

CHAPTER TEN

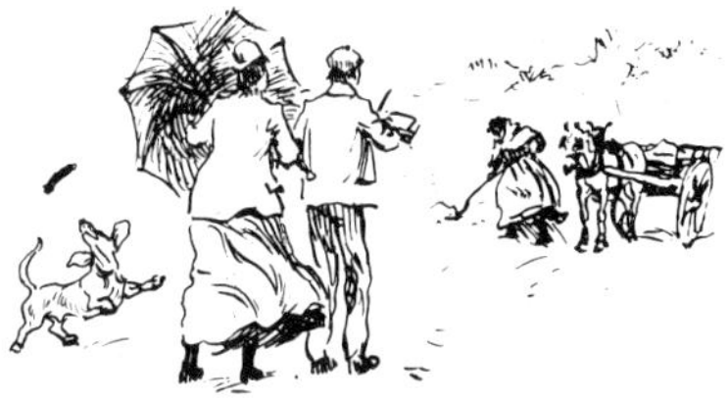

Cornish Interlude

IN THE new year Brian and Dr and Mrs Lancaster set out for Cornwall. They spent a month in a small hotel at Carbis Bay where they enjoyed the privacy of their own sitting room. Brian's impressionable mind was delighted with his new surroundings, and he was fascinated by the Cornish sea which he described as "a lovely green with very white foam, quite different from Porthcawl or Swansea". This was the heyday of the St Ives and Newlyn school of painters and during his stay he met a great many artists, men of a younger generation than Watts, who were beginning to think in different terms about art and painting.

Brian's first letter describes his impressions of St Ives and as usual his observant eye took in much that interested him.

Jan. 8th 1904 — Hendra's Private Hotel,
Carbis Bay

My dear Mother,
I am quite well thank you, had a very comfortable journey. When I got here it was pitch black dark and of course Dr. led a short cut to the hotel up a steep stony path, it was like stumbling along in a nightmare . . . This morning we went into St. Ives by train. It's about the rummiest place under the sun. I don't think there is a single street in which two carts could pass one another. Dr. Lan. pointed out any amount of studios, about the dirtiest little hovels in the place (and that's saying something), they all bear legends on the door such as 'Ye White Studio' or 'Ye Green Wave Studio', which was at the entrance of a passage. We went in, treading carefully amongst filth and refuse, but could only see a broken cow shed and a quantity of washing in a stinking court. There were however a number of decent places with huge windows let in the sides facing the sea . . . We find that artists are busy now and don't like people going over their studios unless they buy.

Love to all
Your loving son
Brian.

Brian complained that the posts were "rather awkward". He had to be sure that he posted a letter before 11 a.m. if his mother was to receive it first thing in the morning. If he posted it later in the day, she would not received it until the following afternoon!

The other day we went to Penzance and Newlyn, it sea misted and driving rain the whole day. However we saw the Art Gallery, some very nice things by Stanhope Forbes and others of the Newlyn School. We mucked about round the

harbour in the rain, but could see nothing for the mist. I can understand the 'Newlyn Grays' now. Saw a dim outline of St. Michaels Mount from the train, think of going over it soon.
Mr. Russell Dowson has just called, very nice old boy, has his studio in a back alley somewhere by some shops by some cottages round some corners somewhere by the market place which is somewhere by the church which is duff in the middle of St. Ives. I hope I shall find it. He has asked me to lunch on mutton chops.

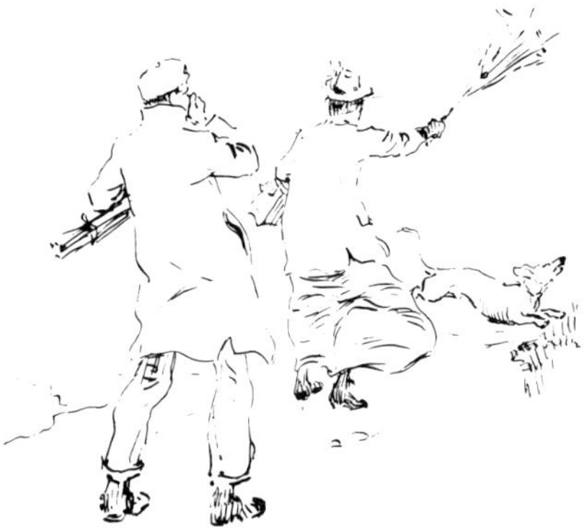

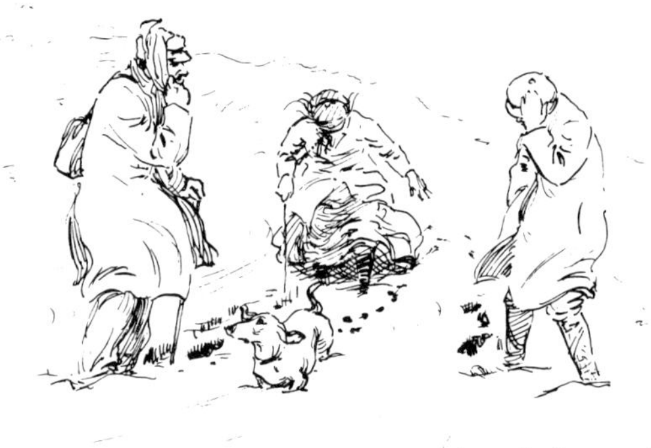

making haste to the ferry through the sand storm.

Brian spent a very happy afternoon in Dowson's studio, watching him enlarging some water colours in oils and gained some useful hints. He was now getting to know other artists.

On Wed. went to Norman Garstin in Penzance, lunched. He then showed us the Art Gallery . . . and afterwards introduced me to S. Sherwood Hunter (painter of figure subjects in Holland, Jerusalum and elsewhere), where we had tea.
Thursday morning went to Newlyn and saw Hunter's studio again in daylight and then Stanhope Forbes who showed me his classes and Studios. Saw the pictures he was trying to finish in time for R.A. — fisherman in boat waiting for Pilchards — and a lot of his studio. Hunter strongly disagrees with Watts about my not being trained. Garstin opened his eyes pretty well too. Forbes also disagrees but wouldn't attempt to argue with Watts.

It was not until the last week of their holiday that Mrs Lancaster discovered that there was an artist, a Mr Girdleston, living in their hotel. She showed him some of Brian's sketches and he was charmed with them, saying that Brian had caught the movement of the sea. He became very interested in the boy and said he would take him into St Ives and introduce him to some of the artists living there. Mrs Lancaster was anxious that they should be aware of Brian's full capabilities, so she wired to Mrs Hatton, asking her to send some samples of Brian's work.

Mr Girdleston was as good as his word and Brian wrote:

> This morning he took me to see Julius Olsson who is considered to be about the best seascaper nowadays. Saw some lovely things in his studio. Girdleston told me he works at an awful rate. He has before now painted a 6 foot canvas in 12 hours that, with a few finishing touches when dry, was ready to be hung on the line at the R.A. I took the few little bits of seas that I had done down here with me. They liked them more or less but of course it didn't give them a fair idea and that why we want some of my horses etc down here with me, because when Arnesby Brown and Alfred East return (from London) after this Academy election . . . Girdleston will take me to see them and I must have some animals to show Arnesby Brown.

Brian knew that his best drawings were of animals, especially horses, which were his first love, and it was only natural that he wanted these artists to see what he was capable of. Eventually he met nearly all the artists in St Ives. There was one called Bromley "who is a water colour man and had the best water colour in the Academy last year". There was Louis Grimes "who had some awfully nice things but seemed rather a queer customer", there was "a young fellow named 'Talmage' and one named 'Hobkink' with his mother, a Red Headed Baroness Ferina-Faron!!"

Brian's drawings arrived from Hereford and Girdleston took him along to meet Arnesby Brown and Alfred East and another artist named Mead.

> East was very encouraging, said he hoped to see me an R.A. some day. Saw some lovely huge landscapes of his that he is getting ready for the Academy. Arnesby Brown had two awfully nice pastoral subjects . . . One of them a drove of cows coming over a bridge (such as you see over the Lugg and similar flat country all round) in late afternoon light more or less behind them; they looked very fine and hot and dusty. The other was a Hay wagon and men and a boy haymaking in evening light full on them, but with chequered lights from trees. But I liked the cows best — Brown thought like Watts that I ought to go on with education now and not take up art to study it in ernest just yet. Mead didn't say much but wanted me to come down and settle at St. Ives, as a good many artists would be only too glad to have me put animals in their landscapes.

The Lancasters had prolonged their Cornish holiday in order that Brian should have the full benefit of meeting so many artists. Their devotion to the boy and their pride in his artistic ability were all important factors in their lives. Mrs Lancaster wrote Mrs Hatton a long account of how Brian had plunged into the art world and of the impression he had made on these established artists. She described Mr Girdleston as a very remarkable, clever man.

> On Monday evening the Doctor and I went in alone to ask him what these artists thought of Brian's work. He said that they were all very encouraging to him, he saw about ten altogether I think. They liked his horses best, one went so far as to

advise him to stick to horses and specialise on them (which would be a great mistake at present). They also liked his seas. They admired his drawing and said it was excellent but they did not like his landscape work, they said the colouring in it was weak, in fact, said Mr. Girdleston, at present his colouring is very poor. I must tell you that the general opinion was that he should study later at some school such as Bushey or Paris. They said he would learn in three months what it would take him years to learn by himself, and that in these days no one would interfere with him or attempt to influence his work. Mr. Girdleston asked particularly how he was being educated and highly approved of Oxford . . . The artists that Brian met on Monday were the men that will be his judges in the future, the present A.R.A.s or R.A.s and one felt down there that there was calm dispassionate judgement. They were kindness itself to him and said he was full of promise, but it was the old story, only education and work will give him his future success . . . promise even at 16 did not always mean fulfilment. They all admire Watts of course but they say also that he is old and apt to be carried away by an enthusiasm.

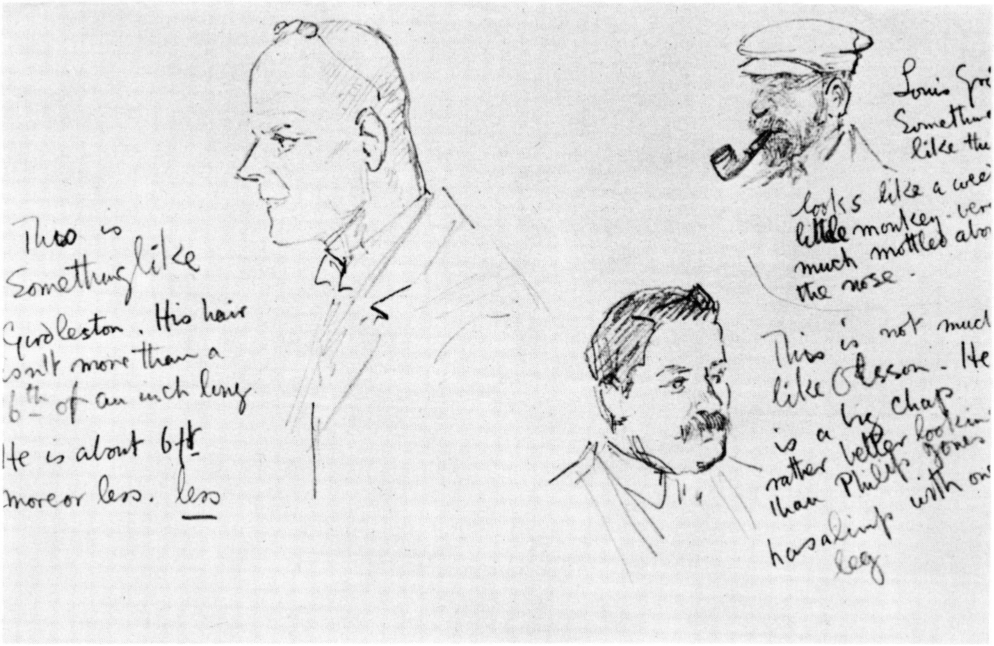

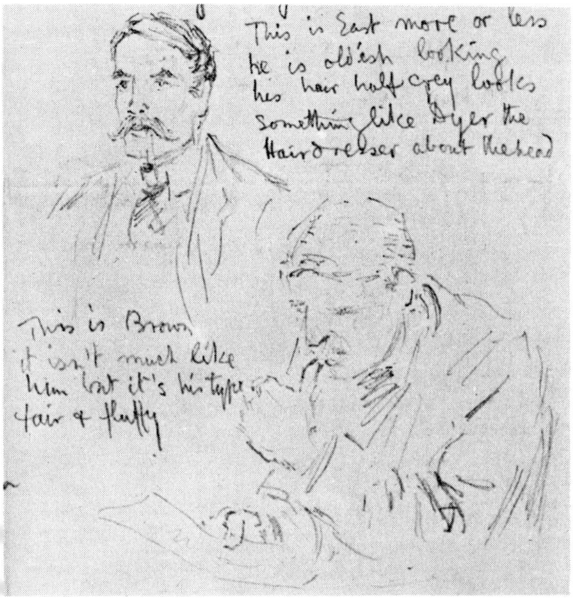
This is East more or less
he is old'esh looking
his hair half grey looks
something like Dyer the
Hairdresser about the head
This is Brown
it isn't much like
him but it's his type
fair & fluffy

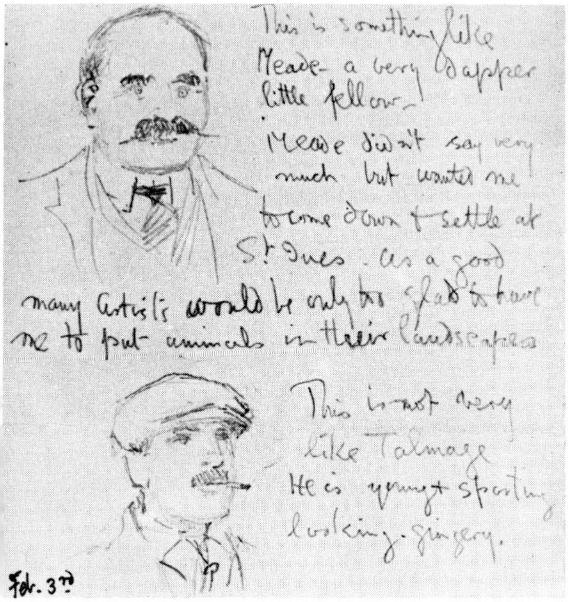
This is something like
Meade a very dapper
little fellow.
Meade didn't say very
much but wanted me
to come down & settle at
St Ives. As a good
many Artist's would be only too glad to have
me to put animals in their landscapes
This is not very
like Talmage
He is young & sporting
looking. gingery.
Feb. 3rd

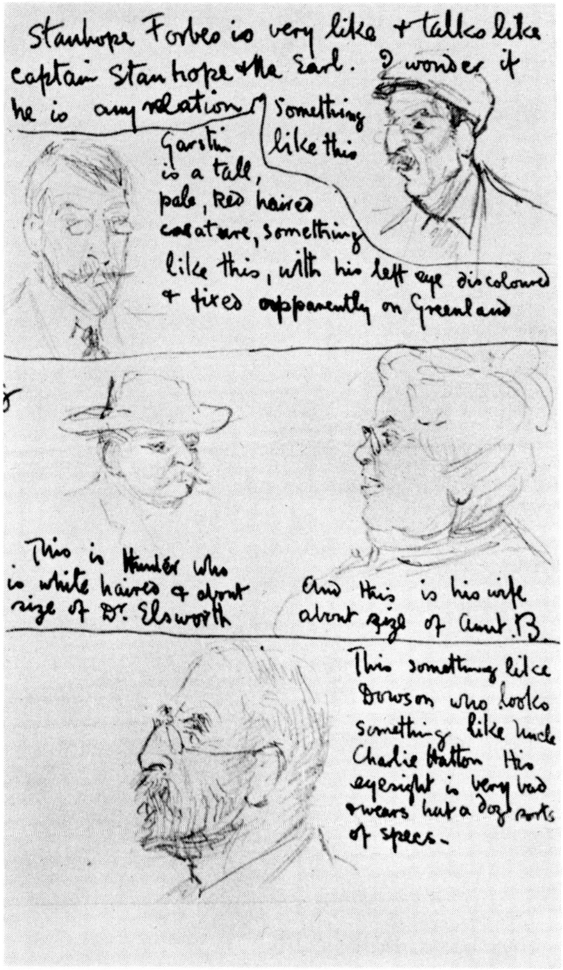
Stanhope Forbes is very like & talks like
captain Stanhope the Earl. I wonder if
he is any relation
Something
like this
Garstin
is a tall,
pale, Red haired
creature, something
like this, with his left eye discoloured
& fixed apparently on Greenland
This is Hunter who
is white haired & about
size of Dr. Elsworth
And this is his wife
about size of Aunt B
This something like
Dowson who looks
something like Uncle
Charlie Hatton His
eyesight is very bad
& wears about a doz sorts
of specs.

In February Brian and the Lancasters returned to Swansea which Brian described as "beastly dismal after blue sea and pretty Cornish scenery". He was not considered well enough to return to school, but his education was not entirely neglected. He asked his mother to send him his Greek and Latin grammar books and settled down to some work every morning, and he continued to paint in oils, and was pleased with the progress he was making.

> The oil is getting on now . . . it is a drove of wild horses and a man heading off one that has got loose, a dark horse in shadow up the road showing dark against lighter ones in sunlight behind.

His more general education continued when the Carl Rosa Opera paid a visit to Swansea.

> Feb. 14th 1904 — Winchester House
> My dear Mother
> I went to Lohengrin on Fri night and liked it very much, only the principal actors were fat and ancient, and some of the scenery was hardly in keeping with the rest i.e. . . . Chippendale table and high back chair like Auntie Ada's, a modern dinner gong and French window with glass — were some of the accessories for an early 10th century period. The way they fought too was remarkable — mainly by clashing their swords against their shields and rushing against one another. However, the singing was *the* thing, though it never made any impression on me, not being catchy enough. However, Faust Sat. afternoon was A.1. Mephistoples was at least 6 ft 6 and as thin as a lath, and most diabolical. The women were quite presentable. In the evening I went with Mrs. L. and Dr. to Carmen which I enjoyed immensely. Carmen herself was awfully good and the tunes more lively. Mrs. L. is singing (?) that awful boating song, most unsuitable for the present state or the weather — making a most terrible din like all the cats in Hell let loose (half the notes on the piano won't strike) so that I can't hear myself write . . . I made some ink sketches of some of the opera caratures . . .
>
> Your very loving son
> Brian.

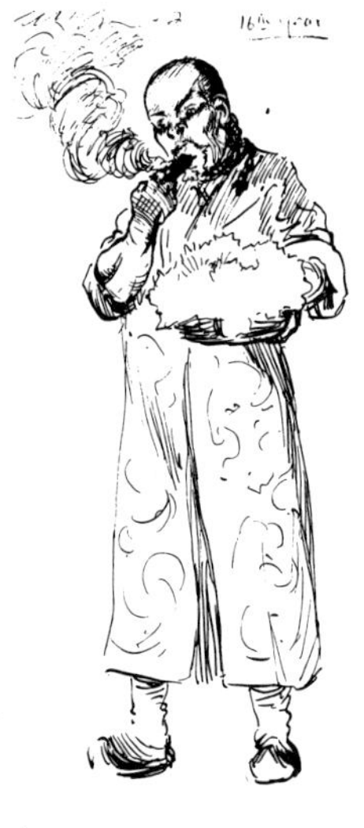

Chung-Ling Soo.

Dr Lancaster might tolerate an evening of opera, but he had a youthful streak in his nature, and for pure enjoyment he preferred to relax at the "Empire". He liked to take Brian with him and together they saw a variety of entertainments which included dancers who whirled about in coloured draperies, trick cyclists, Chargwin the white-eyed negro, Albert Chevalier and a Chinese conjuror who turned out to be an American in disguise.

From Brian's point of view, far more pleasing than all this entertainment was the fact that he had started riding again.

> Feb. 11th 1904
>
> I had a ride this afternoon and feel all the better for it. Had an awfully nice little nag this time went like a bird and could be guided like anything by your little finger . . . I didn't get this gee from Small's . . . but from Bullen's who keeps proper saddle horses (not old cab horses).

Elton had rejoined the household and together they had a spectacular ride.

> March 20th 1904 Winchester House, Swansea.
>
> My dear Mother
> I went for a ride with Elton on Wednesday, went to the Mumbles. Elton rode the same little nag that I rode once and ran away with me. I rode a very decent one too — they both pulled like blazes. Elton's expression was extraordinary, he had acute agony in his arms all the time. Coming home Elton's pony ended by bolting for about a mile. As soon as I knew what was up I pelted after him like fury — all up St. Helen's Rd dodging between the tram cars and making the people scuttle. You should have seen the Bobies stepping gingerly out of the way! however, just as I came up with Elton, he managed to stop her a bit and soon had her all right again. It was the best lark I've had for a long while.

Brian was longing to go home, but his return was delayed by an accident. He was jogging down a slope in one of the parks with his hands in his pockets when he slipped and fell. The result was water on the knee. To cheer him up his mother sent him a magazine which contained photographs of Watts's "Physical Energy" now cast in bronze. Brian's reaction was interesting. He had been brought up to revere Watts but this did not prevent him from having the courage of his own convictions and he did not hesitate to criticise the great man's work. Watts might be one of the leading British artists of the day but Brian, with his discerning eye, felt that there were weaknesses in his knowledge and understanding of the horse.

> I think 'Physical Energy' fair although I can't reconcile myself to the mountain on the horse's neck. I have seen horses with very thick necks stand out in a lump like that — but I think Watts has exaggerated it. It looks like a square box! I think it would have looked stronger to have had a taller horse. The man's legs hang down a long way below the belly rather ignominiously (ahem!) Another thing — as far as I can make out in the photos — the horse is unshod. Therefore the hoofs would be worn down very small — instead of which Watts has made them rather large if anything. Curious too that he has not shown any veins not even the principal ones which always show in the most abject specimens, much more in a thoroughbred animal like that full of blood and sawdust — or — I mean energy. I think it's awfully fine though, the whole thing — the horse's head especially — the horse doesn't appear to have any teeth, only gums!!!

The point about the horse's hoofs illustrates Brian's acute powers of observations and knowledge of his subject. Of course he was regarding the horse and rider in a realistic way, whereas Watts was giving expression of an idea. He described the work as;

> Symbolic of that restless impulse to seek the unachieved in the domain of material things . . . I don't wish my man to be like any model you could find anywhere. I don't wish my horse to be like a natural horse. I want them both to represent the characteristics of the human and the animal.

It was at this time that Mrs Lancaster came in touch with a Miss Thomas, an artist who was a patient in a local hospital. When visiting her she learned that Miss Thomas had studied in Paris with Lezare and with Herkomer at his studio at Bushey, where she had lodged in the same house as Lucy Kemp-Welch and her sister. The indefatigable Mrs Lancaster sent some of Brian's work for her to see, and then wrote to Mrs Hatton, saying;

> She admired all his drawing and pen and ink and pencil work immensely, but not his colouring. She said it was crude, wanting in atmosphere and she believed it would take him years to work out the right results by himself and be a great waste of time, that so much of it was technical — just what most of the artists at St. Ives said . . . She said Oxford would be invaluable to him and she considered it a great mistake to send young people to Bushey . . . that there was no restraint, no one to trouble whether they worked or not, and that way few of the young people could rise above its temptations.

Mrs Lancaster ended her letter with a final comment on Miss Thomas.

> She is a lady very well connected and I was interested in what she said about Bushey.

Miss Thomas' remarks about the Bushey School of Painting may have been justified because Herkomer was now a sick man, but when in his prime he might have been the ideal teacher for Brian. His strong personality had inspired his pupils to hard work but he never believed in authoritative instruction but rather in developing the natural talent in his pupils. As it turned out, Brian did study for a time at an art school (Arbroath) where the resident Master, George Harcourt R.A., had been second in command to Herkomer at Bushey. Herkomer's most outstanding pupil (who eventually took over the running of his school) was Lucy Kemp-Welch and once he realised her potentialities he did all he could to encourage her skill as an animal painter.

There is an extraordinary affinity between the work of Lucy Kemp-Welch and Brian Hatton in their approach to the painting of animals, especially the horse. In her note book Lucy wrote:

> Now as to the actual painting of *animals* which causes a man fully equipped to paint — to forsake all else for this branch of the art — but deep at the heart of him is that something which dictates that he shall do this, that he shall wait and watch with patience infinite for this movement, or that appearance, shall obscure with that devotion to the subject which fears no hardships and will go through anything for the sake of attaining that one scrap of knowledge — and all this before he can paint.

Lucy Kemp-Welch was eighteen years older than Brian and they never knew one another. Had they done so, one feels there would have been complete understanding between them.

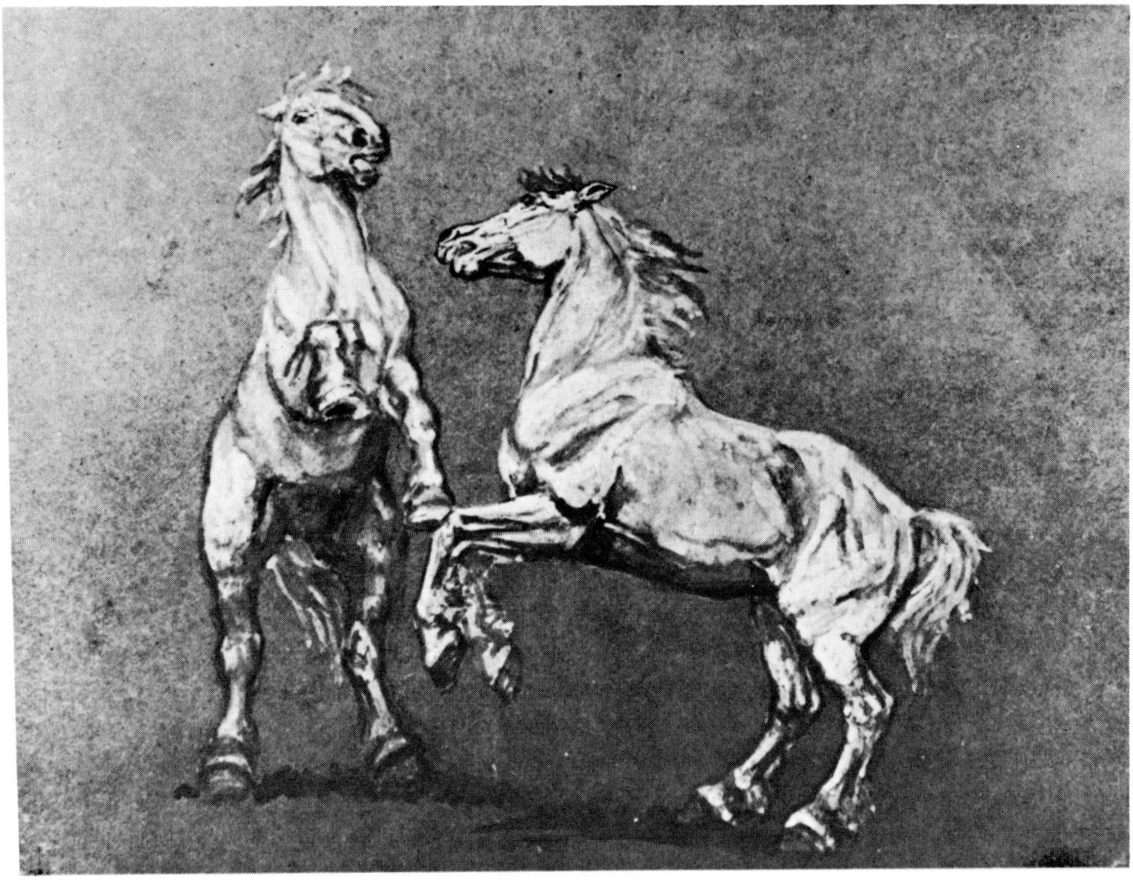

Rearing Horses. White paint on brown paper, 1910

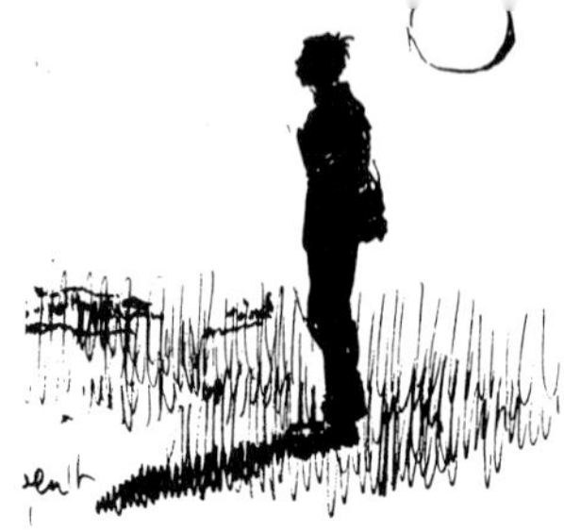

CHAPTER ELEVEN

The Cramming Establishment

BRIAN spent the summer of 1904 at home. He was always happy to be in Hereford and much of his time was occupied painting in the surrounding countryside. In June came the news of the death of George Frederic Watts, which caused much sorrow to Amelia Hatton. She had received a warning letter from Miss Mackintosh, Watts's adopted daughter, which was followed by a note from Mary Watts, saying that they were "watching the end of a beautiful day". Mrs Hatton felt too prostrated to attend Watts' memorial service in St Paul's Cathedral and a fortnight later her grief was aggravated by the sudden death of her father, Robert Keay. She made a note in her diary saying, "A chapter of my life has closed completely". Mary Watts was perhaps the more resilient of the two; she sent Brian a present for his seventeenth birthday accompanied by a letter written in her usual high-minded, emotional style.

> I am grieved when I think that you can have no more direct touch with my dear one. But his words I know will live with you and his profound belief that you will reverently serve art, and use to the utmost the great gifts he believed nature had bestowed on you, will I know be an incentive to do this, if ever one was needed!
> On one of his last days on earth, he told me he would like you to have a little box containing bottles of very precious colours one of *real* ultramarine, and the other of rose madder . . . I think he had very rarely made use of the colours, feeling always his work would be better some day. How I believe he sees clearly, all that he could here only follow as a gleam . . . If what we do here can touch the spirits of those who pass beyond the veil, nothing will please him more than to know you are working as he worked — not for fame or fortune but to do the *best*. He often said to me that you would go further than he. And may these words be true, dear Brian.

It was perhaps fortunate that Brian was endowed with high spirits and a strong sense of humour, otherwise he might have felt overwhelmed by Mary's pious hopes for his future. As it was, he always remained on good terms with her, corresponding with her and paying her visits from time to time.

The faithful Curly also remembered Brian's birthday, sending him a renewed invitation to Cow Leaze and the gift of "a little prayer book". Brian described this prayer book in a letter to his father.

> Curly gave me a tiny little prayer book such as they advertise for bridesmaids at weddings — with the Cherub Choir in silver on the cover and my name pretty big on the back.

Rather a curious present to give to a seventeen year old boy, one might say, but perhaps Curly was unable to think of a more suitable gift.

Brian's parents had been giving much thought as to the best way to complete his general education, and advice on the subject had been forthcoming from many quarters. As we know, Watts had always insisted that Brian should be given every opportunity to broaden his mind in cultural spheres, provided no outside influence should impair his natural gifts, and Briton Riviere had endorsed these principles. Bishop Percival of Hereford felt that languages and foreign travel would be of great benefit and recommended visits to Paris, Rome, Dresden and Geneva. In the end it was Curly who had the last word. Knowing that Brian's parents had long been considering the idea of sending their son to Oxford he took positive action and wrote to his old friend, Mr R. W. Raper, the Bursar of Trinity College, telling him about Brian and asking for his advice. By one of those strange coincidences, Raper already had some knowledge of Brian, owing to a chance conversation with a stranger in a railway carriage. Replying to Curly, he said;

> I am disposed to take a special interest in him for this reason. Some years ago now a man in a train told me of the excellence of this boy's work and produced some of his drawings and I was so far interested that I called on the father in Hereford and talked to him about the boy.

Mr Raper said that he would confidently recommend Trinity as being suitable for a young artist. He had taken the trouble to write and ask for the opinion of Briton Riviere, who had also been at Oxford. Riviere had endorsed Raper's ideas, stressing the point that the real stimulus came from friends and contemporaries, rather than from teaching from above. Raper said that if he was still alive when Brian came up he would do what he could for him. In the meantime he must prepare for the Matriculation examination and qualify for Responsions as soon as possible. Curly sent this information on to Brian, saying that he hoped his father would go and see Raper.

> He can do far more for you in the exam line and every other line than anybody else; it would be a pity to throw away the chance. It is an excellent College too, with lovely gardens.

There was still some hesitation on the part of Brian's parents for the cost of University education was a matter of careful consideration. Curly became anxious and wrote again.

> I was getting perturbed about Oxford. I want you to go to Trinity because Mr. Raper is such a nice man and he is so much interested in you.

It was at this point that an uncle of Mrs Hatton came to the rescue and a decision was made. Uncle Charlie Marr was one of the Ayrshire relations who had always taken an interest in Brian. He wrote a firm, "no nonsense" sort of letter to Amelia Hatton when he heard of the dilemma.

> My judgement is there is no room for argument, discussion or doubt as to what should be done in the circumstances. Brian *must* have the necessary preparation for Oxford and be given every opportunity to fill his proper place . . . It is a pleasure therefore to me to do some little thing in the way of helping him on the road to success and it suggests itself to me that perhaps the nicest way is to ask Brian to undertake another commission for me — to be fulfilled at his own time — even years ahead, as it may be convenient. Please therefore accept the enclosed cheque for 100 guineas on this understanding.

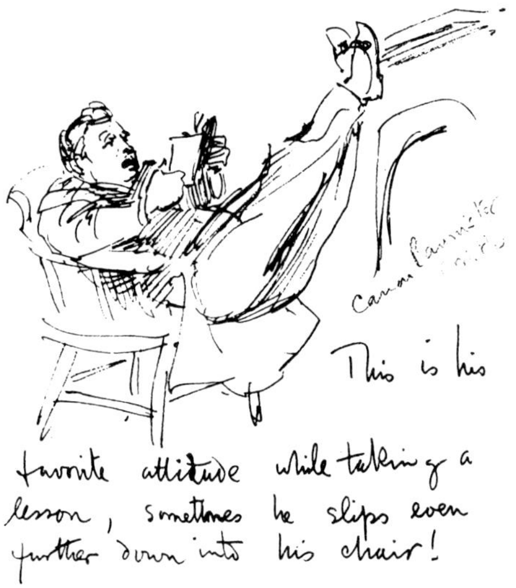

It would be difficult to think of a nicer way of making a gift. Brian would be under no obligation to great-uncle Charlie and in due course he would repay the debt with a picture. For a long time Brian had wanted to go to Oxford, but as his education had been virtually non-existent for some while it was obvious that he would need some intensive instruction if he was to pass Responsions. No time was wasted and in January 1905 Brian went to a coaching establishment at Ewyas Harold Vicarage, which was presided over by The Reverend A. B. Bannister, who was later Canon of Hereford Cathedral.

The time he spent at Ewyas Harold was something of a landmark in Brian's life. Geographically, it was not far from Hereford — a distance of about twelve miles — and the ties with home were as strong as ever, but Brian was encountering in his fellow students a sophistication which was new to him. Although in some ways he was unusually mature for a boy of seventeen, and he had mixed on equal terms with professional artists, he had not had much contact with young men of his own age and there was still something of the little boy about him. He continued on the same intimate terms with his mother, writing regularly and telling her the smallest details of his day-to-day life. Of course one must remember that at the beginning of this century the family unit was of great importance, and for economic reasons alone, parental control continued much longer than it does today.

Brian settled down quite happily, saying that he thought he would get on well with Mr Bannister, and that he didn't find the hours of work too long.

> The boys are rather a flashy lot most of them but some seem as if they aren't so bad. All the talk is about pretty girls and motors! . . . There is no news. *I shall want another dress shirt as we tog up every night*. There is a huge gramophone grinding in my ear.

Like all young people Brian was anxious to conform and stand well in the eyes of his peers, and a little later, when Cousin Mabel was coming to see him, he wrote to his mother, saying, "Tell Mabel if she comes out to be careful what she wears, the fellows are frightfully particular!!"

There was not room to house all the students in the Vicarage so Brian lodged nearby with a Mrs Farr, but took all his meals at the Vicarage. The day began with prayers at 8.20 followed by breakfast and work until lunch time. The afternoons were free and Brian usually spent them on the golf links or walking over the hills. To his delight he discovered that if he went to the top of a certain hill he could just see the water tower at Hereford, with the aid of his binoculars, but the rest of the town was hidden by rising ground. Sometimes they all played hockey in the afternoon, "Old B." joining in, but as they were short of numbers, it wasn't a good game and Brian preferred his freedom, ranging over the hills. There was more work in the evenings, both before and after dinner.

As he became better acquainted with his fellow students, Brian described them in his usual graphic style.

> Jack Stallard of Stallards of Worcester is here, going up to Cambridge. He is going to be a clergyman. He seems very decent but never laughs or enjoys anything very much; sort of quiet little chap. Another by name of Peter Lloyd also seems decent, and so does Allan Campbell. But the others so far as I know them are more flashy and wasters, but all very nicely spoken and gentlemanly to outward appearances. The younger of the two boys whom you saw is a new one and seems a funny sort of ass, talks as if he were cracked sometimes, he stammers too. The other one is only staying till he can come into his inheritance and does no work, only messes about with his motors and dogs, but seems to be very nice. Everyone is called by their Christian names.

(When Brian referred to the boy who "stammers too" he was linking him with himself. He had not quite outgrown this tiresome disability.)

> I am quite well in every way and stuttering has not been in the way at all. I think it may be slightly improving. But I've had no serious viva voce lesson as yet! I have been to church, now not at all a dangerous proceeding as the church was not at all hot . . . We sit in the first two rows, and in a corner slap against the pulpit (which is of old carved oak).

Church attendance twice on Sunday was the order of the day at the Vicarage and a week later Brian was not quite so sure of himself. He had had a bad stomach upset during the night, but had recovered by the morning.

> So feeling quite well I went to church. But when standing up during the psalms felt as if I *might* faint, so walked out quickly.

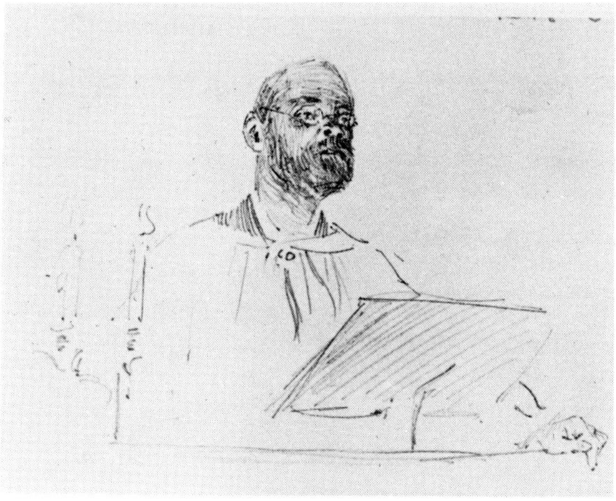

The Rev. Mr Sanderson

Much as Brian enjoyed his walks in the country, there may have been times when he felt the need of a suitable companion and perhaps it was for this reason that he acquired a dog.

My dear Mother Thursday, March 2nd 1905

Thank you for your letter this morning . . . yesterday afternoon I bought a mongrel rough haired whippet for 10/-. The fellow wouldn't take less although I tried to bargain for 7/6. I believe he's a very sporting brute, and a nice good tempered animal, and under 12 months. I suppose I shall want a licence now! I am going to keep him in a box or barrel in Mrs. Farr's garden and she'll look after him.

. . . I don't suppose I shall have any more expenses once I have bought or borrowed a barrel and ½ bolding of straw.

Love

Brian.

March 5th Ewyas Harold Vicarage,
Pontrilas.

I have had rather a fuss yesterday about my dog. You see I bought him on Wed evening from a boy named Gwillam, and that was all right. But yesterday I heard someone had let him loose in the village and that Alfred Prosser (a publican and farmer) had claimed the beast as his and shut him up. So I went down and asked him what he was up to. He said the dog was a stray and had been left in his charge and Gwillam had no right to sell him. So I went to see young Gwillam (who kept carefully out of my way) but I saw his father (who is also a bad lot). He explained a long story about a third person being the owner, who had authorised Gwillam to sell the dog . . . and they would divide profits. And Prosser had had the dog lodged with him and had not been paid for his keep. So when he heard of me being a soft 'un, had tried to make a bit on his account. So Mr. Bannister, who had taken up my cause, put the policemen on to find out if this was true, which he did . . . But as all these men are regular bad lots they may perhaps poison the poor brute for me. He is a very nice dog and well behaved and has already become fond of me. On Friday afternoon I asked a farmer to allow me to try him after rabbits on his land — so Spring caught a little baby rabbit about 3 inches long which I presented to the farmeress with all due solemnity.

Spring turned out to be a splendid companion as well as a good "rabbiter", and he and Brian had many adventures together. On one occasion they met some tough looking men.

> The one with the mule first wanted to buy Spring and then wanted to sell his own dog, which was the most remarkable freak I've ever seen, a sort of cross between a sheep dog and a wolf hound, with great bones sticking out all over it.

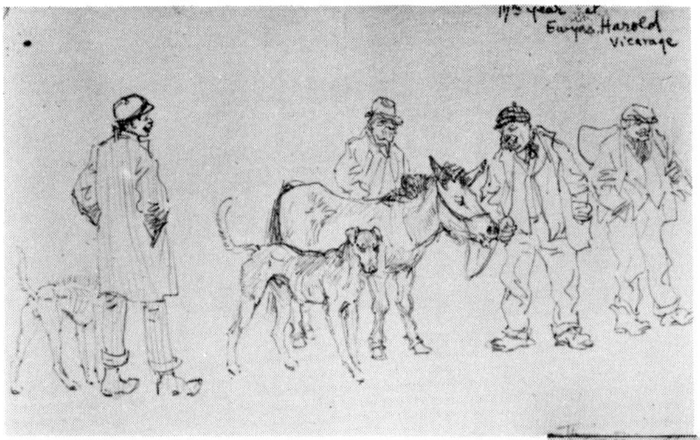

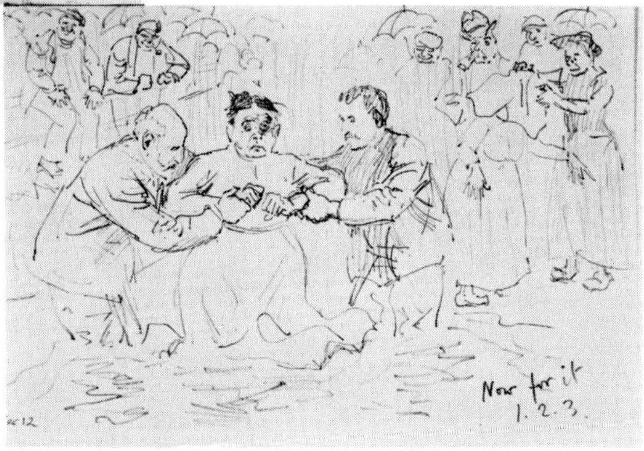

On yet another occasion they witnessed a strange scene.

> This afternoon went to see some Baptist Revivalists being baptised in the Dor brook. Two bumptious Johnnies, who came hopelessly to grief over their h's, dressed themselves in oil skins and began palavering about once having been wicked like those who were present, which was very rude of them, and that now they were 'saved'. Then they walked into the stream and ducked the first woman, who had a tremendous black eye. Several other women followed and one old man. The poor beggars gasped, and could hardly walk up to the bank with their clothes all clinging to them, while one of the baptisers wiped the water out of their eyes with his smudgy hand, and the Baptists yelled 'hallelujah' . . . Spring is very well and nearly did for a cat, which he mistook for a rabbit yesterday.

Brian's sense of the ridiculous gave him infinite pleasure and he followed up his description of the Baptist Revivalists with an account of an evening's entertainment at the Vicarage.

> We had a very amusing evening on Thursday — at least for those who could see the funny side of things. There was a Mr. Rees, a curate from Cardiff, who fairly yelled and worked himself into such a perspiration that it made one hot to look at him. There was also a man from Hereford (brought down by a friend in the village) who recited, his pathetic pieces were killingly funny as he couldn't pronounce, to say nothing of his appearance. But when he came to some French phrases it was too much, and we fairly roared. Then old Palmer, the saddler (whom I have sketched with a red nose) read a piece out of a penny magazine about a drunkard; he read putting such comical expressions into it, that I'm afraid I began to get hysterical.

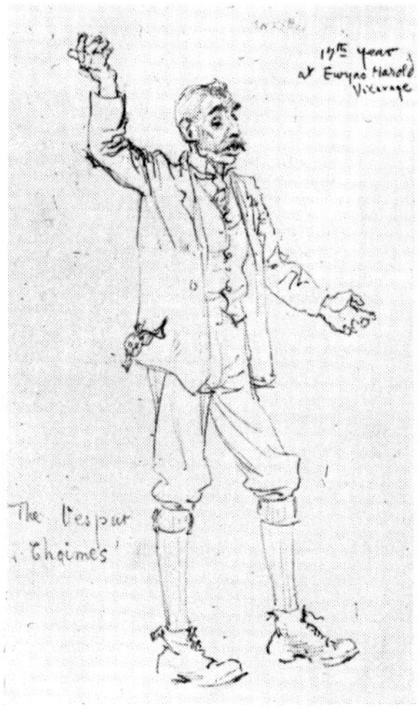

Although his letters were profusely illustrated, the fact that Brian made no mention of painting denotes the fact that his time was fully occupied with work. He began to have doubts about his ability to pass into Oxford and became very despondent. Raper had sent him a message, saying that unless he passed Responsions in June, he wouldn't be able to go into residence until October twelve months. Even if he did pass, he stood a poor chance of gaining a place because the entrance exam was much harder. Brian was not encouraged by the fact that "Old B" maintained that he would not be ready to take Responsions until October.

> Raper says that his own private opinion is that Oxford is unnecessary for me . . . Bit off, isn't it? B. thinks its downright idiocy wasting time on Oxford, so perhaps it is. I don't know. I'm awfully disgusted.

When Brian returned to Ewyas Harold after the Easter break he was very disgruntled, although he approved of the summer timetable.

> It seems as if I've been months already, it's all so blooming stale. The hours are altered somewhat in the summer term; we work for an hour after lunch and then get off until dinner time, at seven sharp, and then work till ten. It is much better as I can get a little walk in the evenings when it is cooler (and the rabbits are out) . . . I am let off maths but the others have to put in an hour every afternoon. Poor blighters!

Brian could see no merit in cricket, and although he did not have to play he was roped in to score for a match.

> Last Saturday's match was the event of my life being the first cricket match that I have witnessed throughout in my life, and I never was so bored before.

Later he wrote;

> Has old B sent his little Billy yet? he said he was going to write to Dad the other day. If he puts down £5's worth of cricket expenses, don't stand for it, 'cause I haven't had any . . . The last one or two nights have been perfectly lovely, I have got out half an hour earlier and strolled the meadows studying the moonlight while Spring studied the rabbits.
> I believe I could paint moonlight a good deal more successfully than daylight, however I haven't tried yet.

Brian seems to have been on good terms with "Old B" and he described "a very interesting" bike ride they had together;

> . . . to Longtown and along this side of the first range of Black Mountains to Pandy and back by way of Abergavenny road . . . On the way back we met an old drunken tramp who had partially undressed himself and had fallen asleep by the road side, much to the consternation of sundry 'pi' old ladies who were driving by.

Mr Bannister decided to let Brian sit for Responsions in July, but was doubtful as to whether he would gain a pass. If he failed to get into Trinity, he thought that Exeter College would be a good second choice.

> B. doesn't seem very anxious for me to work too hard. Strikes me he wants to make a bit more out of me.

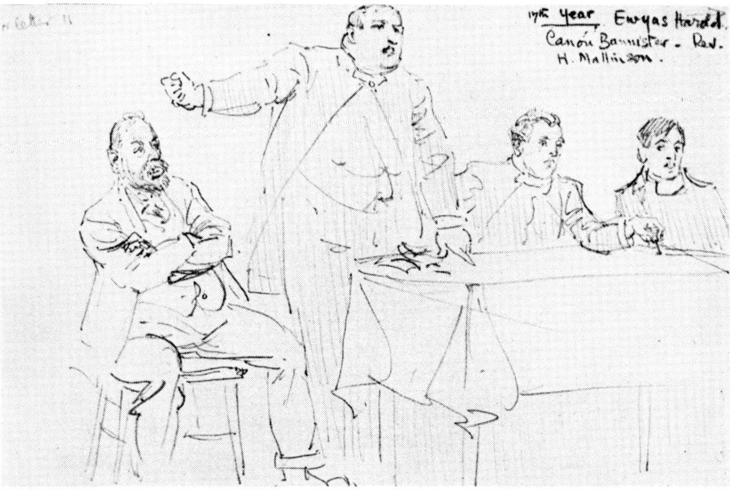

It is probable that Mr Bannister knew what he was doing when he discouraged Brian from overworking. His health had to be watched and perhaps he was showing signs of strain, for he wrote home, saying;

> I haven't been doing much cycling lately . . . I don't think I have been more than 4 or 5 miles any day, which is nothing on a bike. But I haven't been having very good nights lately, do nothing but dream all night long. So I had a good lie down this afternoon and feel much fresher. I think Spring slept more than I did . . . B. has sent up my name for July, so I am doomed!

Mr Bannister accompanied Brian to Oxford when he sat for his exam and had a long talk with him during the journey back.

> July 11th 1905 Ewyas Harold Vicarage
> My dear Mother,
> I had a good talk with old B. yesterday in the train. And his opinion is — that I ought to go abroad (not with my parents, for it is time that I learnt to stand on my own feet!!!) But since I explained to him that this was at present impossible, he said I ought not to hesitate to go to Oxford for a year, and that Exeter was a very good College which would take me on Smalls. Also that going to London, even with good introductions, is not the same as Rome or Dresden, etc., as they are not so cosmopolitan in London and I should only move in a little circle etc. etc. B. has written to Raper to find out my marks on each paper and any details he can get.
> I somehow 'feel' (as Mrs. Lan would say) that what he says is right. And if Dad could possibly manage it without great self-sacrifice to himself and home etc., I should like to go for a year . . . I feel very well and much brighter here. I think I am going up to the Glebe (B's shooting) now with Gilby and Spring to see if he could spring on a rabbit. I should like you to settle up and decide soon so that I shall know what I am working for.
> Much love to all, your loving son,
> Brian.

Once again Brian showed his concern for his father and the rest of the family. Only if it could be managed "without great self-sacrifice", did he want to go to Oxford. He had recovered his spirits now that the exam was over and could enjoy some sport with Spring once more.

> The other day Gilbey and I went out and shot 5 rabbits and an old hen who was loafing about and which we carefully hid in the bracken.

Although his letters were liberally illustrated Brian had not mentioned doing any serious drawing for some time, but now he was busy designing a triptych. His father had recently collected some carved panels of oak, and a local craftsman was engaged to fit them round the walls of the Mount Craig sitting-room and to design and make a mantlepiece. Over this was to hang a triptych* drawn by Brian and worked by his mother in gesso and then to be coloured by Brian.

*Brian's design in charcoal on brown paper exists in his gallery in Hereford.

> I have roughed out a design the other night for your mantlepiece. I don't know what you will think of it, but I don't think the middle bit goes very well with the two outsides. I must try and think of something better for the middle. But I don't get much time for meditation now! The thing half way up the middle bit represents a thick wattled hedge with climbing roses etc., a la Burne-Jones and their saplings on the near side of it. The idea of the hedge was to hide the lower part of the bloke with the scythe . . . Does it strike you as being at all suitable? I rather like the two side panels . . .
> We made the duce of a noise in church this evening, fairly bawled (as Ailsa would say) the hymns and quite upset the choir. Old B. quite sarcastic to us about base voices singing treble parts etc.

Brian did not pass his exam in July for he was taking it again in September.

> Old B. seems to think I shall pass this time, I only hope he is right. Hope you will hear from Raper soon, as I expect it will mean Exeter.
> *Mon.* Had your letter today, greatly delighted about Trinity and old B. greatly surprised.

The letter which so "greatly delighted" Brian told him that Mr Raper had written to say that it had been decided that Brian could take up residence in Trinity College in October, on special conditions (for one year only) provided that he passed the necessary examinations. He would occupy one of Mr Raper's spare bedrooms.

Brian still had reservations about his ability to pass the exams.

> I hope to goodness I shall pass. Mr. B. thinks I ought to just do it if I don't put in a lot of absurd howlers and don't say twice 2 are 5. But of course I shall do it wrong like I always do . . . I think I had better stay at the Mitre alone, it will do me good.

Brian passed Responsions and the stage was now set for him to go up to Trinity in October.

CHAPTER TWELVE

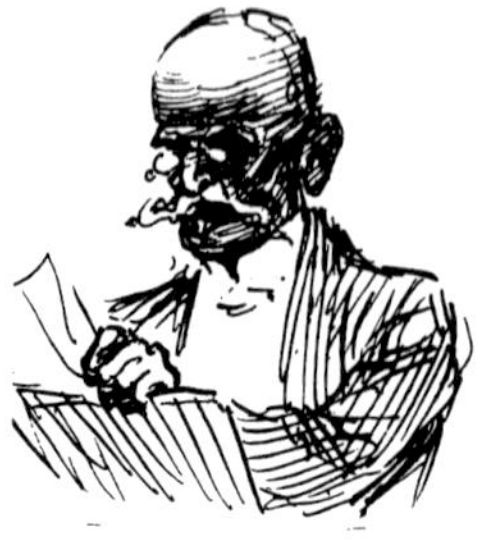

Oxford

BRIAN was unable to go up to Oxford at the beginning of the autumn term, owing to an attack of bronchitis, however he made a quick recovery and his first letter from Trinity is dated 6th November, 1905.

My dear old Dad
I've just been matriculated, rather fun, as the old Don didn't quite know if he ought to admit me as I don't propose to do the ordinary work. However, after a consultation with the President, I was taken to the Vice Chancellor who swore me into membership of the University, etc, all in Latin, which he kindly translated for my benefit, and having handed me a book of statutes in Latin, and a paper with some of the important items in *English*, let me go. The junior Bursar is going to make me up a programme of lectures for me, which will be ready by Wed. Meanwhile I am to study the drawings of Raphael etc in the Art Gallery. All the dons are awfully motherly old maids, none of the sharp official character about them.

Love to all
your loving son
Brian

P.S. This is Mr. Raper's pen, so please excuse scrawl.

Brian's links with home were still very strong and he wrote to his parents several times a week, sharing with them his first impressions of University life.

Nov. 10th 1905 Trinity, Oxford
My dear Mother,
Your letters are very welcome, not that I am homesick or any such rot, but its nice to have something to read at breakfast time. Curly was here at about one o'clock for a little while . . . One of the first things he said was that he supposed as soon as I left Oxford I should go into someone's studio, but he rather pooh poohed Herkomer, as being a fadist and experimenter . . . [he] said though that I *must* go to Italy soon. He is very smart today in a suit like my cap and white waistcoat and flashy tie, looks quite a symphony of grays, his hair has got much whiter since you saw him I think . . .
I don't know if I told you that we don't dress for dinner in Hall, which is a blessing, only slip on our gowns and gobble . . . The grub is quite good and wholesome. 3 or 4 courses but no one ever seems to wait for the savouries. Hall consists of a big room, panelled and hung with portraits of the College celebrities, with a raised dais at one end where the Dons dine, and 3 or 4 long tables going the length of the hall where the undergraduates gobble. Unfortunately I was put at the end of one of them and had to serve some of the dishes, which I did very successfully without fainting!

Mr. Raper told me to put 'Mr' on my cards, but all the cards that I've seen have no Mr. on them. I must see if it's *very* bad form, if so I must see about getting the plate altered or something . . .

Your loving son
Brian

P.S. I've bought a cap and gown, 8/6 the lot. It seems I've only got to wear them on special occasions and after 8 p.m. thank heaven.

Brian, who had come up to Oxford under "unusual treatment", was something of a problem to Raper. He personally doubted whether the young artist would gain any advantage from University life, although he did not declare his views after Briton Riviere's fervent advice that Oxford was essential. Raper did his best to help Brian to reap the benefits of University life, and he housed him in his own suite of rooms. Brian could not have come under the influence of a better person.

R. W. Raper has been described as "Oxford Don, man of taste and of affairs, friend of friends". He was a scholar, deeply versed in the classics and in the literature of his own and other lands. He was a cricket enthusiast and a protector of the traditions of his College and University. His wit and wisdom are preserved in the letters he wrote to Brian and his family, written in such microscopic handwriting that no letter ever overlapped the first page. One of these letters has survived.

Trinity College
Oxford

Dec. 20
1905

Dear Hatton

Very many thanks for the drawing of Guy Benson. I did not write at once because I sent it on to Mrs Benson and I thought that you might like to hear what a mother thought. She was away from here and so I only got her answer this morning. 'Such a pretty little drawing of Guy arrived by post yesterday morning and I think I can trace your handwriting on the envelope. How did you manage to get it done and who is B.H.? do gratify my curiosity. The likeness is quite caught particularly the mouth wh is excellent.' (may I add my own criticism— 'much wh I don't think you drew at the time but put in from memory a little thick' this is not to detract from my gratitude but to give you the only defect I discern or seem to discern) Again a thousand thanks. With best wishes for Xmas and the new year and looking forward to your continued peaceful presence.

Yours very ty
R W Raper.

Raper exerted a lasting influence as a counsellor, friend and aide among the men and women of his time, and to Brian he gave generously of his friendship, wisdom and advice, following his career with interest until his own death in 1915. He allowed Brian to paint him in oils* (as well as make several pencil drawings of him), a privilege he denied to everyone else.

*The small portrait hangs in Trinity College, as well as a head and shoulders in pencil.

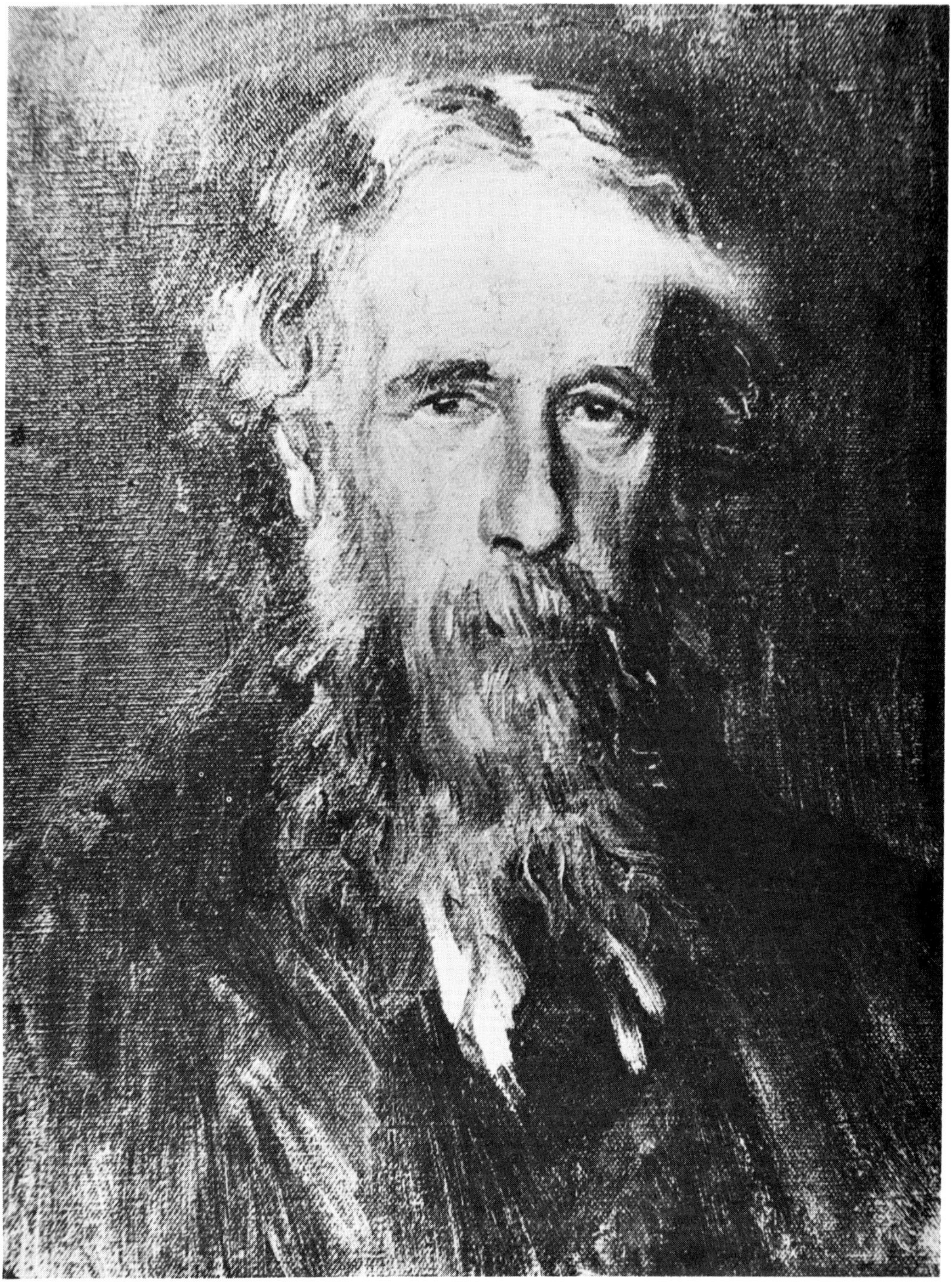

R. W. Raper: Bursar of Trinity College, Oxford.
Oil, 1912. 13½″ × 10″ *The President of Trinity College, Oxford*

Raper helped to guide Brian in his studies and he readily fell in with the suggestions Raper made.

Nov. 7th

This morning I had a talk with Mr. Raper, who doesn't quite see why I should come if I don't take a degree etc. But he knows a Mr. Thomson who is very good at anatomy and has written an excellent book (which Raper has lent me, quite the best I've seen, lots of photos etc) and he thinks I ought to have some instruction from him, to which I readily agree. So . . . at 11 a.m. I went to the Taylorian Gallery and studied Raphael, Michael Angelo, Turner, Durer, Rossetti, Francis Hals and a host of others for 1½ hours.

There was a branch of the Slade School operating in Oxford, and before contacting Mr Thomson, Brian decided to see how he would get on there. Two sessions were enough for his independent nature. He spent the first morning doing a study of a man's head from life, "for the old boss to see what I was up to". The Slade professor told him to come again the next day to have a talk about anatomy. This was not a success.

Went to Slade Professor this morning again, don't think he's much good, too old and fussy and South Kensingtony, tried to teach me anatomy by drawing from the cast, found it hopeless and depressing, shan't go there again.

Brian could see no virtue in working from a cast. Considering the fact that he had been drawing from life from the age of two and had a fair working knowledge of anatomy, his attitude was perhaps well justified. He did, however, return to the Slade, attending life classes twice a week. Whatever he thought of the tuition, he knew the value of a live model.

I shall soon be able to do heads à la Rossetti I hope. But I bar the antique and always tell the old boy I've got a lecture and can't get off!

For Mr Thomson Brian had real respect.

I went to Mr. Thomson this morning, he's much more the right sort and talked sense. I am going to lunch with him on Sunday, and talk matters over. He of course agrees with Stanhope Forbes and Co. i.e. that I should learn in a week, what would take me years to find out all alone, and it need not necessarily take away any originality . . . Thomson said that he knows nearly all the Academicans and lots of outsiders too. (He is Professor of Anatomy at Academy Schools now) and he rather doubted if Herkomer would be the right sort or if he would have me, as he has no settled studio anywhere now.

Brian duly went to lunch with the Thomsons;

. . . found them very nice easy going sort of people. There were two other freshmen there; one a Scotch laddy (rather raw) from Trinity and another fellow from Keble; a mixed assortment of girls, two of Thomson's and a girl who was staying with them and does designs for advertisements etc, mostly things of girls á la

> Gibson and Stanlows . . . quite brilliant little bits some of them were . . . I think Thomson is a clever little cock and can teach me no end of anatomy and perhaps of painting, but he's so beastly modest and always makes out he's only an 'amateur' . . .
> Thomson was very pleased with the pen and inks of the gypsies and gave me great praise for them, especially the one with the 'at. Of course he couldn't resist calling them Herkomerish and Walkerish etc which rather annoyed me. He is going to get me a model and he will demonstrate anatomy on him etc.

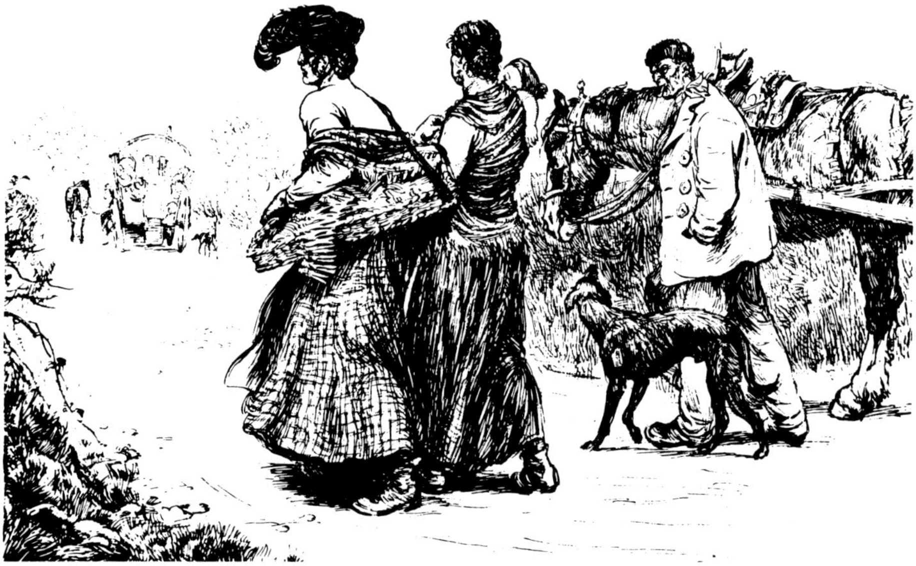

The Gypsies on the Road
Pen and ink, 1906-7. 9½″ × 11½″ *Brian Hatton Gallery, Hereford*

It is clear that Thomson very soon summed up the potentialities of his new pupil for a few days later Brian says;

> Thomson wants me to help him in drawing plates for a book on anatomy of the horse in some future time perhaps.

Brian was beginning to enjoy the lighter side of University life. Nearly every day he went out to a breakfast party and once a week he returned hospitality in his own rooms.

> I fed my honoured guests on fish, then devilled fowl and bacon, tea or coffee, toast, butter and marmalade. All of which is the usual thing with the exception of eggs and bacon, or kidneys and bacon, or hashed pheasant . . . the whole affair lasts from about 8.30 to 9.45 but of course that means a smoke afterwards

for those who smoke. The conversation is usually very high class, i.e. personal remarks about the way in which the different personages eat or don't eat, etc, also sport or current events of paramount importance viz. college events. We rarely allow ourselves to be dragged into arguments about theology or suchlike vulgar and commonplace subjects . . . There are to be celebrations of 3 'Twenty-firsters' tonight in this quad, that will mean a frightful din and free drinks all round, chairs burnt etc, rather exciting . . .

Much as he enjoyed the social life of Oxford and the companionship of his friends, Brian, the visionary, still desired periods of solitude. On one such occasion he wrote:

Have been a long walk along the canal and out on the Broad meadow (or some such name) one big meadow about 2 miles long and ¾ mile broad. Perfectly flat with a river on one side with sailing skiffs and canoes etc, and on the other side the canal and barges. Rows of willows and poplars in the distance and the towers of Oxford on the horizon, it strikes me that that is where Tennyson got his idea for the Lady of Shalott. It reminded me of it at once only I didn't see the castle on the island.

Brian joined the Union where he could borrow books, be supplied with writing paper and ink and have his letters stamped free of charge, as well as having the privilege of joining in debates. All this for the sum of £1.10 a year.

The Union is awfully nice, and I do all my writing here now, you can get your College address and whatnot on the paper . . . It is very amusing to watch the different expressions of the men writing opposite me:
Drat, the man on the right has just gone, he was doing his accounts. I'm sorry for him if they were in such a state as mine. I always forget to put down the various items until a week afterwards, consequently one or two (?) get occasionally (!!) left out . . . A great gaunt Don has subsided beside me now. Lord how he sniffs. Am going to dine with Raper and a select company in the old Bursar's rooms tonight. Shall sport my dress clothes for the first time.

Very soon Brian was attending a lecture given at the Union by Lord Roberts.

He had a very small voice but I was well up in front and heard every word. It was on the N.W. frontier of India, and very good, especially towards the end. This is an attempt at him, he has a huge braincase and large ears and is very well made and set up, on a miniature scale.

Nov. 13th 1905 Oxford

I am going to attend my first lecture tomorrow morning at New College, on Henry VIII's reign I believe. These old dons are very sleepy, I believe they would have been quite content to let me live as a gentleman at large for ever more, so I just ran round and stirred up old Blakiston with the result that about an hour afterwards one of the lecturers, a certain Rev. M. W. Paterson, who seemed rather a jolly sort, came to my room with a list of lectures and we marked some that looked useful. History and two a week on social questions or something of the type, altogether about five of 'em.

Mr Raper also had some suggestions to make about Brian's academic studies.

> 14th Nov.
>
> Old R. seems quite interested in me! had a long talk last night says I must know more about mythology etc, therefore must read some of the old Greek authors in English. He's going to see about it.

Brian's days were very full now, what with lectures, the Art School and Thomson as well as his social life and his letters describe all those facets of his existence.

> Did a lecture this morning. No end of men and women there. I took no end of unreadable notes with a pencil which wouldn't mark! and tried to pretend I was busy! . . . Have just been to a Rembrandt lecture where I enjoyed myself very much. Am simply inundated with invitations to grub with different men and having them to me. Went to watch Trinity beat Jesus, Cambridge this afternoon . . . I've been to lunch with Patterson, a young don, and have been sketching his dogs, an Irish Terrier and a Spaniel of whom I am going to do him a little pen and ink. Went to the Slade this morning . . . They've got a girl this time who is infinitely pleasanter to draw, though not a Venus, than the beery bob we had last week.

At the end of November, Brian received "an awfully nice letter" from Mary Watts, inviting him to spend a weekend with her at Limmerslease. She was anxious for him to see some of Signor's studies in chalk which were shortly to be removed, thinking they would be helpful to him. Brian immediately accepted. His fellow guest was head of a big Canadian bank and was described by Mary in a letter to Mrs Hatton as "the most cultured man in Canada" and a collector of pictures and etchings. She continued.

> I should like you to have seen his face when I showed him Brian's sketch book. His first words were almost Signor's, 'The schools have nothing to teach him'.

Mary had a long talk with Brian about the merits of art schools and said that she believed there was something to be gained from the regular work and the atmosphere, also from the blunders of others. She gave Brian an introduction to a fellow undergraduate of the name of Hahn* who she described as "a heaven-born art critic and lover of art".

Brian was rather dubious about meeting Hahn, saying that he didn't sound a very lively sort of person, but hoped that he wouldn't turn out to be too bad. A few days later he went to tea with him.

> He is German and very nice but frightfully aesthetic or whatever you call it. Goes into rhapsodies over Burne Jones's life by his wife — scarcely healthy in his mind I should say. He's too young to talk such drivel about Burne-Jones and Watts, though very good drivel of its sort, accompanied by plenty of action. He indulges in walks and hockey in the afternoons so I expect to have the pleasure of a walk with him some time! If he jaws much about the scenery I shall go mad or

*This eccentric young man, Kurt Hahn of Christchurch, was later to make his name in England as the founder of Gordonstoun and the Outward Bound Schools.

contradict him I'm sure. Can't stick having things explained to me which I can see well enough with my own eyes. But perhaps he's not so bad when you get used to him. He was so nervous when he came and introduced himself to me that I thought he was going mad the way he danced round the room — rather an uncomfortable five minutes for both of us.

Although the term was nearing its end, Brian still looked for a daily letter from his mother.

Nov. 29th 1905 Oxford Union Society

My dear Mother
Glad to hear from you this morning. I get so accustomed to a note every morning that I miss them frightfully . . .
I had a party of seven this morning, all senior men with the exception of one. I didn't find out until morning chapel that it was not the thing for freshers to invite senior men out. But they all came and seemed to rather enjoy it.
Yesterday evening I went to a smoker at Hertford . . . [it] ended in fine style with a bonfire in which several chairs and tables were consumed, teapots etc. One man (slightly squiffy) tried to jump it but only succeeded in sitting in the middle and getting burnt. A few windows broken, likewise many sets of crockery etc . . . I missed the 'Freshers Drunk' at the beginning of term. I believe only two fellows got squiffy and they were both Bishop's sons!!

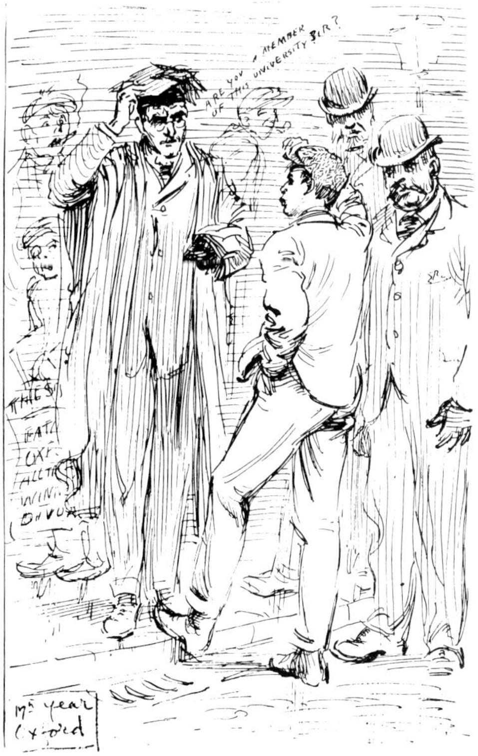

Dec. 2nd
I've only done one morning chapel this week . . . so consequently was 'hauled' this morning. I was simply bursting when I interviewed the Dean and put it down to the beastly Oxford climate that made me so sleepy that I couldn't get up in the mornings. The poor old Dean (who is very nervous) blushed very much and tried to look severe, but only told me to do 5 next week instead of 4 . . .
I was progged last night, it was so foggy I ran into the prog just 5 yards from my own gate, rough luck, rooked me 5/- next morning for being without cap and gown.
Love B.H.

On 4th December Brian sent his mother a post card saying:

Will return on Monday DV & WP.

So ended his first term at Oxford.

CHAPTER THIRTEEN

Halcyon Days

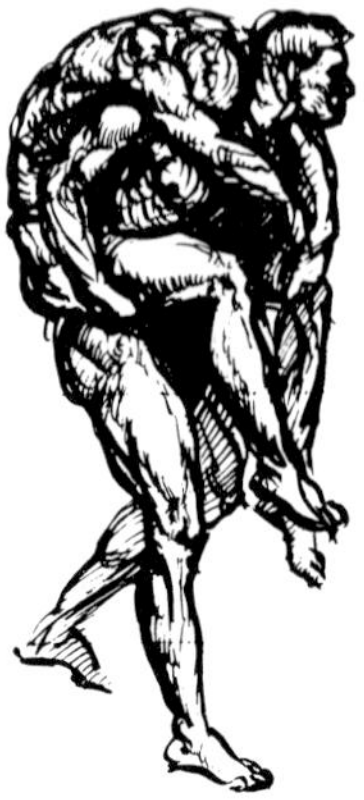

WHEN Brian returned to Oxford in January 1906 he continued to write to his mother several times a week, but now the letters are interspersed with post-cards. He began the term with one of his unpredictable indispositions. This time it took the form of gastritis, or possibly an attack of appendicitis? He suffered bouts of sickness all through the night and by 5 a.m. he was in such acute pain and misery that he called Raper who sent for a doctor.

Jan 30th

. . . Raper has been very kind and so has the scout in looking after me, and altogether I feel very comfortable, eating Brands essence and warm milk. Am going to have some bread and milk or something a bit more substantial presently.
Hahn and Chapman have just been in for a while. Hahn is going to send me round a few comic books and papers to enliven proceedings . . . Can't think what started this business as I have eaten nothing nor been bumped into nor felt a chill . . . Have been sleeping all morning. Much love to you all. Something always happens to upset my plans but thank goodness it isn't much this time.

Jan 31st

My dear Mother,
I knew you wouldn't be able to resist telegraphing in spite of my protests. I am up now and have been entertaining friends all the afternoon. Hahn & Co like The Turnip Cutters very much. Am getting on first rate though have lived on bread and milk today.
Am of course expecting a worried and worrying note from you in the morning. But for goodness sake sleep at night and . . . don't worry.

The picture which Brian referred to as "The Turnip Cutters", which was admired by Hahn and his other friends, had been drawn by Brian during the Christmas vacation. Eventually it was chosen by the British Museum as an example of his work and is now in the permanent collection in the Print Room.

Brian soon regained his health and settled down to the routine of University life. He added French to his curriculum for it was always in his mind that one day he would go to Paris to study art. He continued to work with Thomson who, although he was not permitted to take an art class, as this was not his province, allowed Brian to study with him as a special favour.

> Thomson showed me how he had seen some students working abroad somewhere, viz. to tie the charcoal on to a piece of wood about 3 feet long and work on a big scale standing as far back as possible.
> I found it difficult at first to hit the paper in the right place, but the result seemed to please the little man.

It was during this term that Brian became acquainted with Gerald Siordet of Balliol, and a close and lasting friendship grew up between them. Brian admired Siordet's artistic ability saying, "From what I can make out he has great imagination, but lacks knowledge to carry it out. Awfully nice man".

Later they were sharing a model and Brian was helping him with perspective. Two other close friends were Ralph Enfield and Oswald Chapman and he continued his acquaintance with Hahn whom he found to be a stimulating companion, even if they didn't always see eye to eye.

> Just off to spend an evening with Hahn. This is his last term. No doubt in an hour's time I shall be entangled in weighty argument about something or nothing ending in a fight.

The bumping races at the end of February delighted Brian and exercised his descriptive powers.

> Have been down to the river this afternoon. Shouting and running with the Toggers (i.e. Torpids = college 8s without sliding seats) The bumping races began today . . . Our second Togger nearly bumped, but silly fool caught a crab at critical moment and we got bumped instead. 1st Togger held its own well. About 10 or 12 boats are started at equal distances behind one another. The tow path is congested with people running (sometimes over their shoes in slush) and firing guns, rattles and other instruments.

> March 11th
> I went to see the Light of the World by Holman Hunt this afternoon. Rather disappointing, I thought, it looks so like an oleograph, especially about the white gown. And the face is very com-com, the whole thing seems to lack simplicity and therefore dignity, though of course it is a most wonderful piece of work and very soft, not glaring like the ones you saw in the Ashmolean. It's not very big either.

The last letter of term was written in a light-hearted tone;

> We all joined hands and danced round the Dean . . . poor man did look a fool he tried to smile but blushed instead. Old Raper was in great form, they wanted to chair him but he wasn't having any . . . We had a piano out and danced a bit, a tight man played in marvellous style, arms and legs, towards the end half the notes had gone and it sounded like a banjo. Someone climbed out of a window and managed to put a cast of Venus de Milo in a hitch about half way up the buildings. We made a collection — 2s 2d (all in coppers) and presented it to the Dean in a jerry.

When the summer term started Brian left Mr Raper's rooms and moved into digs at 57 St John's Street. He told his mother that the rooms were very nice and bright, "papered with red and lots of cushions" and that the old girl who ran them was very obliging. Mrs Hatton continued to write to Brian every day. She too had taken to using post cards, but as she was not always very discreet, Brian found it necessary to reprimand her.

Turnip Pullers Resting.
Pencil, 1906 *By courtesy of the Trustees of the British Museum*

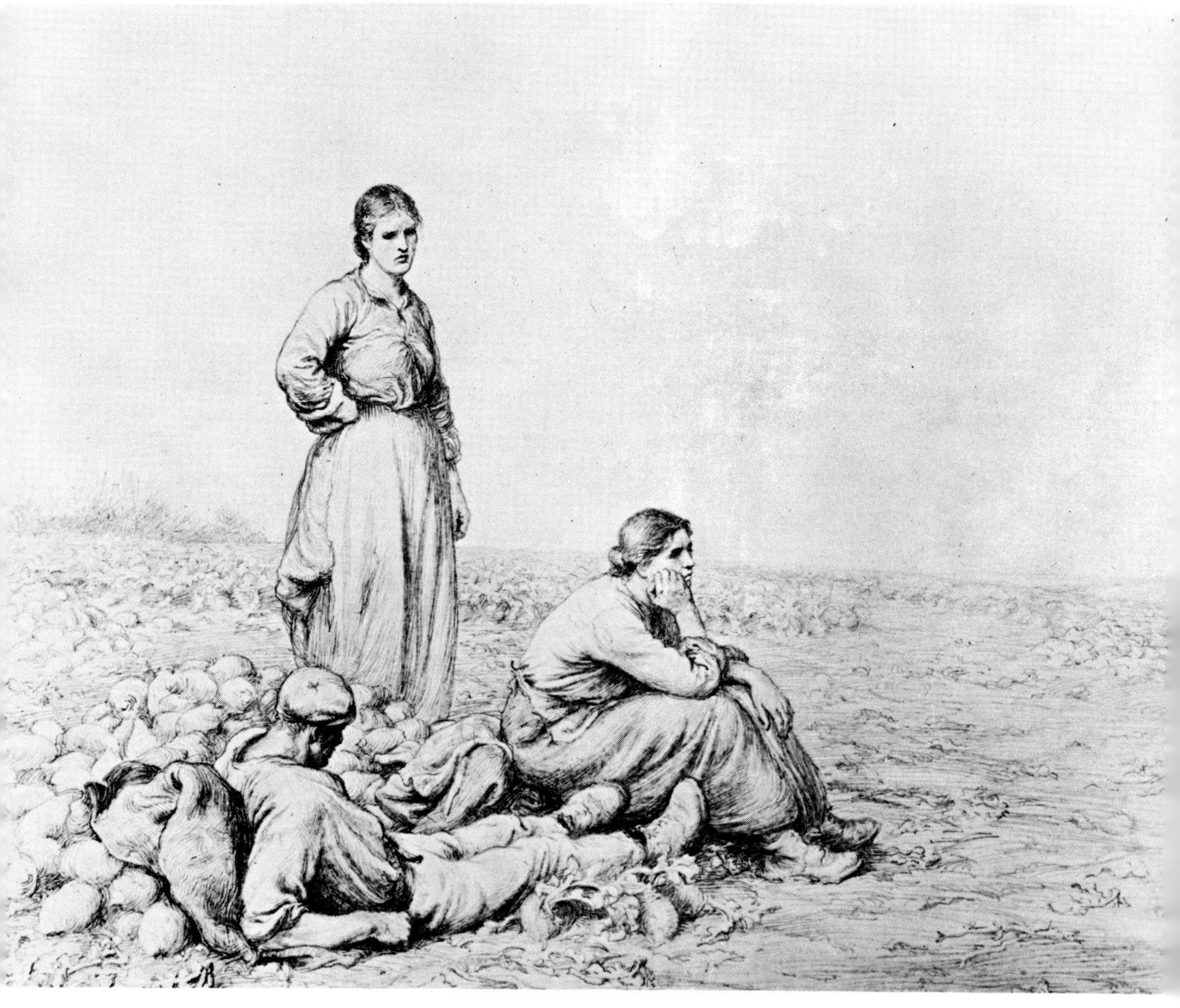

> You do put some most undesirable things on my P.C.s because of course the servant reads them all when she brings them up. So if you feel that you must keep on reminding me 'to take care of myself' or 'to put on more things this changeable weather' etc, please enclose them in an envelope but better by far to leave them out altogether as I don't take the slightest notice of them.

Brian made the most of this, his last term at Oxford. He attended numerous lectures mostly connected with art or literature. They included "Classic and Modern Epic Poems", "Greek Sculpture of the 5th Century B.C." and Thomson on "Surface Anatomy". The latter was really intended for medical students but Brian found the lectures helpful. The margins of his notebooks were always liberally sprinkled with sketches. He read copiously, sometimes in the Bodleian but more often in a boat on the river. Much of his reading consisted of Homer, Ruskin, Keats, George Borrow and More's *Utopia*. He was enchanted by the beauty of Oxford and the surrounding countryside, especially the river.

> April 21st 1906 Union Society, Oxford
>
> . . . Oxford and its surroundings are beginning to look very pretty now that the trees are coming into foliage, especially the pear blossom in our front quad . . . Have been slacking and reading on the river this afternoon, quite warm and nice and also did a little sketching . . . Saw a heron the other day when out in the 'Knu', and several wild ducks etc. We have found a stream that no one appears to know of or frequent. It is very pretty and home of many wild birds etc.

The "Knu" was the name that Brian had given to a canoe that he was sharing with Siordet. He loved to find a secluded spot under the sheltering trees, where "its quite possible to do a certain amount of reading when moored against the bank propped up with plenty of cushions. Have done quite a lot of Utopia like that [!]".

> May 1st
>
> This morning I suppose the choristers greeted the 1st May from the top of Magdalen Tower with a hymn etc at 5 o'clock a.m. . . . I spent the afternoon on the river by myself, and I must say I preferred being alone as I could just cast anchor and sketch and read etc without consulting anyone.

Like all creative people, Brian sometimes needed solitude but he also delighted in the companionship of his friends. He describes a happy occasion when he, and several companions, spent the whole day boating up the river, stopping for lunch and tea at a cottage. However "they were slackers and we didn't get nearly as far as we ought to have". Brian remedied this lapse by paddling the Knu some nine miles to Abingdon and back.

When not on the river, he took his recreation bicycling in the countryside, sketching or going for a lone walk.

May 27th

I went for a long walk this afternoon by myself which I enjoyed very much. The breezes are so refreshing but it came on to rain . . . I met a gentleman with a patriarchal beard and equally long hair, a sort of ancient Briton. He could have passed for Michael Angelo's Moses very well. I felt inclined to stop and sketch him, but he seemed uneasy and showed the white of his eyes. So I judged it safer to pass on . . .

A man from Balliol looked me up yesterday, named (I think) Lowinsky. He had heard that I daubed, so introduced himself as an artist who had studied under Brangwyn and does charcoal heads life size dontcherknow. He swaggered about my room until I could hardly keep my hands off him. He is going to ask me to brekker some day soon.

Music was always an important factor in Brian's life and with the early encouragement of Dr Lancaster he had developed a liking for the theatre. On one occasion he had to make a difficult choice between music and drama.

Joachim is here next Wednesday afternoon, if it is not too dreadfully expensive I shall go and hear him, which means of course that I shan't be able to go and see 'Pansy's Breach of Promise Case' at the theatre!!!

No such decision had to be made when Benson's Shakespeare company came to Oxford or when he went to see Martin Harvey in "The Cigarette Maker's Romance". He commented, "He's awfully good but the rest of the company frightfully poor".

Brian enjoyed Eights Weeks and the ensuing gaiety which he described as "a small Henley". Enfield's family came up and there was a dinner party at the Mitre and Brian entertained Enfield and his sister to tea in his rooms.

She is a quaint little bird, used to be at Somerville Ladies College here and looks somewhat like it too.

During the last week of term Brian and his friend Chapman went to spend the day with Miss Landau at High Wycombe.

June 5th 1906 Oxford

My dear Mother,

We had a splendid day at Piper's Corner yesterday. We started at 8.15 from Oxford and got back at 8 p.m. . . . Miss Landau started a sketch of me!! in black and white chalk on gray paper. We had two sittings of about ½ hour each. But although she worked tremendously fast it wasn't finished. I can't say it was very like me, a ¾ view: Chapman says I wasn't looking nearly so thin as she depicted me, for which I am heartily thankful, for she tried to make me look aesthetic and hollow cheeked, when I was feeling particularly bloated after lunch. Moreover I am nice and plump at any time . . . Mrs. Zellner (Miss Landau's mother) told me that, on very good authority and by a man whom she could trust etc etc, she has been told that Hospitalfields is a rotten place, not because Harcourt's system of painting etc is bad but because he is scarcely ever there . . . and that the students were a rotten lot and the whole tone and morality of the place was bad! She wouldn't tell me all that she had heard but gave me to understand that it was all very shocking!! However she has offered to write to Mrs. Watts about it so we will await what she says first. Of course Mrs. Watts would not be likely to know the ins and outs of the place at all . . .

Much love to all
Brian

Mrs Hatton probably felt rather disconcerted at Mrs Zellner's description of the Hospitalfields Art School at Arbroath for it was practically decided that Brian should enrol there in the autumn. Mary Watts had favoured the idea of his studying under Harcourt and had advised a reconnaisance visit to the school during the Vac. Mary probably became uneasy when she received Mrs Zellner's letter, for she immediately sent a telegram to Brian, asking him to visit her on the following Sunday at Limmerslease. Brian willingly accepted the invitation.

11th June 1906 Oxford

My dear Mother,

I have returned from Limmerslease this afternoon after a most enjoyable time there. I spent all Sunday morning looking at the drawings in the Gallery which has been built near the pottery and which is being enlarged and added to, to take some of Mr. Watts's sculptures including the original gesso of Physical Energy as soon as it comes back from being cast. Of course I slipped the key of the gallery door into my pocket (its about nine inches long) and forgot all about it, until I came back here, so have just sent it off with my apologies. That's me all over, missing link somewhere.

The pottery business is getting on no end. They are making, among other things, an elaborate mantlepiece, with symbolical figures all round. Mrs. Watts got me to do the hands of two of them. She stood as model for the 1st lot. Of course I did them in more or less sort of style (never having done any before) but I think helped her a bit. She finds that the boys can do the faces pretty well but nearly always fail with the hands.

On Sunday evening I did a little sketch of 'Dear Miss Mackintosh' much to the delight of her fiasco* 'Mike' whom you met in London. However I made the lower half of her face too big and wasn't able to alter it this morning as the 'dear thing' was 'indisposed' . . . Mrs. Watts wants me to have his book on the anatomy of the horse which I have brought back with me. I should think it's very valuable, all in old English and most beautifully engraved plates.

Mrs. Watts thinks a winter in Egypt would do me more good than all the art schools in the world, and also set me up in health. And then when I settle down to serious art, if I like she would tell me all Signor's little tricks of painting etc, which she knew so well. There was a very learned and businesslike Canadian staying there who thought that I should not go to an art school, and gave Poyntor as an example of academic teaching. But Mrs. W. will think it over and wants me to do the same and take good advice about it etc. She will give me an introduction to Harcourt that I might see his school.

Can't write any more now. Much love, Brian.

*Fiasco was a family word for "fiance".

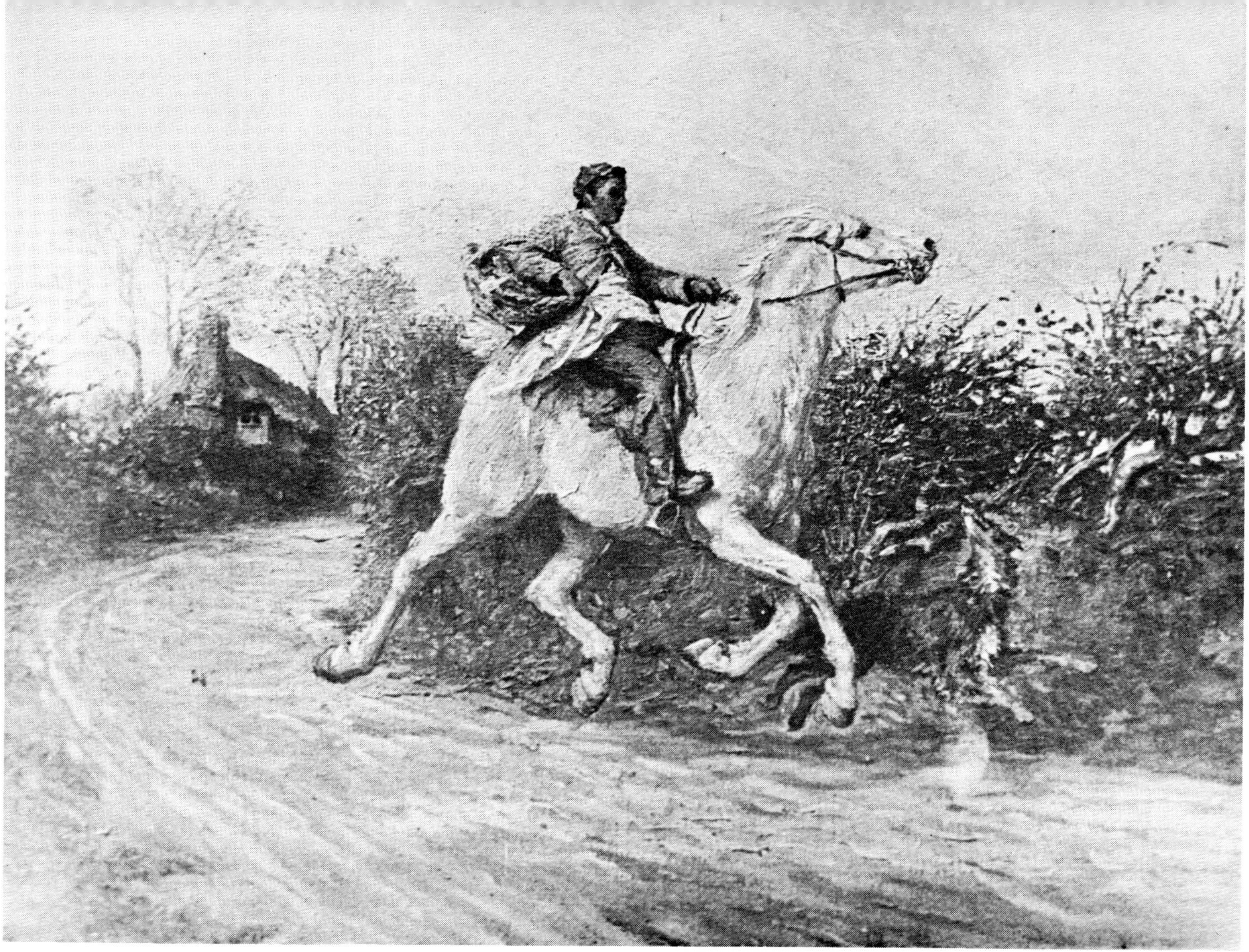

The Butcher Boy and his Dog. Oil, 1910. 10¾″ × 14″ *Mrs Ralph Symonds*

Mary Watts was indeed a very talented woman and with the aid of her pottery school she had taught and inspired village people to carry out work of a very high quality. The most interesting example of her creative ability is the Mortuary Chapel at Compton, erected by her with no assistance other than that of the local builder and blacksmith and a group of villagers trained at the pottery school. The interior of the chapel has a rococo richness perhaps unsurpassed by any other English church. Every inch of the walls and vaulting are covered with a relief decoration in the style of *art nouveau* described by Mary as "glorified wall-paper". Winged messengers, a tree of life, seraphs, angels' heads and an intricate tangle of Celtic knots are moulded in "a solid plastic material called Gesso, its substance plaster of paris in which a fibrous material is soaked". It was in that medium that Mary was working when she asked Brian to help her model the hands of the symbolic figures for her mantelpiece.

Brian had no regrets about leaving Oxford. Some weeks before the end of term he said, "I am beginning to get bored with Oxford and especially with the men of my own year at Trinity. They are all either a very sporting and betting set, or else very flat and uninteresting". However, he remained faithful to his special friends and invited Enfield to visit his family. He told his mother that Enfield would be bringing his cello with him and he gave her a vivid description of the expected guest.

> You will probably receive a shock when you see Enfield!! He is very very short and dark with a great bristling moustache!! and tiny little stumpy legs!! And is never seen without a great pair of goggles and a huge pipe in his mug!!!!!

In July Brian paid a return visit to the Enfield family who lived at Burton Joyce, near Nottingham. He wrote a descriptive account of a day out with Ralph.

> We went about 20 miles by train to Mansfield and then cycled about 8 miles to Edwinstow where we had lunch (11.30 a.m.) and then a mile on to the forest where a huge oak tree is called Major Oak or Queen's Oak. It is supposed to be the largest known oak in the world and it certainly is tremendous. 32 feet round the narrowest part of the trunk and 67 feet round the roots. As soon as we got there it came on to rain so we sheltered for about ¾ hour inside, where 16 people can be squashed in . . . arrived back in time for dinner in excellent spirits tho' somewhat damp.

It was typical of Brian that he should leave his dress coat and boots behind when he left the Enfields, but perhaps the fact that he had made sketches of various members of the family made up for this misdeed. From Nottingham he went to stay with Great Uncle Charles Marr who lived at Chislehurst. This massive, genial man, who had helped with Brian's fees when he was at Eywas Harold Vicarage, under the pretext of commissioning a picture, was deeply attached to Brian. He went out of his way to make this a memorable visit, even planning "a wee jamboree on the Continent".

Nearly every morning started with Brian going for a ride — "splendid horse and a groom as well behind". He visited the Chislehurst Caves, played golf with his uncle and made a red chalk drawing of his head. Together they spent a crowded day in London.

> We went first to the Constitutional, where we met Harry Thomson who took all off to the Zoo . . . He knew all the keepers and they took us inside some of the cages and places where the sea-lions were and some of the big birds. The Zoo was very crowded after the Eton and Harrow match . . .
> After spending about three hours there we had dinner with Uncle C. at the Athenaeum and then Thomson took us to the Arts Club where we had coffee, and he introduced me to Spielman, who chatted for a minute or two. He spoke very highly of Harcourt and Arbroath. Uncle C. is awfully bucked because it is all free!!! He keeps repeating it!!!! So after going to one or two more clubs we got back here at about 9.30 p.m. . . . Am going up to Town by the 3 o'clock train to see the Flemish exhibition at the Guildhall . . . and then meet Uncle C. at his office.

The "wee hurl" on the Continent was Brian's first trip abroad and Uncle Charlie kept the destination a secret until they were about to start. They went first to Amsterdam and then to the Hague, where Brian wrote to his mother to tell her how they were getting on.

> 21st July 1906 Hotel des Indes
> The Hague
>
> My dear Mother
>
> I am not writing you a long letter but I thought you would probably want a line to know how I am getting along. Yesterday we left Amsterdam and went to the Island of Marken by steamboat, along the canal and back by Zuyder Zee, then on to here by train. Today we had 'Brunch' at 12 midi!! And then we pottered round the Paul Potter's bull and several Rembrandts etc, and then became inflicted with a guide who drove with us to the Palace in the woods, where the Peace Conference was held, and then we drove on to Scheveningen or some such place which is very fashionable and on the coast about 4 miles from here. We have just come back.
>
> I am extremely well and not tired at all, the air has been very fresh and bracing since we have been over here. Uncle C is most attentive to all my little wants and in a terrible funk of you if I get the 'stuffing' taken out of me.
>
> With much love to all
> Brian

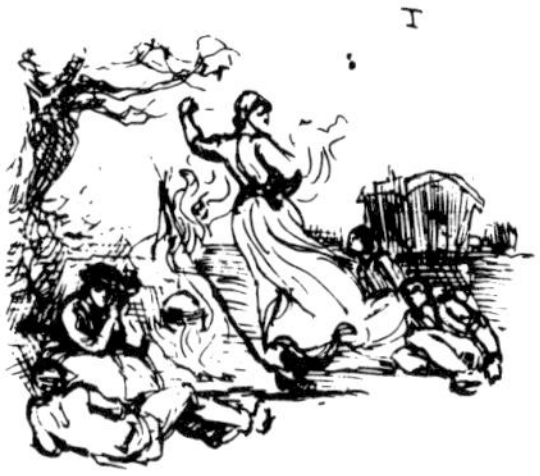

CHAPTER FOURTEEN

Arbroath

IN AUGUST 1906, when Brian was just nineteen, he went to Hospitalfields, the art school at Arbroath, situated on the east coast of Scotland, north of Dundee. Hospitalfields was built in the Victorian Scottish baronial style and stood on the site of the ancient hospital of the Abbey.* It had been opened as an art centre in 1902 and was run by a board of trustees. The resident master, or governor, as he was called, was George Harcourt, R.A. the former pupil of Professor Herkomer.

Most of the students were taking a four year course, but Brian went first as a "visitor". However, after a few days, Harcourt told him that he had a vacancy and asked him if he would like to stay until Christmas — possibly longer. Brian accepted with alacrity. In the past he had not felt the need for instruction in either drawing or composition, both of which came naturally to him. However, he had not as yet come to terms with the art of working in oils and it was here that he needed help. Unfortunately he soon began to doubt Harcourt's ability as an instructor.

> Harcourt spends the whole day fooling about with his children, a boy and two girls, all under 7 years old. He neither seems to work on his account or instruct the students. It is a great pity as we only see him on an average for about 20 minutes a day in the studio and then he never does much. His brother lives here too, a dreadful individual (called 'Bushey Bill', he comes from Bushey) who also dry-nurses the kids all day long . . . Harcourt only paints about 2 pictures a year now, and he paints exceedingly quickly. But I suppose his £500 a year has made him lazy. But he is awfully nice and kind and a clever step-dancer!!

One of the nice traits in Brian's character was his generosity. He seldom criticised any one without also referring to their better points. A few days later he says;

> I got old Harcourt into conversation last night and wormed out a few tips about oils. He tells one a lot more out of work hours than in, if you can catch him.

Brian soon settled down and put in a good day's work and he ceased to complain about lack of tuition.

> I work from about 9.30 until 12.45 in the morning and in the afternoon from 2 till 4 . . . Harcourt showed me how to etch on copper plate last night. I did a little man and a geegee (as per usual!) Tonight he is going to show me how to bite it and take prints.

*Hospitalfields was owned by a descendant of the Philorth family of Fraser who married Patrick Allan, a painter of humble origin whose mission in later life was to help struggling artists. This benevolent scheme was administered by leaders of Scottish art, and living and tuition were free for the students.

Later he said that etching was a dreadful business. The drawing was the least part of it, but one had to have an immense amount of paraphernalia — "lamps, screens, needles, varnishes, grounds, inks, burnishers, a press for printing, acids and baths and goodness knows what besides". He said that he was getting used to oils and progressing slowly.

> Harcourt makes one get one part absolutely right before going any further. There is no hoping it will come right in the second coat because there aint going to be no second coat!! . . . I have bought myself a painting overall as I get so mucked up. The first day they were all so fascinated by its cleanness that someone labelled me
>
> Hatton
His
Shirt

Brian often spent the evenings on the golf links, the cost being three pence a round, and on Saturdays, when there were no formal working hours, he would explore the countryside on his bicycle or go for a ride on a hired horse. Needless to say, he found time for sketching, delighting in the changing landscape. "The effects of the sunshine and shadow on the corn is wonderful." He avoided going to the kirk whenever possible.

> I find the Scotch services very dull and uninteresting. Everything is done for one. There's not even an amen to be said by the congregation and the Sermons are very long.

At the end of September the whole school spent a week landscape painting at Auldbar which was about ten miles from Arbroath.

> The scenery is rather fine. The other students come out by train in the morning and back again about tea time, which means that one misses the evening effects etc. So a man named Anderson and I have taken a room close to the scene of action for 12/- each per week!! and very good grub too. [Its] about ¼ mile lower down the line at a small farm house with a mill adjoining.
> I am painting solidly from about 10 a.m. until nearly 7 p.m. with about ten mins interval for a lunch and sandwiches and pastry and ½ hour for a meat tea at 4.30. But I am thriving and not at all too tired — standing all the while too.
> I and another man have started a very ambitious landscape in which I am rapidly becoming a hopeless cropper, but it is all practice and it is more exciting to do an interesting composition, which is beyond one's powers, than a simpler piece which may be more suitable . . . I am struggling away in oils of course . . . The daughter of the house, we were told, was exceedingly clever at playing the organ. One night we asked her to play on a little asthmatic thing they had there. And then — well then we wished we hadn't because she sang too, or at least tried to! Without opening her mouth! All through her nose!!! We could hardly contain ourselves and keep up a respectable appearance in front of the fond parents.
> She sang 'Take this message to my Mother' and 'Bluebell' etc.!

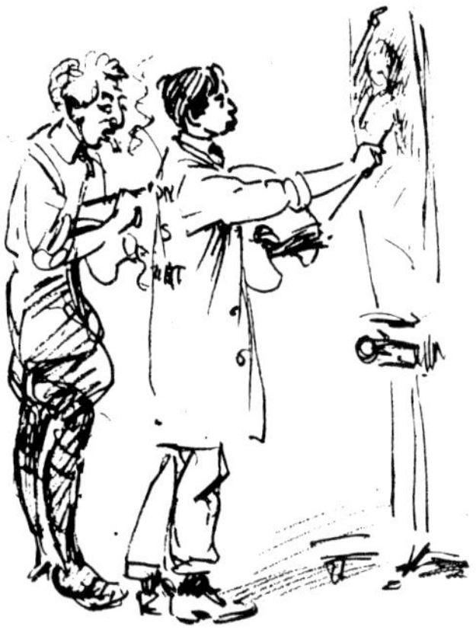

Brian kept up with his old friends and mentions receiving letters from Mrs Lancaster, Mary Watts, Curly and some of his Oxford contemporaries. Curly had been suffering from a bad attack of jaundice and Kurt Hahn had been ill for some time with a curious malaise which he described as "sun-stroke". He was unable to work and spent much of his time in a darkened room. Brian wrote;

> Hahn is just going to have an operation 'to remove some superfluous fluid in his head'. It is not serious, so he says. 'And *then* I will begin my *life*.' Typically Hahnish.

Kurt Hahn's operation was certainly a turning point in his long and eventful life, which culminated in his founding Gordonstoun, The Outward Bound Schools and the Atlantic Colleges.

As the winter closed in, outdoor painting ceased and Brian, who loved to work outside, felt rather frustrated.

> We are having a figure model tomorrow again, it will be a pleasant change after the sickening old men's heads that we do week after week. Just great furry lumps of grey beard with a cherry end of a nose sticking in the midst thereof. As per sketch.
>
> It's a lovely moonlight night. I have just been along the seashore.

One evening all the students went to Dundee to hear a lecture given by Herkomer. Brian was most impressed by the quality of the lecture which he described as "excellent". When it was over they all foregathered at the hotel where Herkomer was staying, and spent an hour with him, drinking champagne. Brian remarked that he talked so splendidly that one quite forgot his conceit!

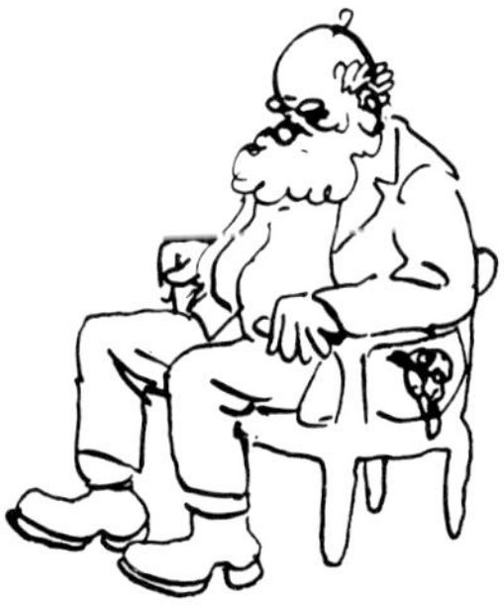

Christmas was drawing near and Brian sent etchings to all his friends this year, as he had no time to do anything else, but he was not in sympathy with this medium. He described it as "beastly dirty inky work. I fairly hate it". He said that his oil painting was becoming a little easier although he was still far from satisfied with the results. He was now looking forward to returning home but he begged his mother to stop fussing over him.

> Please don't get hot water bottle for my bed as soon as I come home. I have never had my bedroom window shut yet . . . it is always *wide* open . . . For heaven's sake don't burden me by sending a travelling rug, I shall have enough to look after as it is, and the trains are always over heated.

As it turned out, Brian did not go home for Christmas, as his sister Ailsa was ill with diphtheria; instead he went to stay with some relatives who lived in Killochan Castle near Girvan. Compared to the gaiety at home, he described Christmas evening as "very flat", with everyone in bed by 11.30. However, he enjoyed some rough shooting and riding and returned home at the end of the year. He didn't go back to Arbroath until the end of February, owing to some indisposition. The long train journey was something of an ordeal, and he was sick twice before reaching his destination. Once back in the bracing air of Scotland, he was soon in good health and spirits and he received a warm reception from his friends on arrival.

> 4 of the old students met me at the station amid loud applause and saved me porters and tips.

A few days after his return, Harcourt and all the students went to Edinburgh on a picture viewing expedition.

> March 17th 1907 'Spittly
> My dear Mother
> I got your budget on my return from Edinburgh last night. I enjoyed it all thoroughly. Up at 6.30 a.m. and in bed at 12.45 a.m.! There were some very fine pictures at the annual show, some of them on loan, Sargent's three 'Misses Hunters' and Clausen's 'Ploughing', an early example, and two very wonderful little specimens of D. Y. Cameron's work. Also Orchardson's portrait of Sir Walter Gilbey. It is quite a relief and an eye opener to see the different qualities that are to be obtained in paint under different handling, after the stale old life studies, etc.
> After seeing the Scottish Academy and National Gallery, I and another chappy went to Peter Pan in the afternoon. It was very charming and original, and after tea some of us went to the Empire which amused us until it was time to start for the train home.
> Am very fit — much love
> Brian.

One of the trustees of the art school, Miss MacDonald, had become interested in Brian's work. She asked him to do a design for a block calendar which was to be printed by Raphael Tuck and sold for charity, price 1/-. Brian agreed to do so, but was rather annoyed when she turned down his illustration, saying that it wasn't suitable for the classical quotations she was going to use. They were to be taken from the writings of such people as Confucius, Plato, Cicero, Bacon and Goethe.

> She might have told me all this before; however she was very nice about it and gave me a good tea. So I must have another shot I suppose. She expected to pay me for the design; but I am going to have as many calendars as I like instead and original drawing and copyright etc. So if I do it you won't be hard up for Xmas presents!!

Brian did indeed make another drawing for the calendar with a group of classical figures, which was published under the title "Daylight and Truth". Miss MacDonald said she thought it was "perfectly beautiful . . . I never dared hope that I should be able to get such an exquisite design". The calendar was sold in aid of The New Hospital for Women, London N.W. and of the Orphanage at Aberlour.

Brian's independent nature was frustrated by routine and he got bored with painting the same model day after day, even if she happened to be a good one.

> This is her last week and we are all pretty sick of her after 5 weeks every day. Although she's a very excellent model and poses for Marcus Stone and Bernard Partridge, etc. . . . Please send by return my painting coat that Dad got for me. My old one is now in pieces.

When the new model arrived, he remarked that her feet and toes were perfect, "like Trilby's", but she was "rather out of drawing in parts". He would have preferred a male model for a change. He felt that his work was progressing as he was now "not so nervous of the paint".

In April two or three old students returned to Hospitalfields for a weekend visit and this was an excuse for a "rag", which Brian enjoyed.

> Yesterday morning we all togged up in anything and everything ridiculous we could find and met the old students at the station and drove them out on a lorry!! Through the streets of Arbroath!! me driving in my pink shirt and pyjamas and a burnt cork moustache and imperial!! The others too were just as bad, or rather worse. A very high Highlander with an umbrella and red nose, etc. Several people thought it a circus procession. I further enlivened proceedings by acting postillion occasionally.

It was about this time that Mrs Hatton became interested in Oliver Lodge's writings about the spirit world, and Brian had brought one of Lodge's books back to Arbroath with him. He remarked that all the students and the Harcourts had been dipping into it, and that he himself was about to read it a second time. Brian had shown signs of being mildly interested in the occult when he and Dr Lancaster used to amuse themselves with a planchette board, but to him it had been little more than a game. Now it would seem that his mother had suggested that they might get in touch with each other through telepathy. Brian's reply was a splendid example of his healthy, commonsense attitude to life.

> I don't think I'll try the telepathy dodge just yet, as it could entail a very highly strung and nervous condition of mind and body, whereas I want to enjoy the healthy animal side of this transitory existence as long as possible! You don't mind do you?

Term ended early in May and Brian went off to pay some visits before returning home. He went first to Oxford to stay with Raper where he had "a very pleasant time". He went to see his old friend Professor Thomson and discussed Harcourt's teaching methods with him. Brian had found them uninspiring but Thomson said they had some good points, "viz it teaches you to match tone etc swiftly and accurately. But dammy, painting doesn't end there!

From Oxford Brian went on to Compton to stay with Mary Watts. He wrote home asking his mother to send him a lot of painting equipment as Mrs Watts had said he could stay as long as he liked and hoped he'd do a little work.

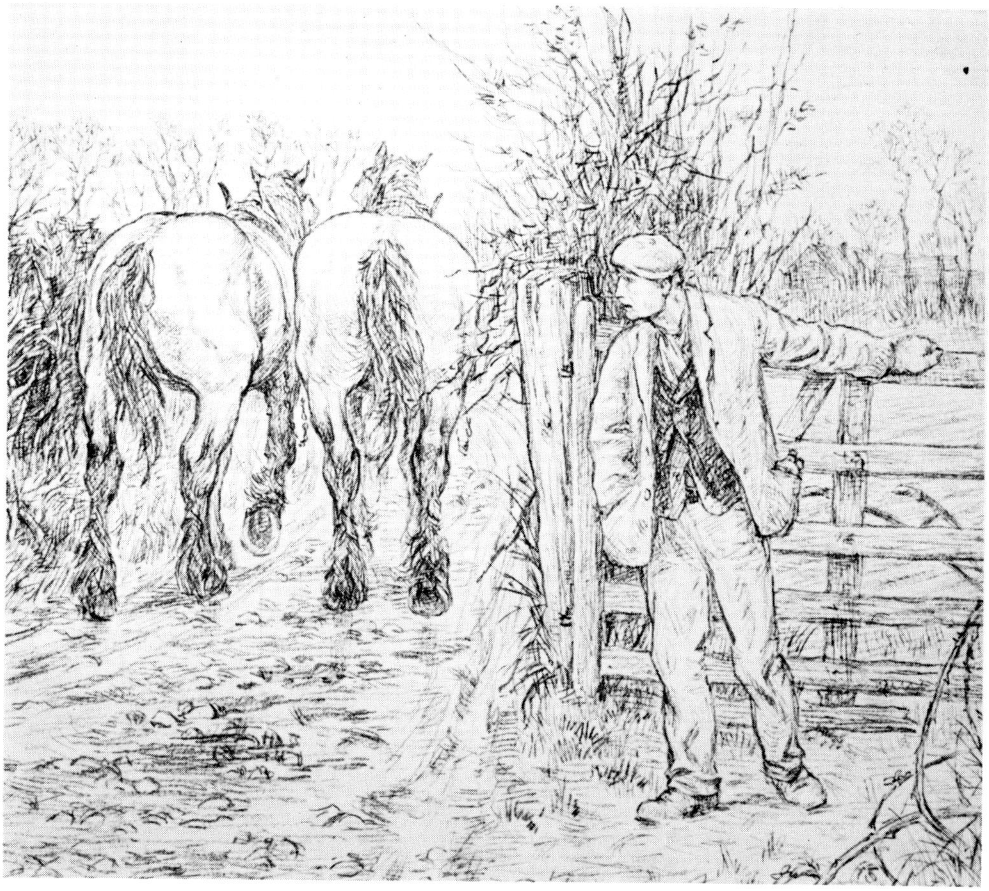

Horses and Man at Gate.
Pencil, 1910

Brian Hatton Gallery, Hereford

> 4th June
>
> Mrs. Watts doesn't think much of Arbroath teaching as it doesn't cultivate the taste for the beautiful etc, also one doesn't get enough time for studying sufficiently carefully. So I am going to put myself under her wing for a few days and see what happens. I'm going to do a little modelling till all this stuff arrives.

Two days later the painting material arrived, but Brian had another request to make.

> Please send me a pair of black evening socks with white embroidered fronts . . . Wearing the same patterned socks day and evening looks as if I didn't change 'em!!

Mrs Hatton must have had a busy time coping with Brian's requests. The socks arrived safely and also some riding breeches.

> I am riding one of Mrs. W's ponies, it is very good but too quiet for me. I borrowed a pair of spurs yesterday off the coachman and they kept him a bit more lively!! . . .
>
> I am copying a little nude study, one of the few which Mrs. W. says he painted from the model, but he has an imaginative outdoor background. I am doing it in the underpainting method and glazing with more or less pure colour on the top. It gives a quality which cannot be obtained any other way.
>
> [Mrs. Watts] has crowds of visitors every day to lunch and tea. I get awfully bored and fed up with passing things. I wonder she doesn't go cracked with being polite etc to so many people.

Brian's next visit was to Miss Landau at Hughenden, where they worked together in her studio at Piper's Corner, painting heads. He returned to Compton and spent a few more days with Mary Watts before going home at the end of July. As usual, he left something behind — his mackintosh this time, which Mary duly forwarded.

Brian returned to Arbroath at the end of August without much enthusiasm, for he was very dissatisfied with the lack of instruction he received. He was considering converting the coach house at Mount Craig into a studio and working at home in the not too distant future. As it turned out he was to leave the art centre with undue haste before the end of the term. He had never got on well with Harcourt whom he considered to be lazy, evasive and generally lacking in manly qualities. Harcourt probably resented Brian's outspoken nature and the fact that the young man could easily outwit him if drawn into an argument.

Only a few letters cover this period, but it was natural that Brian's close links with his mother should be loosened, now that he had reached manhood. In November he mentioned the fact that there was to be a fancy dress dance at the end of term. Then followed a letter which so distressed Mrs Hatton that she took to her bed for a week.

Private Dec. 1st 1907 Hospitalfields.
My dear Mother,
I am sorry that I have to tell you a most painful and unpleasant piece of news (i.e. unless your wonderful sixth sense hath divined it already!) To cut a long story short, there has been a pathetic little tragedy enacted at 'Spitaly during the last two days.
Act I Last Friday a cold frosty day, 3 men go riding.
Scene I Departure from White Hart.
Scene II Return to above with symptoms of a cold on yours truly (which is not surprising considering about 8 students are snuffling).
Scene III The interior of some place with Scottish remedies flying around!

Act II
Scene I Arrival at 'Spitaly of one student in a merry mood and encounter of same with G. Harcourt Esq. in the narrow path. The last named smells a rat (very distinctly)
Scene II Bedchamber of student with occupant wrapt in peaceful slumber. Failure of H. to elicit satisfactory responses.

Act III Next morning.
Scene I Harcourt's studio. Wrath of authority descends upon unlucky student's head, who is happy at having lost his cold. Apology of latter gentleman.
Scene II Evening of same day. Harcourt deliveres with his own hands a very carefully composed letter to student requesting that under the circumstances he should tender his resignation to himself in writing and so save reporting it to the trustees! Moreover that he should take himself away same day this first week in December. Acquiescence of student. Much sorrow is expressed on both sides.
Curtain.

How's that for quick work! Eh! I am quite sure that you will understand my feelings about the matter, in which self reproach for being a damned fool and sorrow for causing you and Dad so much trouble and anxiety and grief share the foremost place. Besides the awkward position it places me in with regard to Uncle Charlie (who would be wild if he knew) and others . . . I will wait until I get your reply to this before starting south. Will you please enclose £1 for emergencies . . .
Don't you think it would be best for everyone if you and Dad kept very quiet about my getting squiffy. You can just say that H and I had a row and we thought it better that I should leave . . . Because the real reason is that H. & I have had two or three slight differences of which I have said nothing, but which have made him have a knife in me ever since my first term . . . And by degrees I found I was in a pitched battle in which I did not spare my energy. I apologised afterwards, which he accepted, but not in spirit. And whenever things incline to go wrong, he is always ready to say something spiteful to me. Once or twice I have

snubbed him pretty severely when his blether was beyond the limit. He went very red and shut up. The fact of the matter is that he is about the laziest hound in existence and will do anything to save himself trouble, which means he does nothing . . . He is the slave of a bad-tempered wife. All very unfortunate for him and everybody in the house. He never speaks out and says what he means and never looks anyone in the face.

His plan for giving me a letter of dismissal is typical of him. Moreover I wasn't badly drunk and rode home on my bike, but felt drowsy when I got into the warm house after the cold air. The reason I went so far was because I successfully tried the remedy for a cold which I caught driving at Blairgowrie. So you needn't think that I am going to the bad or anything like that! as the taste of whisky always makes my gorge rise. By the way the other fellows I went riding with were very decent fellows, one being T.T. and the other kept well within bounds.

I think my costume for the dance will be 'The Invisible Man' à la H. G. Wells!!

. . . Much love — hope you are all well

Your loving Brian

P.S. . . . Had a very polite little tea party with the Misses MacDonald yesterday. How quickly things happen!

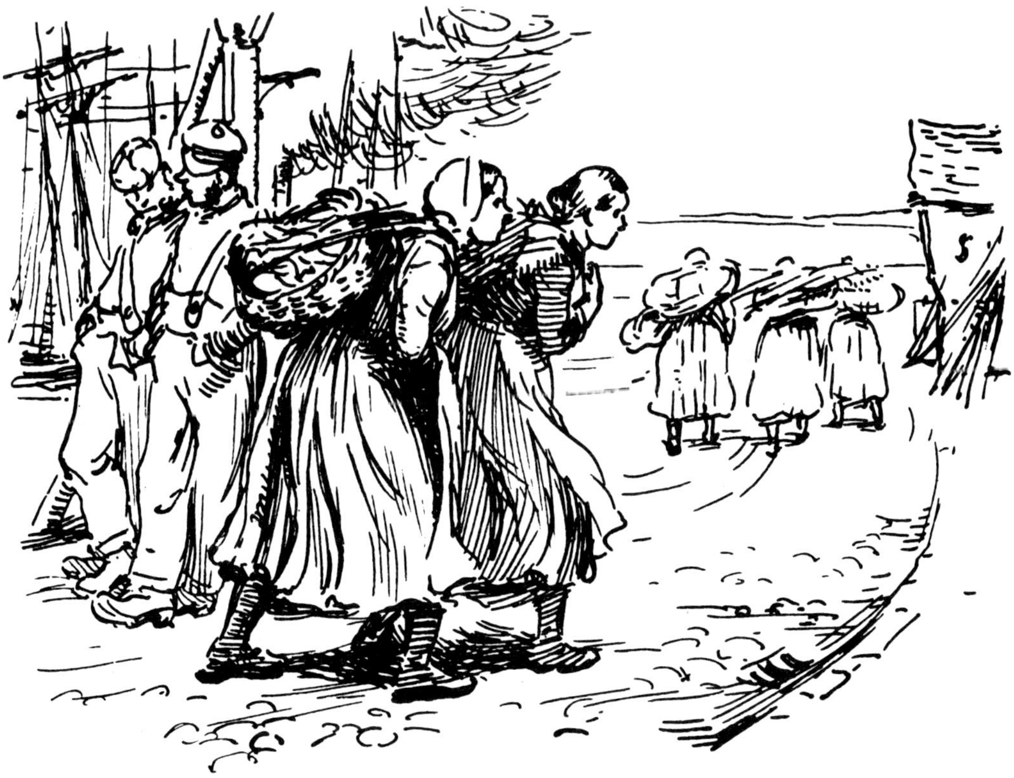

It was unfortunate for Brian that he should be in the unenviable position of the family idol. So much interest, so many hopes were centred on him, that the slightest misdemeanour on his part was bound to have wide repercussions. It must have been difficult for him to break the news of his fall from grace to his mother and he evidently found it less embarrassing to describe the incident in dramatic form. Having got over that hurdle he then reproached himself for causing his parents so much trouble and with his usual generosity he went out of his way to exonerate his companions whom he describes as "very decent fellows". It is only natural that he should ask his parents to refrain from spreading the story "about my getting squiffy" all round the family.

It does seem absurd that a little indiscretion such as this should have resulted in the termination of Brian's residence at the art school. Had it taken place at a University it would have been of no consequence. However, Harcourt seized this opportunity to get rid of a pupil he disliked. Brian had a definite advantage over him, for he never had any difficulty in expressing himself and even as a little boy he had been able to outwit his schoolmasters when it came to a wordy battle.

Brian wrote one more letter from Hospitalfields. Apparently his mother had hoped for a reprieve for him but he says;

> I don't think there is any havering in this business. It is all cut and dried in dead earnest. Although the Gov. pretends that it will not have to be reported to the Trustees, at any rate in detail, yet I know that he spent nearly the whole of Saturday with the MacDonalds (who are the working Trustees). I thought it strange that he should suddenly have enough spunk to take the responsibility of 'sacking' me into his own hands . . . I think it will be better if I write a little letter to Miss MacDonald, I can put it better. It is a rather uncomfortable thing to talk about especially to a lady.
> The only thing that I care about is worrying you. Please take it as calmly as you can for your health's sake and consequently for the sake of the rest of the family.

Miss MacDonald was evidently a woman of good sense who was able to see the incident in its true proportions. She wrote a reassuring letter to Mrs Hatton saying how vexed she was at this unfortunate trouble and begging her not to grieve over it.

> So far as I can make out there was nothing seriously wrong, and I am rather at a loss to understand Mr. Harcourt's action in the matter. Personally I must say that I am extremely sorry that Mr. Hatton is leaving Hospitalfields. Of course I always admired his work immensely and we were all very pleased to make his acquaintance . . . When you see your son he will be able to explain all sorts of things one cannot say in a letter and I shall be very glad if I can ever help him at any time, and I hope you will not sorrow over this incident as I cannot see that it is at all serious . . .

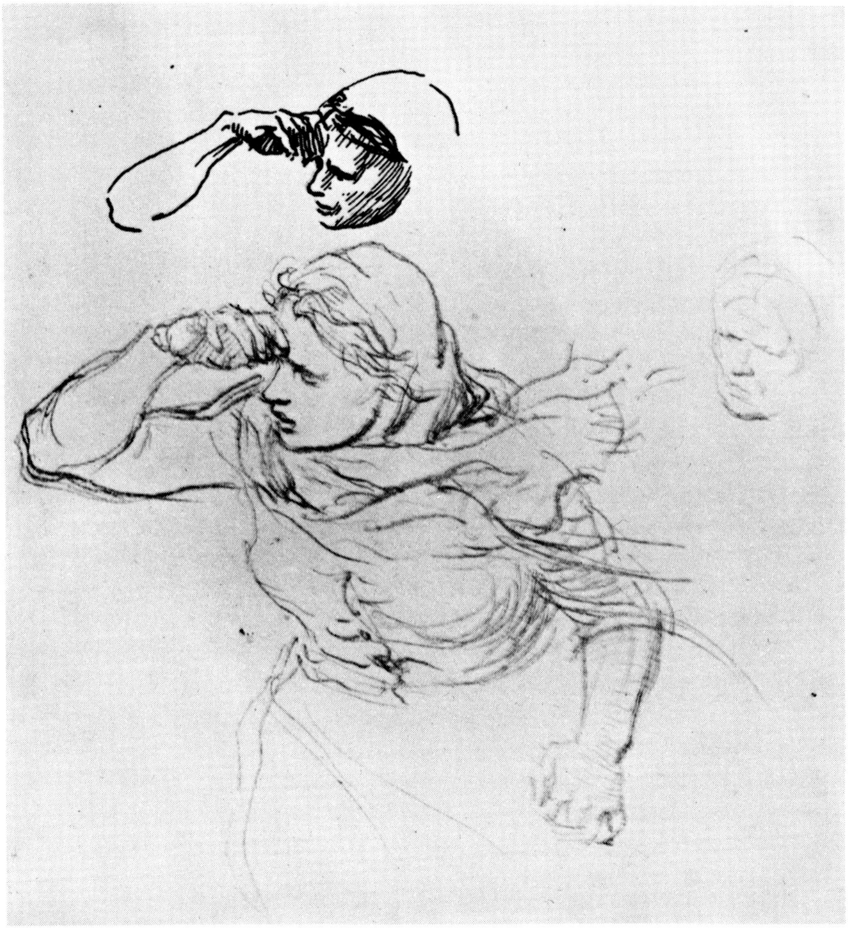

It is quite easy to see whose side Miss MacDonald was on! Uncle Charlie Marr was even more outspoken. If anything, this incident had enhanced Brian in his eyes and he wrote a firm letter to his niece.

> 16th Dec: 1907
>
> There is no sense in magnifying such a trivial incident to mountain size. Old Harcourt ought to have head well punched for acting in such a very inconsiderate manner, and his action shows a bad disposition on his part. My strong advice to you is to say nothing more about it to anyone, and moreover I advise you still more to stop thinking about it. The incident in itself is one that any *man* would regard with benevolent consideration . . . because it was the result of boyish inexperience and in no way associated with the idea of vice. I can't even think there is much to regret, as Brian will be better away . . .

Uncle Charlie was probably right in his summing up of the situation. It is hard to assess just how much benefit Brian gained from the time he spent at Hospitalfields. Although there was but little instruction, models and materials were supplied free of charge and Harcourt certainly gave him some help with oils, a medium which perhaps he had neglected for too long. If no paintings of outstanding merit mark this period of Brian's career, his undeniable ability is revealed in two exquisite sketches of fishermen's wives.

When he got home, Brian busied himself sending Miss MacDonald's calendar to all his friends. Curly thought the design was "quite lovely", but "wished the little date arrangement was at Jerico", as it prevented him from framing it. Thereupon Brian sent him a proof of the drawing, which delighted him.

> 8th Jan. 1908 Cow Leaze
> Dear Brian
> I returned yesterday and found the proof. This is of course to my mind more beautiful than the reproduction and worth the best frame going. Thank you very much. I heard from Princess Louise today and she says 'Brian Hatton sent his lovely drawing which pleases me much'. I knew she would admire it . . .
> I was stopping at Farringford last week and Lord Tennyson* enquired for you.
> We so much admired your drawings here.
> Best of luck for coming year and again thanks.
> With love from your affectionate
> A. Collins

*This was the second Lord Tennyson.

CHAPTER FIFTEEN

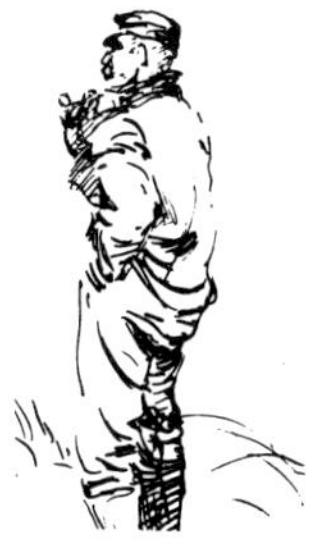

Egyptian Venture

IN FEBRUARY 1908, Brian went to stay with Uncle Charles Marr at Chislehurst. His intention was to do some work in the National Gallery, for copying old masters was considered an essential part of an artist's training. Brian looked up his old teacher, Professor Leslie Thomson, in London and they lunched together at the Arts Club. The professor promised to give Brian an introduction to Sir Charles Holroyd, the Director of the National Gallery. He advised Brian not to be in too great a hurry to start copying, but to take a good look round and make sketches of compositions of pictures. Brian followed his advice and eventually decided he wanted to copy Titian's "Christ and Mary Magdalene", a picture which greatly appealed to him.

> With the exception of Christ's legs and Mary's hands!! . . . I say, how would I do for an art critic? If all else fails it may be a last resource!!

A student applying for a ticket to work in the National Gallery had to submit a signed and authenticated specimen of his work. Brian just sent one of his sketch-books and received a ticket by return of post. However, a week or two was to pass before he started work. As so often seemed to happen when he was starting on a new venture, Brian was overtaken by illness; in this case a sharp attack of influenza. He had left Uncle Charles' comfortable house and moved into rooms in Chislehurst. He wrote to his mother, begging her not to fuss and start telegraphing for news.

> The old landlady is kindness itself and looks after me as well as you could (tho' you may not altogether like to think it!). She is an excellent cook and understands just what I want in the way of eggs, milk, fish, chicken, barley water and all the rest of it — fire in bedroom etc . . . I hope I have satisfied you that there is no need to spend sleepless nights on my account!

Uncle Charles visited Brian every evening and stayed for a chat. Although he appreciated the young man's artistic gifts and was anxious to give him all the practical help he needed, he did not pretend to know anything about art himself. Brian wrote;

> I am re-reading Clausen's aims and ideals again. I thought the first chapter might interest Uncle C. as it seemed simple and explained why a picture is great etc., and treated of truth to nature and photography etc. He read two pages and

> asked me if I could understand it! Then said 'Good Lord' and said he 'had no use for these high-falutin ideas and phrases' and, catching sight of Watts' Nude Study, remarked 'how abominable a woman looks without her clothes on'. So he's a very instructive patron to have!!

As soon as he had recovered, Brian started working in the National Gallery.

> March 13th 1908
> I have been working there today and have finished laying in with burnt sienna and amber and white (on Leslie Thomson's advice). Much to the amazement of a fussy little old man who is working nearby, as it seems to be more usual to lay in with colder colours; but I notice that scarcely any of the copyists ever succeed in getting the warm glow of the originals — Taken as a whole they are a 'very poor lot' — nearly all old maids or there abouts, a few old men and one or two young ones who are pretty slack. Very few of the copies show much ability!! (ahem) but their authors seem highly delighted with them.

As well as copying, Brian wanted some instruction in modelling from Professor Lanteri who taught at an art school in South Kensington. He approached Lanteri who told him that he must first apply to Mr Spencer, the Principal. Brian had rather a difficult interview with Spencer who told him that before joining the modelling class students had first to do three months on architecture — Brian argued that as he intended ultimately to be a painter, not an architect, this would be a waste of time.

> He [Mr. Spencer] seemed rather pig-headed and urged me 'not to be silly' and that architecture was 'all for my ultimate good' . . . However I held out as politely as I could and eventually he has allowed me to join Lanteri's classes for this term . . . I found Lanteri very nice, he held quite different views on the subject and thought that architecture would only be useful to a sculptor, not to a person who only does a little modelling to help his drawing and painting etc.

Brian started off by taking an exam which lasted for six days. He had to copy a bust and the more advanced students were very helpful, showing him how to measure up and to handle the clay. He was duly accepted as a pupil and enjoyed working from live models. He learned about armatures and stands and made progress with the clay. On Uncle Charles' advice, he moved to London to be nearer his work. He took rooms at 25 Princes Square, Bayswater, where he was joined by his cousin, Geoffrey Vevers, who was now a medical student at St Thomas's Hospital.

Brian enjoyed the amenities of London. He went to a Private View at the Institution of Watercolour Painters and, at the National Portrait Gallery he found a whole room devoted to portraits painted by Watts. Money went a long way at that time; he ordered a new suit which was to cost "£3.10 at least". He had his first ride in a taxi and said that it was certainly the quickest means of getting about London above ground. But on a hot evening, when he felt the need for fresh air and a rest, he preferred to ride on the open top of a bus for an hour or so — "it only costs about 4d". He fell in with his Oxford friend, Oswald Chapman and together they planned to see a performance by the new dancer, Maud Allen.

> If she is good, she would be worth my while to see, I might get some hints. I remember an excellent drapery dancer at the Swansea Empire once when I was too young and engrossed with sheep and horses, to appreciate it.

Chapman asked Brian to do a red chalk portrait of his (Chapman's) mother, who lived in Bryanston Square. Brian accepted the offer, but told his mother that "She is very difficult and rather plain so the issue is extremely doubtful".

By the end of June, which was half term at South Kensington, Brian decided he had learned enough about modelling and that it was time to leave London and return home. At Mount Craig the coach-house had been made into a studio. The conversion, which included the introduction of north windows, top lights and blinds, was made to Brian's precise specification. A movable throne was installed and the studio was ready for use.

Marjorie Hatton.
Red chalk, 1908
Brian Hatton Gallery, Hereford

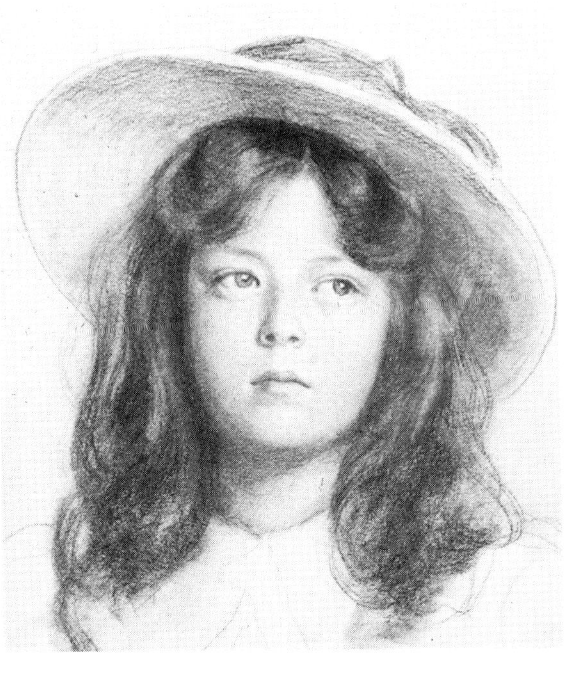

Ailsa Marr Hatton.
Red chalk, 1908.
Brian Hatton Gallery, Hereford

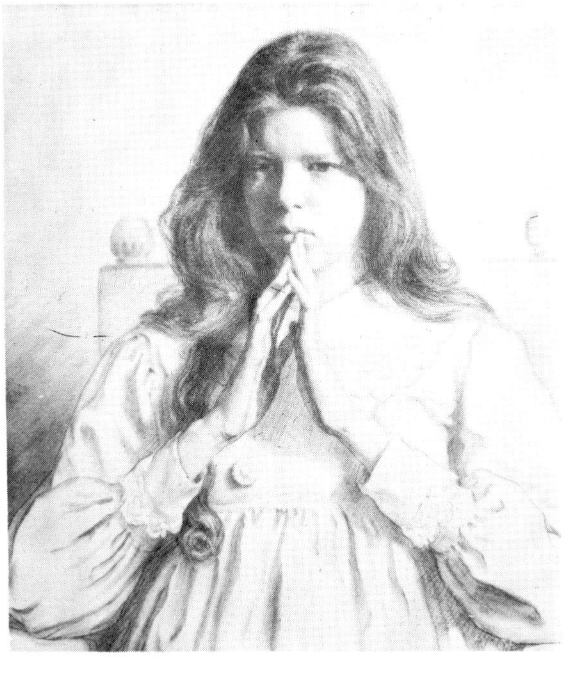

From early years Mount Craig had been sought out as the home of the young Hereford artist. Lawrence Housman, Mary Watts and many other prominent visitors to the city, as well as every liberal candidate at election time, found their way to Broomy Hill and were taken all over the house; first to the dining room and the drawing room, then up the stairs to the principal bedrooms, to see Brian's pictures which hung on the walls. Some would be entertained to lunch or tea, and others with a whisky and soda or with some of Mr Hatton's coveted local cider, kept for over twenty-five years in a special corner of the cellar. Now the studio became the focal point of the household. When not busy on other subjects, Brian would require his sisters, now in their early teens, to sit for him. But before long he was on the move again.

For some time Mrs Watts had been endeavouring to give Brian the opportunity of a visit to Egypt. She and her husband had spent some time there during the winter of 1889 and although Watts had not been well enough to do much painting, he considered the fellaheen workmen ideal models with their lithe figures, strong square shoulders and long shoulder blades. The archaeologist, Professor Flinders Petrie (later Sir William Flinders Petrie) was a friend of Mary's and was now engaged on an archaeological dig at Memphis. Mary conceived the idea that Brian might be attached to the Professor's party.

Professor Petrie, a man of forty-five, was one of the leading archaeologists of his day. His book *Pyramids and Temples of Gizeh*, published in 1883 had brought him to the fore as an Egyptologist and from then on his life's work was to fill in the blanks in the history of Egypt. In less than twenty years he traced the history and civilisation of Egypt from a remote antiquity until it ended under the Romans. He revolutionised the ideals and methods of archaeology, making the past live and proving that accurate knowledge of the past is of vital importance in the understanding of the human race.

It is understandable that Mary Watts should consider that it would be greatly to Brian's advantage to become a member of the Professor's encampment;

> with delightful work going on and the companionship of educated men and women . . . better than hotel life — simpler and less expensive.

Professor Petrie, however, did not take quite so kindly to the idea, although he felt obliged to fall in with Mary's wishes. He wrote rather grudgingly, saying;

> Please understand that we do not wish people in general to know that we have anyone with us who is not on our work; as we might run a hotel on the applications we get. But your friend and the Signor's of course I cannot say nay to.

And so it was arranged, and in November 1908, at the age of twenty-one, Brian set out for Egypt in the company of Professor and Mrs Petrie. They travelled via Bologna, Rome and Naples and then took ship for Alexandria. From Rome Brian wrote to his mother.

22 Nov.
Sunday Night

Hotel Navarro
Via Cavour
Rome

My dear Mother,
. . . I did the crossing very nicely, it was quite smooth. But I was a bit Jonah on train next day, had to rush off in middle of lunch. Since then I have been quite all right. I didn't sleep much on train first night, but made up for it last night at Bologna. We left early this morning.
Monday night. I got up at 9.30 and got to the Vatican and saw the Sistine Chapel — just marvellous. Unfortunately the Raphael cartoons were closed so I went round to the sculpture part and saw a lot of old friends . . . After lunch I went with the Petries to San Sacramento (or else some other church and the festival is called Sacramento — I get fuddled!) Anyhow it consists of 3 churches built over each other in layers. The bottom one, house of Clement, now under water, but the middle one containing wonderful old frescoes, was illuminated today on occasion of the festival. Petrie explained everything. We then walked past Coliseum and Forum etc to house where he lectured on what he had found last year at Memphis — most interesting . . . No time to write more, must get off to bed. Wednesday we leave for Naples. Much love. Am very well.
Brian.

During the passage from Naples to Alexandria, Brian, never a good traveller, spent most of the time in his bunk, existing on a diet of apples. "I was only 'Jonah' a little to start with."

From Alexandria they took the train to Cairo. The party consisted of the Professor and his wife and two assistants, named Wainwright and Mackay, and, of course, Brian, who says;

> Mackay is another of the Wainwright sort and goes on to arrange the building of huts tomorrow. I like the P's very much, they have been very decent to me all the time; they are certainly somewhat unconventional, especially Mrs, but she is very decent and kind all the same. The other two are quite good sorts too, and very wrapt up in their work. Apparently the party is complete. There may be some visitors later on at Memphis but we shall be at Thebes for a couple of months first. I find the coinage frightfully muddling.

They spent a week in Cairo and Brian did all the usual sight-seeing, visiting the Pyramids, the museum and various mosques and bazaars and he rode on a donkey to the tombs of the Caliphs. He was very intrigued with the swift sunsets.

> The sunset does not last long, but it gives a beautiful rose madder tinge to everything just before the sun goes down; while the sun is actually sinking an inch or so off the horizon, everything seems to be in shadow, which is somewhat strange to me as the sun is still visible.

On the 4th December the Petries went to Luxor. Brian followed next day with Wainwright who had to take the equivalent of £400 in gold coins with which to pay the workmen in camp. The four hundred mile train journey took fourteen hours.

> . . . and all for the modest sum of £1.1½. 2nd class! But it was a most disgusting journey owing to the dust and sand blowing through every chink and crevice and smothering everything . . . We gradually became snowed up about ½ inch deep in sandy dust in which condition we ate cold chicken and dry bread and oranges. Luckily I slept most of the afternoon and arrived in remarkably good form though somewhat encrusted! Wainwright has safely delivered the £400, a weight off his mind as well as his person.
>
> Today we met the P's who are staying with friends here and went to Temple of Luxor most of the morning and this afternoon to Karnak, with its three square miles of temples and excavated buildings and avenue of sphinxes, etc. The architecture is simply colossal, I've never seen anything approaching it elsewhere. However I can't always give it my unalloyed admiration, the proportions are somewhat clumsy. The sunsets however are *the* most wonderful thing out here. I shan't describe them but I shall of course try to paint feeble imitations! . . .
>
> I am writing this before dinner, after dinner we intend to see Karnak by moonlight, being full moon tonight. And tomorrow afternoon we hope to go across to the camp. It is the other side of the Nile, under the hills.

A few days later Brian said that they were all established in camp which was about two miles from Luxor and situated at the entrance of a "Waddy" or gorge. The true desert began on top of the cliff beneath which they were sheltering. The living accommodation consisted of one long hut built of sun dried bricks plastered with mud and thatched with maize stalks. It was sub-divided into bedrooms and dining room.

> The north wind keeps the temperature cool enough for winter clothing although the sun is in reality a good deal hotter than it appears to be . . . We need piles of blankets as the nights are surprisingly cold. The worst feature of the place is the dust . . . On a windy day the air is full of it and little columns of sand are seen whirling along in the distance . . . We none of us wear collars but a handkerchief if necessary, nor socks either if we go among the deep sand.
>
> The natives are always ready to take advantage of you. This morning I was doing a sketch of a waterwheel, worked by oxen, when the owner demanded 'bakshish' . . . When I laughed, he of course laughed too and offered a donkey for hire for which he eventually accepted half the price he asked first of all.
>
> I haven't sketched the men at work yet. There are some fine specimens among them and some good heads too. The only native who is allowed in our courtyard is the cook who is exceptionally clean and enlightened (having been cook to the P's for 15 years). But even he isn't allowed in the bedrooms. They are all just alive — alive-oh.
>
> The cook tries to teach me a few words every day . . . he says I have a good accent!! The men found two tablets of the 11th Dynasty this afternoon, with which Petrie is very pleased. (I think they are most ghastly atrocities).

The 50 or 60 workmen lived in huts in an enclosure on the hillside. Petrie had a reputation for looking after his workmen. He trained them until they became experts at archaeological digging and he never allowed them to run a risk to life or limb. He never had a fatal, or even a serious accident in all the years of his active work; if there were a risk, he took it himself. He allowed no interference by local authorities between him and his men, thus warding off those who usually made the wage-earner his prey.

Brian soon settled into the camp routine. Although one day was much like another he didn't find life dull; for he could always find something fresh to paint. Of course there were various hazards to be overcome.

> I have been sketching in the maize fields this morning, they are harvesting now, but the moment I took my cigarette out of my mouth the flies fairly swarmed onto my face, it is always the same where there are Arabs and animals about . . . The dogs are a great nuisance . . . they fly out and bark at every stranger. They are savage, untamed beasts that look like wolves, and bark all night long. There are plenty of foxes and jackals about too, but they are very timid . . .
> I have no difficulty in getting nude models, there are one or two men in the camp who don't mind stripping in a secluded place and the shadoof men always work practically nude. Idle men are always willing to stand for bakshish and usually the little girls do not mind, though they are rather shy. I haven't tried the women but I expect they would object . . . They pull their head shawls across their faces and hold them in their mouths when they meet a strange man, so that one only gets a view of one eye and half a nose . . . It is wonderful to see the tremendous loads they carry on their heads — even quite little children too.

Brian got on very well with the Petries and was soon making sketches of them. He particularly admired Mrs Petrie, saying:

> Mrs. P. is a regular corker. She makes a point of being extremely independent and won't accept help from anyone (suits me all right!). She is of course a hot suffragette! tho' not militant. Her costume out here takes the biscuit. Usually a blue native gown, such as the poorer class men wear, and a sort of small motor cap, plenty of bare throat and ditto leg, no stockings of course! . . .
> I am doing a pencil sketch of Mrs. P. in the evenings now. I have done one of the Prof too, but he is too busy to pose and I could only catch him for a few minutes while talking and digesting after dinner. Mrs. P. wants me to do as many as I can of him. He won't sit for his portrait at home. He did once when Mrs. Watts asked him to, but the result wasn't up to Mrs. P's expectations! . . .
> The other day (Mrs. Petrie) suggested that I should exhibit the sketches I am doing out here at their exhibition at University College, London, that they have every year of the result of the winter's work out here. She seemed to think that she was conferring a great benefit on me. But what do you and Uncle Charlie think and what would Mrs. Watts think about it? . . . I simply smiled and said 'thank you' when she proposed it. It might add to the interest of the exhibition (to which about 6,000 people go yearly) which lasts a fortnight or so.*

*Brian did exhibit his sketches as Mrs Petrie suggested. He also illustrated an article by Arthur Weigal, Government Inspector for Upper Egypt, and another by Dr C. G. Seligman, both of which were published.

As time went on Brian began to meet people and partake in diversions outside the camp. He and Wainwright went to lunch in Luxor with Mr Weigal.

> Mrs. Weigal, who is a very shy and stiff little person, pumped me as to whether I would care to give her lessons in painting! but I sheered off on the score of incompetency, etc! . . . She has studied a little here and there and is fond of painting but hasn't got time to do much and is also too shy to show what she does do! The usual style! . . .
> The last two nights we had visitors to dinner. Last night an artist named Tyndall and the night before an Egyptological artist (i.e. one who copies the painting in tombs etc) named Davies and his assistant Unwin . . . [Unwin] wants me to go to Athens with him and perhaps Venice on my way home . . . He talks art with a big A!! I must see if his work is equal to his talk!

A week later Brian writes;

> The artists here are pleased with my pencil sketches . . . I have been taking our giant navvy over to Unwins in the evenings and we sketch him by lamplight in a tent . . . The model has apparently taken a dislike to Unwin and would rather pose for me alone! Shows his good taste, you see! Unwin is certainly a conceited sort of drawing room young man, but his architectural drawings are very good though his figure sketches don't seem up to much. Lately I have been painting a girl of 11 or 12 who minds some sheep and goats not far away. She is an awful nuisance. Continually getting 'much-radi' [unwilling] and going away and pretending to cry and asking for more bakshish in the middle of a sitting . . . Presently I spied another girl who stood like a rock and allowed me to finish.

Mrs Hatton wrote to ask Brian if he would like her to send him some books, but he replied that he spent the day painting, eating, walking and sleeping and had no time for reading.

> I probably walk 5 to 8 miles a day and occasionally go tramping 10 to 12 at least. The other day I went up the Farshut pass over the hills behind us. It brings one out on the peak of the highest hill after two hours steady climb and pretty rough going . . . I don't know how camels and donkeys manage it but they do. From the top one gets a magnificent view up and down the Nile valley, of which I did a little sketch. I walked a couple of miles along the desert which is undulating and covered for the most part with black flints, many of these chipped by neolithic and paleolithic man. I brought down a pocketful . . .
> We are expecting Dr. & Mrs. Sulliman* tomorrow; they are going to join us in order to learn Arabic and to learn to manage natives, for excavating next year. Mrs. P. goes home to her baby next Tuesday week. And soon after we shall be going down to Memphis . . . Our cook has had indigestion for two days, so he wants to be sent home to die! He points to his tummy and says his heart is breaking.

Brian had been on good terms with the cook who took him to Luxor during the Islam festival of Beiram.

*Dr and Mrs Seligman.

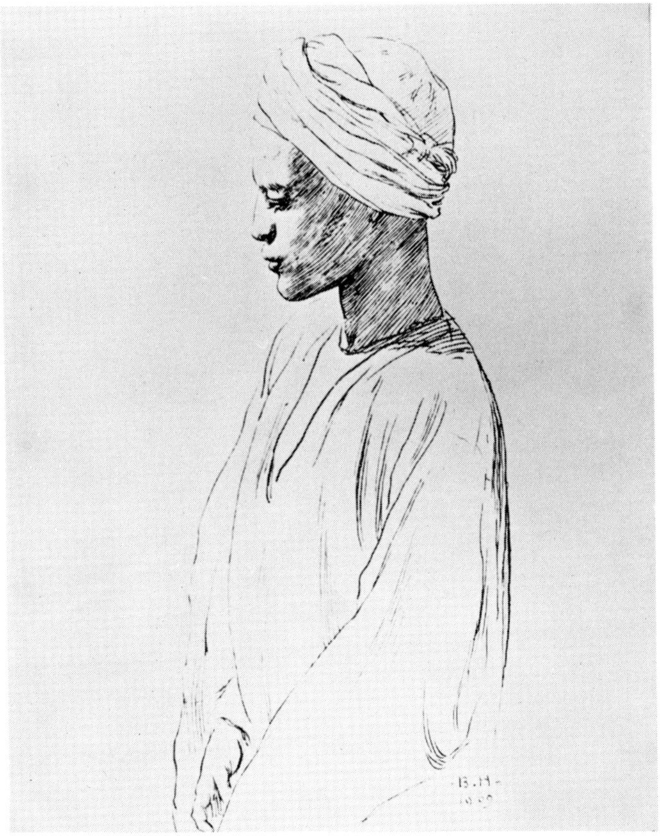

Egyptian Boy.
Pen and ink, 1909
10¼" × 6½"

. . . commemorating Mohammet's cheap return journey to Heaven, so that he was able to describe the place to the faithful.
First all the people, dressed in their best, assembled in the cemetery and brought offerings of drink and bread to their dead relations. It was a noisy cheerful gathering, no-one seemed depressed. Then there was a service for the men. After the service two men played at quarterstaff very prettily for a little while, and then the big Daerwish arrived and a big Zikker was inaugurated, i.e. two lines of men are formed who repeat first a few verses of the Koran and then the 9 names of God to a sort of chant, swaying their bodies meanwhile . . . This gets gradually faster . . . the men getting more and more ecstatic as the blood gets into their heads . . . The action is very violent and 5 minutes of it would kill a European but these chaps keep on for hours. Every now and then a man shrieks out and falls in a fit or a faint, but no one takes much notice . . . The Zikkers are almost the only form of entertainment the Arabs have. The Darwish rolled about in the middle and tried to weep, in order that he might have a vision of the Prophet.
I watched this bobbing crew until I became half seasick and came home to lunch. So much for Beiram.

CHAPTER SIXTEEN

Home Again

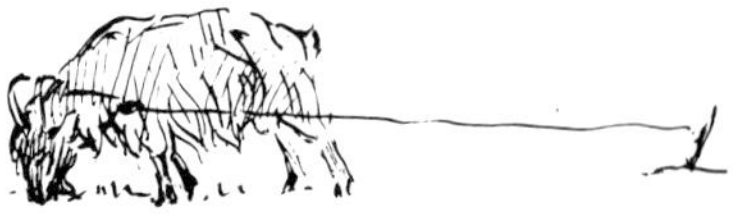

TOWARDS the end of February, Professor Petrie gave up working at Luxor and moved on to Memphis; Brian who was anxious to finish some sketches, stayed on for another ten days while Mackay was busy packing up all the treasures that had been found in the dig. When the work was finished, they both moved on to the camp near Memphis.

> 23rd Feb. 1909 — Mitrahinsh, Bedrashein
> My dear Mother,
> We arrived here at sunrise yesterday morning, after a sleepless night in the train. We have quite settled down in our new home . . . We are in the midst of a forest of palm trees . . . This is a far superior order of mud house with a verandah and small windows with *glass* in them! also doors on some of the rooms!!
> The country here is quite different from the other place and on the whole I think I like it a trifle better. Though the people may not be quite so artistic; they are several tones lighter in colour. There are many Bedouin encampments near us, about as dirty as you could wish, but picturesque. They come down and cultivate the land at this season, and then when the Nile overflows depart into the desert again. There are camels ad lib here, much larger, heavier animals than the weedy beasts up country. At present there are hundreds of strings of them (6 or 8 to a string) carting Sabbak, i.e. manure, which consists of any earth which contains salt. So they are making heavy inroads into the masses of roman mud-brick work that abound, much to Petrie's delight, as it enables him to get at the older buildings underneath. And he gets his work done for nothing!
> The other day I took a donkey and went to the Pyramid of Sakkara and to several sculptured tombs nearby, also the Serapeum, where the sacred bulls were buried . . . We can see no less than 11 pyramids from our house . . . This is the only place in Egypt where there is a forest of palm trees.

It is interesting to note that Brian now wrote an extremely good grammatical letter. From the earliest days he had been a graphic, humorous writer, undeterred by his difficulty with spelling. Now, perhaps due to his general development, his letters had taken on a new quality.

Numerous visitors turned up at the camp, some of whom were subscribers to the excavation fund.

> Yesterday we had Seton-Carr, the big game shooter. He gave me some tips for vermin! Paraffin is the thing for the little invisible lice that every native possesses! Fleas are getting plentiful now, so I am using plenty of insect powder. The greatest thing is to catch 'em on the hop.

Fleas and lice were not the only hazards they had to contend with; sandflies, mosquitoes, gnats and various other bugs abounded, but perhaps worst of all were the dust storms.

> I have been bottling myself up in my room all the afternoon on account of a beastly dust storm . . . The dust here is dirty and chokey, much worse than the clean desert grit. However, it has gone down again now (5 p.m.) leaving some of our men still coughing and sneezing.

The evenings and the early morning were the best part of the day and every month, during the moonlight period, the bedouins had a fantasia which was fun to watch. Music with a monotonous rhythm accompanied the dancing, which consisted of exponents "waggling various parts of the body independently of others".

Brian's health, never his greatest asset, had been good all the time he had been in Egypt, but when March came, the dust, the sudden changes in temperature and possibly a stray germ, were too much for him. He was sketching early one morning when a cold wind got up. Being engrossed in his work, he ignored it and the result was a "chesty" cold. After a few days, when he showed no signs of improvement, Professor Petrie advised him to go to The English Winter Hotel at Helouan, which was situated high up on the Arabian desert. Helouan, noted for its pure air, was considered to be the health resort of Egypt, and the hotel had some of the characteristics of a nursing home, as the proprietress was used to catering for invalids. The doctor diagnosed bronchitis and arranged for an English nurse to visit Brian twice a day to administer poultices and a variety of medicines. Unfortunately, all this treatment did nothing to alleviate a very bad cough, and eventually it was discovered that he was suffering from whooping-cough!

Brian remarked that "this little turn" was a great nuisance, as it interfered with his work and caused him to miss going on an interesting excursion. Seton-Carr (the big game hunter) had taken a liking to Brian and had asked him to join him on a camel expedition into the desert near Fayoum. It was hard to have to lie in bed and think of what he was missing.

> I am losing all my magnificent sunburn, lying here . . . There is no news that I know of except that Lord Roberts and Hall Caine were seen parading about the other day. Also that there is a missionary lady staying in the hotel who sends me 'good' books, which I don't read!

A week later, Brian was a little better and spending the whole day in the garden for he was always a great believer in fresh air.

April 1st — Winter Hotel, Helouan

. . . I spend my days sitting about in the garden reading or amusing myself with a little monkey who lives here, and who always ends by biting me! Occasionally I get little interludes in the way of kind ladies inquiring after my health, and old gentlemen giving me a detailed account of their ailments and symptoms . . . One day the female missionary made an attempt on me but she did not receive sufficient encouragement to induce her to try again! Don't see how anyone could be 'saved' by an American accent of such thickness as hers.

Several people have been trying to pump me as to what is wrong with me; they find it hard to believe that bronchitis would keep on so long! . . . But I have to stick to my guns or else I should get turned out onto the desert to shift for myself if the good people realised there was anything infectious in the place! It is every man for himself in this world!!

April 11th

. . . Today is Easter Sunday and it so happens that the Greek Easter falls on the same day this year. So last night the streets were filled with Greeks heralding the day until about 3 o'clock in the morning, serenading, and yelling and shouting that 'Christ is risen!', and thereupon letting off rockets, as emblematic of the rising I suppose. Anyway, what with small and large firearms and various other noisy implements they managed to put any thunderstorm to shame. Then at 6 a.m. the Roman Catholics began ringing bells etc for early mass. So you may guess there was not much sleep for the wicked last night!

Brian was due to leave Egypt at the end of April. He could not know that before so many years had passed, fate would lead him back to this country and he would experience another Easter day in very different circumstances.

Brian had kept in touch with Unwin, the artist, and now they decided to travel in company, breaking their homeward journey in Greece and Italy. They met in Cairo to make final arrangements and then Brian went on to spend a few days at Ramleh, a suburb of Alexandria, before they set sail for Piraeus. His cough was still troublesome and he hoped that the sea air would help to ease it.

April 20th 1909 — Hotel Beau Rivage.

This hotel is right on the sea front and my bedroom overlooks the sea, which is a wonderful greeny blue here . . . I think the sea air has eased my cough considerably . . . I am starting tomorrow afternoon 4 p.m. on the Osmanish for Piraeus, i.e. of course unless something very unusual turns up, which pray God it won't . . . I lunch with Unwin tomorrow in Alexandria after meeting him at the station and then we go on board.

It seemed that Brian had no regrets at leaving Egypt; indeed, he was anxious to get away. His usual high spirits had been lowered by his tiresome illness and he was depressed by the fact that he was not bringing home all the paintings and drawings he had hoped to make. Now he wanted to get back to Hereford, "dear little Hereford". Of course the Egyptian sojourn had been a great experience and had opened his eyes to a wider world. As for the Pyramids and the temples, the excavations and the links with the distant past, he summed up what he felt about it all when he visited the three square miles of temples and sphinxes at Karnak saying that, "the proportions were sometimes clumsy".

It was the visual world which interested Brian; the proportions of the buildings rather than their antiquity. What appealed to him in Egypt were the sunsets, the rolling desert, the Arab workmen, the donkey boys and goat herds. His pencil sketches of the natives interested the other artists "as something new".

Brian and Unwin had an uneventful passage to Piraeus. They spent five days in Greece sight-seeing, before taking ship for Italy. Brian had no reservations about the rightness of Greek architecture, and stated simply, "The Acropolis is the finest thing I've seen yet".

The sea trip from Piraeus to Brindisi was "very delightful for once. The voyage through the Greek Archipelago was most pleasant, we stopped at Corfu and landed for two hours".

From Brindisi they took the train to Venice where they spent a week, "seeing no end of pictures and churches". Through Mary Watts, Brian had an introduction to Lady Lazard, the widow of Sir Henry Lazard. She entertained the young men in her beautiful palace and showed them her fine collection of pictures. They had intended to stay longer in Venice, but the weather was cold and dull, so they decided to go on to Munich, where they had yet another introduction from Mary Watts, to Mr and Mrs Adrian Stokes. They were both artists, and of Mrs Stokes, Mary said, "She is charming, an Austrian, and as I dare say you know, paints also beautifully in a simple spiritual way".

Brian called and saw Mrs Stokes at work in her studio. After Munich the young men had another short respite in Bruges and arrived home in time to enjoy the beauty of an English May.

On his return, Brian found his mother in poor health. Indeed, much of the time he had been in Egypt, Mrs Hatton had been away from home, staying with relations in Dumbartonshire, or on a visit to Llandrindod Wells. Her complaint had been diagnosed as "nerves", and Mary Watts had remarked that "nerves are terribly difficult to repair, when once they get wrong". It was after Brian had returned that the doctors prescribed a rest cure, the normal treatment at that time, and in July Mrs Hatton was installed in a nursing home in Church Stretton, where her family paid her frequent visits. She returned home and all seemed to be going well. It was therefore a terrible shock to everybody when she died suddenly. Ailsa and Marjorie were staying in Helensburgh at the time and when the news was broken to them, they were told, "Your mother's heart just ceased to beat".

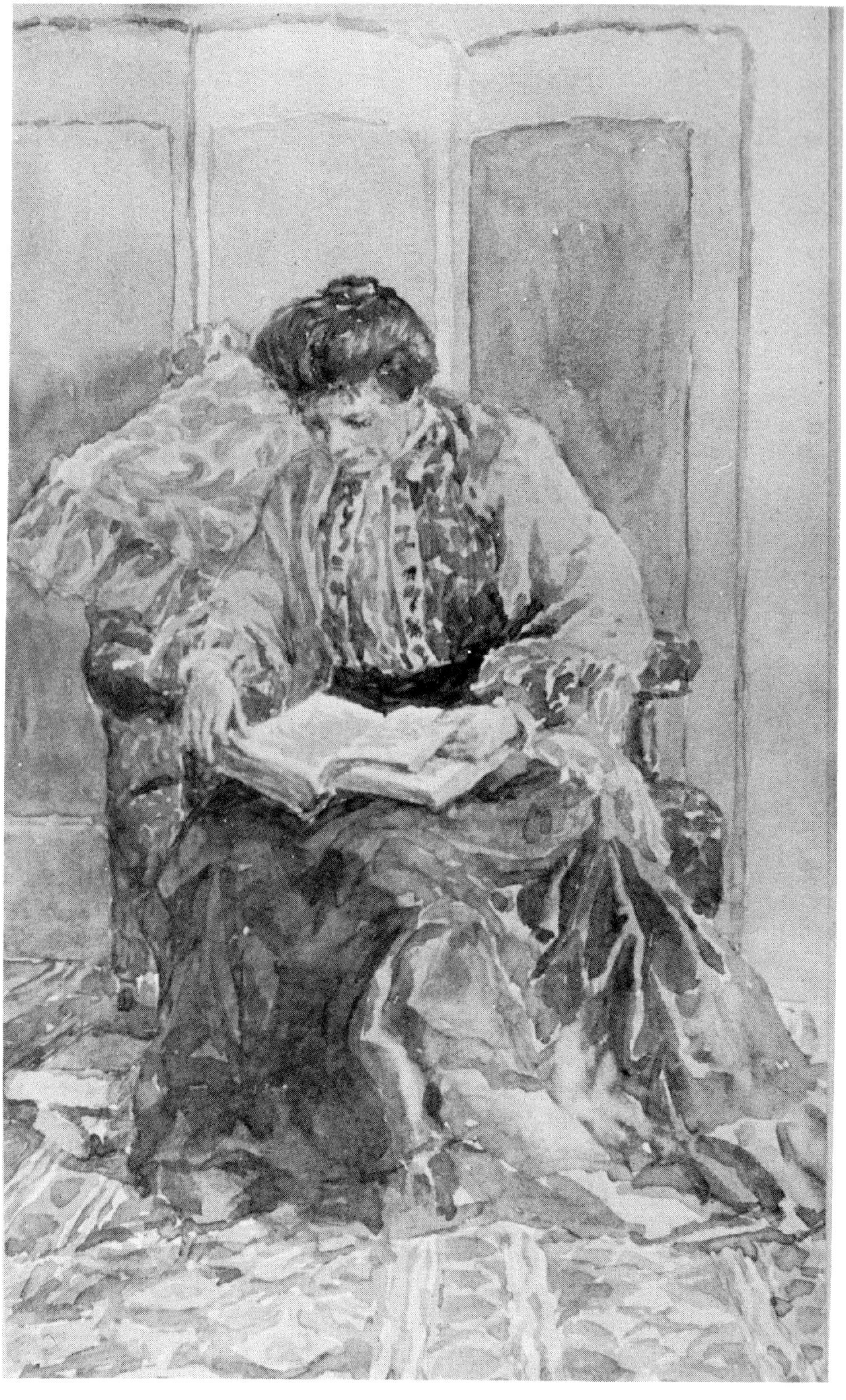

Amelia Hatton's death was a blow from which none of the family fully recovered, but her influence was lasting. Gentle and self-effacing as she was, she had been the mainspring of this closely knit family. Her brother-in-law, John Robinson Harrison, described her as having "one of the finest natures I have known . . . her life was gentle, her nature too deep to be understood by many". Mary Watts wrote to Brian saying, "It was dear and kind of you to write at once . . . She had quite an unusual mind I felt, so wise and direct. I always felt better for being with her".

For Brian, whose artistic potential his mother had recognised and respected at an early age and whose progress and character she had nurtured with such thoughtful care, the loss must have been irredeemable. All his life she had been his closest confidant and friend. After her death he paid her one last tribute. He went into the room where she lay and made a very beautiful drawing of her. He inscribed it simply; "Mother, July 27th 1909".

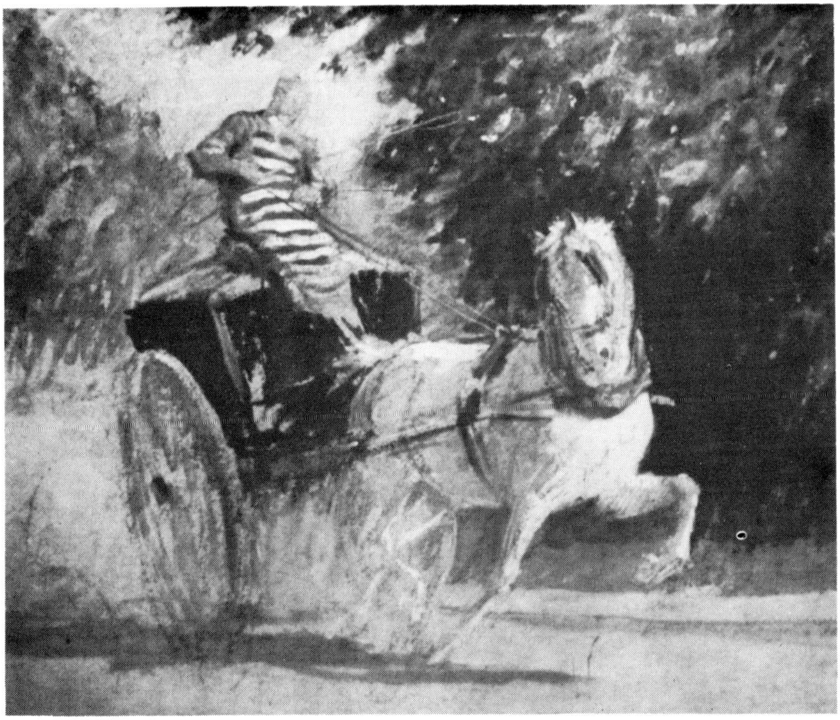

Butcher Boy. *John Davies*

⇦ Mrs Hatton (Brian's mother) Water colour, 1903. 8½″ × 5″

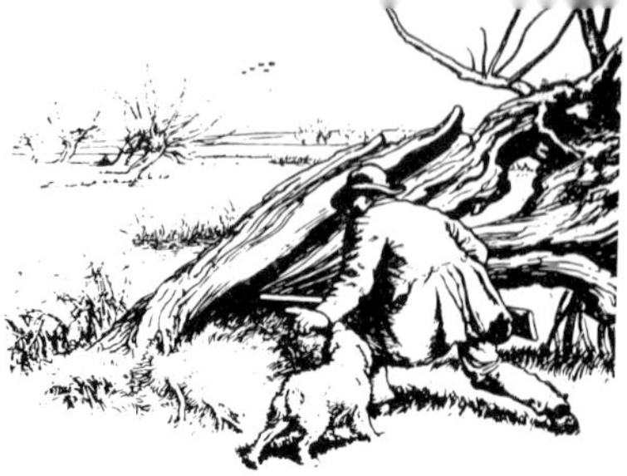

CHAPTER SEVENTEEN

First Commissions

AFTER the death of Mrs Hatton the well-loved cousin, Mabel Maddison, who had lived at Mount Craig since her High School days, took over the housekeeping and the care of the family. She continued to do so until her marriage in 1919 to a Herefordian, Edward Landon of Bullingham Court. Although of course she in no way took the place of his mother — indeed, she was more like an elder sister — Brian felt a great affinity with Mabel, and when away from home he kept up an intimate correspondence with her, describing his day to day affairs.

He continued to work in his studio and in the surrounding countryside. Visitors came to view the work and often to purchase landscapes and animal studies. Whenever the gypsies called with their lace and pegs and brooms, they were invited into the studio and sketched. They were always surprised at being paid for what they called "only sitting down and getting a rest".

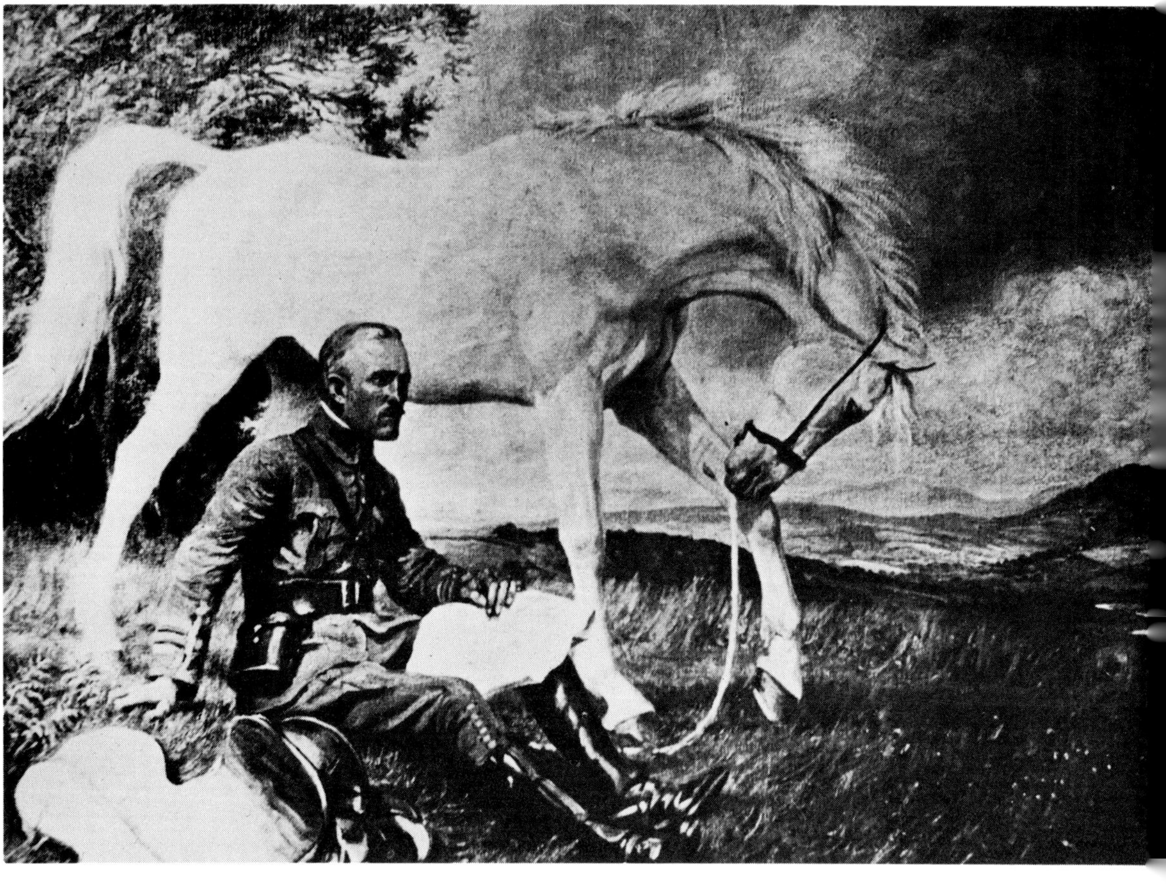

In the spring of 1910, Brian obtained his first commissions. Personalities of the town and county came to the studio to be painted, drawn in pencil, pastel, or red chalk. One of the first was John Percival, Bishop of Hereford. Another commission was for a portrait of Sir Reginald Rankin and his Arab horse, "Dervish". This was a remarkable picture for a young man at the beginning of his career; the composition is indeed original and if anything, the grey horse takes predominance over his master, who is seated on the ground beside him. In order to emphasize the wild freedom of the Arab, Brian has painted him unsaddled, pawing the ground. At the same time, he has painted a fine portrait of Sir Reginald. One can sense the pleasure the artist felt while working on this double portrait of man and horse, and indeed he was delighted that he was not forced to part with it until the sitter had finally agreed to pay for the frame.

Another early commission was a portrait of Colonel Mackay J. B. Scobie, of the Hereford Regiment, a presentation to him from the officers of the regiment. This was put on exhibition in a shop window in the town and later Brian was permitted to have it with him in London for a time as an example of his work.

In the autumn, Brian went to Newcastle Emlyn in Carmarthenshire to paint a portrait of Charles Horne Lloyd Fitzwilliams of Cilgwyn. This was a challenge which Brian seized upon, for his subject was a man of character with all the qualities that Brian most admired. An excellent horseman, he was a man of immense stature, both physically and in his personality. He was 6′ 7″ tall, with an elegant figure, a curiously long tapering head and a magnificent moustache; a true countryman who excelled in field sports, he was the idol of his eight sons and two daughters and loved and respected by the men who worked on his estate. One of his sons, Captain Edward Fitzwilliams, had been stationed in Hereford, where he came in contact with Brian. What was more natural that he should ask him to come and paint his father's portrait?

As it was to be a life-size portrait, Brian worked on an 8 foot canvas, using a pair of steps to reach the top. Fitzwilliams wore hunting pink and Brian posed him standing at the foot of a fine oak staircase. He said that he was a very genial old boy "and had quite entered into the spirit of it". There were days when no work took place and they all went hunting, Brian riding one of his host's horses. Mrs Edward Fitzwilliams, who had been away on a visit, returned to join the household, much to Brian's consternation. "I wish she hadn't come as she rode the only available horse out cubbing, so they gave me a thing the size of a rather undersized sheep-dog upon which I waddled about."

It was decided to put a hound into the picture so Mr Fitzwilliams went off to the kennels and borrowed one from the pack, called Lexicon. They had a certain amount of trouble in making him hold the right pose and Brian complained that he was "very niffy!"

Major Sir Reginald Rankin, Bt., and his Arab horse, "Dervish", at Bryngwyn, Herefordshire. Oil, 1910 *The Lady Jean Rankin*

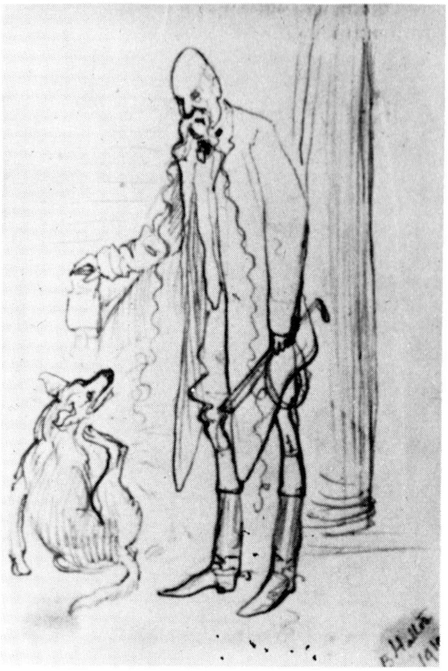

Caricature of portrait.

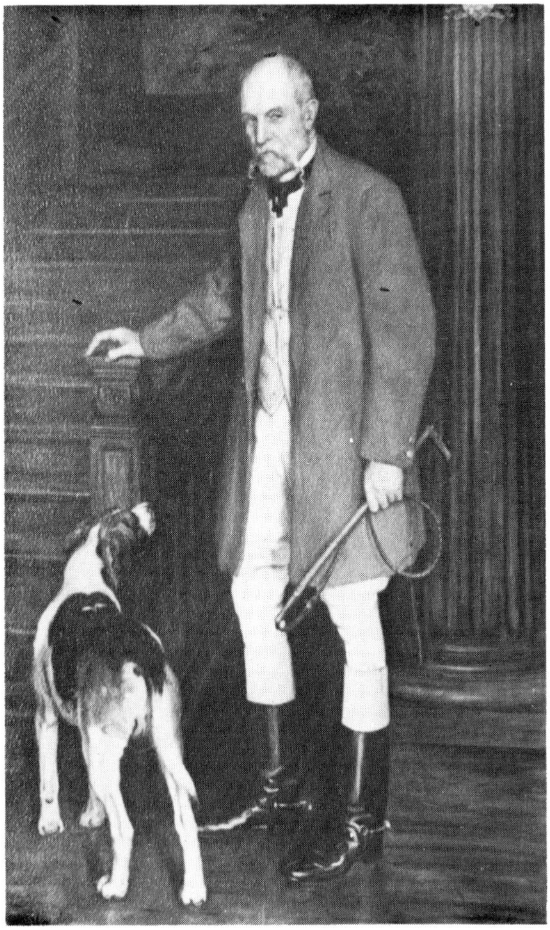

Charles Horne Lloyd Fitzwilliams of Cilgwyn.
Oil, 1910. Full length

The picture was completed to everyone's satisfaction and Brian went home. After his departure from Cilgwyn, there was found in a drawer in his bedroom a delightful caricature of the portrait, sketched on a piece of stamped writing paper. It emphasised all Fitzwilliams's outstanding features; his pointed, egg-shaped head, long straggling moustache and very thin legs. One can almost sense the smell of the hound at his feet, scratching himself with abandon. Quite contrary to taking offence, Fitzwilliams was delighted with the humour of the sketch which he had framed and hung in his study.

Commissions for portraits continued to flow, but Brian decided that he needed a break from this kind of work. After all, even when he was a small boy he made up his mind that he wanted to be "an all round man". For some time he had been planning a visit to Paris and in November 1910 he decided that the time had come for him to go. He wanted to visit the Louvre and the Luxembourg and to work at the Academie Julien. When he arrived in Paris, his old habit of keeping in touch with home persisted and every few days he wrote to Mabel.

Thursday (Nov:) Hotel du Univere & du Portugal
Paris.

My dear Mabel,
I have arrived here and I think it seems quite comfortable. Certainly the dinner I have just had was very good and the wine quite passable. There are several American and English people here, but mostly aged females, so I have not made any acquaintances yet!! The Mâitresse is quite kind and affable . . .
I met Unwin in the tube yesterday and went to lunch with him . . . Tomorrow I go out prospecting.

Brian spent a month in Paris. After visiting the Louvre, he said that there were "miles of pictures" and that one needed weeks to see them properly. At the Pantheon he saw Rodin's "Penseur" and some frescoes of J. R. Laurens, who taught at Julien's Studio, "first things of his that I have liked". Brian was soon enrolled at Julien's and also doing some copying in the Louvre. To improve his French he took some lessons.

I have found a very nice little man who knows English well but wants his accent corrected. So we exchange tuition! Unfortunately the lessons are short, half hour each way, but long enough in the evening after working all day.

Brian ran into an old Oxford friend called "Calder", who was honeymooning in Paris. They all dined together and visited the theatre, and Calder advised Brian to move into the Latin Quarter, which would have the advantage of being cheaper. However, Brian decided to stay where he was, his only complaint about his hotel being the lack of a proper sitting-room or lounge, but "French people don't seem to understand these things". Brian did, however, see something of the less conventional side of Paris before he left.

Nov. 30th 1910 Paris

. . . Last night I and two other chaps (sort of dilletante artists!) made a little expedition to Montmartre. We sampled a low music hall and two or three cafés. It was rather entertaining. The two johnnies knew their way about pretty well and amused me immensely by making sketches of types in huge sketch books in every fresh place. They were frightfully pleased with their results, which were the most hopelessly feeble caricatures under the sun. Needless to say we did not return to our quarters in time to get much beauty sleep. But it is no use coming to Paris without seeing Montmartre at night.

Brian returned to Hereford in time for Christmas. The following year, 1911, is remembered for its long, hot summer, and also for the Coronation of King George V. Brian spent much of his time painting at home, often working at commissions; occasionally he went on visits to London and elsewhere. A chalk portrait of Aunt Anne Keay was hung on the line at the White City Exhibition and Brian went to see it.

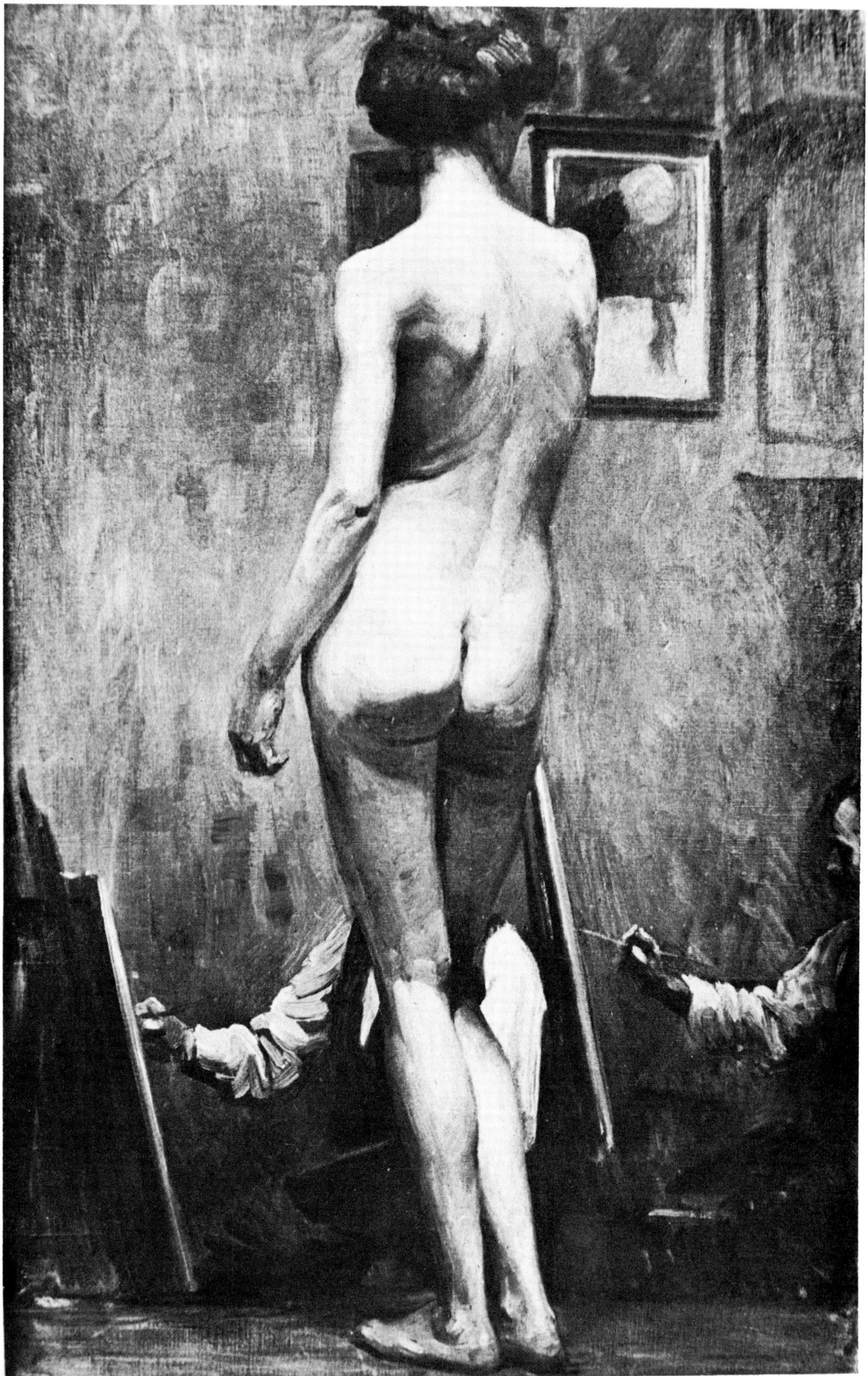

May 25th 1911 — 25 Princes Square
Bayswater, W.

My dear old Dad,
Sorry I have not had time to send you a line before, but no doubt you will have no misgivings as to my safety!
I found my drawing of Aunt Anne hanging on the line in a very good position . . . I had walked all through the galleries without finding it and had come to the conclusion that it wasn't there. But I just struck on it at the last moment in a room with oil paintings, not among the black and white . . .
Yesterday Geoff and I called on Col. Collins digs' and found him at home (to our surprise). He seemed pretty well, but very busy with Coronation arrangements etc. He will do his best for me with the Princess and wants me to send her some of my work . . .
I lunched with Enfield today (he is in some gas company now) and afterwards shunted my cards at several people's houses, whose inmates I fortunately found out . . .
Geoff and I went to the Empire last night, some good dancing there. I think it quite probable I shall take a studio next September, but will see what Sir W. Richmond advises on Tuesday. Shall go to see R.A. and other exhibitions tomorrow.
Much love to all. Ain't this a chatty letter!
Your loving son, Brian.

As everyone knows, the career of a professional artist is a hazardous one. So much depends on trends and fashion and the whims of a fickle public. Brian had made his mark in Hereford and the West Country but now he was eager to move to London and find his place among the established painters of the day. It would surely be helpful to have a patron in high places to focus attention on his work, which must ultimately be judged on its merits. Perhaps for this reason Colonel Collins suggested that Brian should send some of his recent work for Princess Louise to see. Brian complied with this request and chose the portraits of Bishop Percival and Nicholas Heins, and an oil of Lugg Meadows on a foggy day and two pencil heads.

Brian had an introduction to Sir William Richmond, R.A., who had offered to give him some advice after seeing some of his work. Brian left some pictures with him, while he and Gerald Siordet went off on a little jaunt to Whitby. On his return, Brian found an encouraging note from Sir William, advising him to start working in London. Brian expressed his gratitude and said that he would start looking for a studio, "but of course it's all a question of L.S.D. and up to the present I have no certainty of getting any commissions".

There were others who were not so encouraging and feared that Brian's work might suffer when he came in contact with "modern painters". As we know, the impact of the French Impressionists had not met with whole-hearted approval in England. When Brian had been on his way to Paris, Mary Watts had said;

⇦ Julien's Studio, Paris.
Oil, 1912. 31¼″ × 21″ — *Brian Hatton Gallery, Hereford*

> I feel sure you would gain much from going there, so much to see and hear and learn, and so much even to avoid . . . I do not think you would want to join the post-impressionists.

Briton Riviere also wrote a letter of warning.

> I feel that a move to London is almost inevitable for you as time went on and I hope that now you are strong enough in your own convictions and beliefs, to escape being drawn into any of the artistic extravagances and fashions of the day, which have been so much to the fore in these times. Chelsea is a hotbed of these peculiar ideas, but you must brace yourself to a search for artistic truth. I know that Watts was very anxious that you should be permitted if possible to develop naturally your own natural gift, with no violent external influence, but the outer world must some time be faced and handled.

Brian was not unduly worried by these warnings. He had never been easily influenced by anyone, even his mother, although he was always prepared to respect other people's ideas. He was now twenty-four and much as he loved Hereford he did not want to become a provincial artist. It was now time for him to move to London, and after deciding to team up with Gerald Siordet he started looking for a suitable studio. He found one in South Kensington called "The Bronze Door" and in January 1912 the two young men moved in. Friends and family rallied round, providing furnishings and curtains and from home came linen, cutlery and a cookery book. Aunt Ada Vevers gave him some tapestry to hang on the walls, while Uncle Charles gave him £10 with which he bought a chesterfield and an arm-chair.

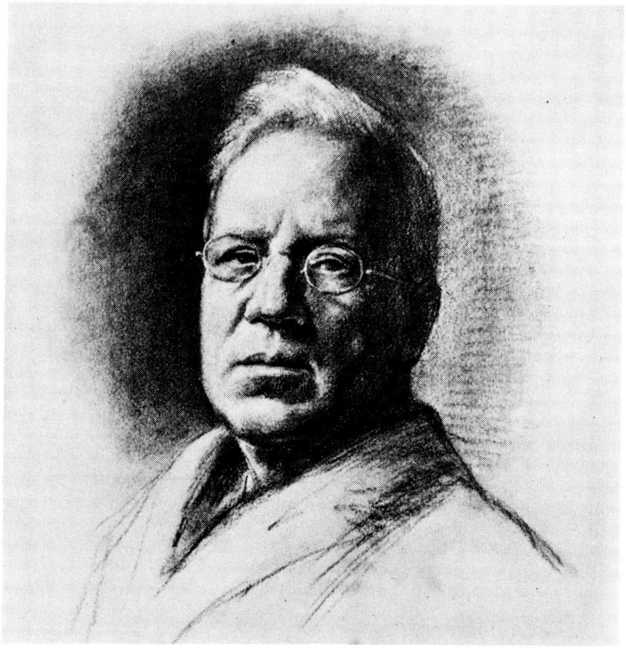

Nicholas Heins of Hereford.
Red chalk, 1909. 23″ × 19″
Brian Hatton Gallery, Hereford

Feb. 1st 1912

The Bronze Door,
1A Cathcart Road,
South Kensington.

My dear Old Dad,
Siordet and I spent our first night here last night. We are quite comfortable, though I did find my bed a bit hard! No doubt it will flatten and soften a bit with a little lying on. Geoffrey came to help us to 'unpack and hang pictures', he was only good at getting in the way. Siordet took a little rest every five minutes in the new armchair, which he found suited the bend of his back. Today we breakfasted well, and I made a very nutritious lunch off ham, bread and mustard, with cheese, butter and marmalade galore. There is quite a good little Italian restaurant near here, where they also send out meals as well. It is cheap too. Siordet has brought a cart load of books out of store. He has filled one book case and will have to buy another now . . . I seem to have found a very good woman, i.e. if she goes on as she has begun. She is clean and sensible and a hard worker and can cook too.

Your loving Brian

There was one disappointment which Brian was to suffer when he moved to London. He would see no more of his old friend and patron, Colonel Collins. Just before the turn of the year, "Curly" died at the age of sixty-six. Over the years Brian had continued to send him drawings and water colours and now he made enquiries about getting them back. Curly's nephew and heir, Mr Leo Collins, kindly agreed to his request and Brian collected about a dozen pictures.

One of the first things Brian did after settling into the studio was to seek membership of the Chelsea Arts Club, where he soon made new friends. Writing to his father he said;

I have met some members (Chelsea Arts Club) who have promised to find me a mount for a day's hunting within a reasonable distance of London, so please send up my kit. Mabel will see to it. Coat and breeches and hat guard. Boots with garter straps, and spurs with black straps. Also crop, flask and sandwich case. If you can spare a boot jack, so much the better. And while you are about it you might as well send leggings too and spurs with brown straps . . . By the way, I don't seem to have brought my Herrick. Please send it on with the other things.

Poor Mabel! She must for ever have been packing up parcels for Brian — and such awkward shapes and sizes too!

Other useful contacts came from the Arts Club.

Last night I was invited to go to a private sketch club where they had a model for quick poses. I think I shall go every week; it is good practice and worth the shilling each man subscribes towards the model's fee . . .
We had a great night last Monday at the Club dinner. Many notabilities were hors de combat at the end of it!! The atmosphere was fearfully smokey and rank, which gave me a headache next day. Please note it was the atmosphere which caused it!

With Gerald Siordet or Geoffrey Vevers for company, Brian frequented the theatre, seeing Pelissier's Follies at the Empire, the Diaghilev Ballets, and a performance of "The Miracle", which made a deep impression on him.

> Siordet and I went to see The Miracle the other night. We thought it was wonderful, the grouping and colouring were splendidly carried out, with the exception of a hideous purple light that was played onto the Virgin most of the time. But I thought the nun's acting rather ridiculous and she couldn't dance for toffee. We unfortunately missed the beautiful Madonna;* Lilian Braithwaite is taking the part now and she has about as much idea of it as a great cow.

Friends and relations came to visit Brian at the Bronze Door, and although he was willing to let people see his work and to make new contacts with a view to commissions, some of his visitors were less welcome than others.

> March 6th 1912 The Bronze Door
> I have just had Auntie Ada and Mrs & Miss Dickson round here to tea. It was fearfully dull and Aunt A. very officious. She sent me a note beforehand requesting that I should either drape the lay figure in something more than a night shirt or remove it to my bedroom. Needless to say I did neither. As a matter of fact, only a prudish woman of evil tendency would notice it at all, as it was well behind my desk . . .
> I hope you are pleased with the suffragettes. They have succeeded in getting themselves very much disliked even by their sympathisers. All public museums and many exhibitions are shut on account of their irresponsible actions.
> If you haven't sent off my hunting things, please include boot lifts and stocks *clean* and *ironed*.
> It is the big Arts Club Ball this evening at the Albert Hall. I shall not be there. I am now a full member and they all drank my health the other night, but I refused to be drawn into making a speech.

Brian's unwillingness to make a speech may have been due to the fact that he was still troubled by his stammer. He went to see a woman in Hampstead who gave lessons on the control of stuttering and he signed on for a course of six lessons. He said it was darned expensive, but she seemed to know what she was about, "but I doubt if I shall get much benefit. However, we shall see". His old tendency to fainting had not entirely left him either. While lunching with Aunt B. he said he distinguished himself by "doing a faint, but not a very bad one". He put it down to indigestion and said that he was really quite fit.

Brian was now hard at work and too busy to go home for Easter. He was painting a hunting scene in oils and he had work on hand that he wanted to prepare for the New English Art Club. Aunt B. was sitting for a head and shoulders portrait, but he said the prospect of painting her was rather daunting.

> I know she will not be pleased unless she is flattered and spoke shaved a great deal. But she won't get more than a little of that sort of thing from me!

*The "beautiful Madonna" was, of course, Lady Diana Manners.

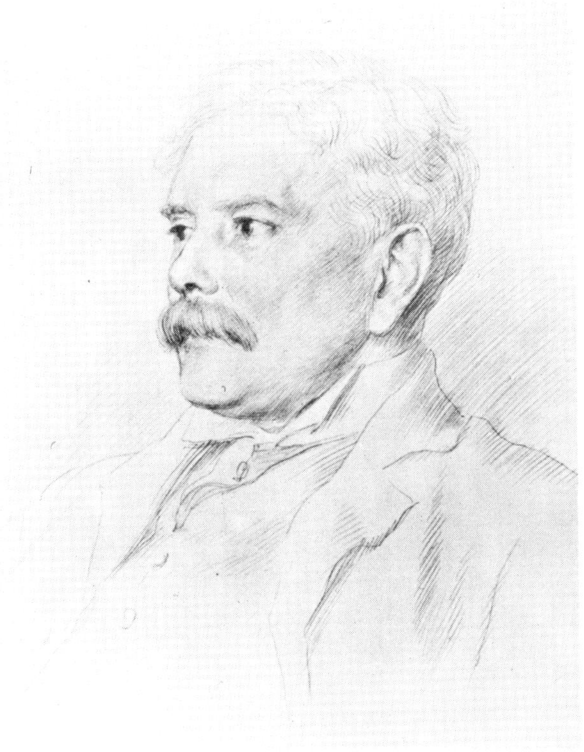

Sir Charles Oman, M.P.
Pencil, 1913 *C. C. Oman*

It was, however, Brian's old friend, R. W. Raper, who gave him his first real break. He invited Brian to visit him at Oxford and graciously permitted him to make an oil sketch of himself; a rare privilege as he had refused to sit for anyone else. Brian was distressed to see how ill and shaky the old man looked; however the portrait was a great success. It even satisfied Brian himself, and he said that he hoped that one day he would be able to turn it to good account.*

Brian repaid Raper for his kindness by making a sketch of one of his lady friends who came to lunch.

> It had to be done quickly, and after a heavy champagne lunch, so no one was more surprised and thankful than I that it proved a likeness! He wants me to paint a portrait of another lady whom he rather admires, if he can negotiate the business part without giving offence to the husband. He wants to pay for it himself.

A few weeks later Brian told his father that "old Raper" was sending some ladies to him to be sketched, in order to advertise his work. Raper would pay a nominal sum of three guineas each.

> It's very decent of him. He is also trying to get me orders in Oxford, but he is so darned slow and secretive that I am afraid he will peg out before he brings anything to a head.

*The portrait now hangs in Trinity College, Oxford.

Brian added a rather sad little ps to his letter to Mabel.

> Did you see in the Hereford Times if Drinkwater's mare 'The Gift', did any good in the Ross point-to-point? If I had been at home I should have ridden her!

"If I had been at home . . .". Brian's heart was always in his beloved Herefordshire!

Raper's efforts did eventually succeed and in June Brian was back in Oxford, to "do more drawings of his lady friends" of which there seemed to be a limitless supply, and to start work on a portrait of Professor Odling,* the professor of Chemistry which had been commissioned by All Souls. Other sitters were the young Carola Oman and her father, Professor Oman.

The pictures Brian sent to the Academy were "chucked", but he exhibited at the New English Art Club where the Cromwellian portrait of Gerald Siordet (Praise God Barebones) was placed in a central position and another work hung on the line. By mid-summer he was busy with commissions. "Have just finished a pastel of Mrs. Clive's little girl and am to do a pencil sketch of Mrs. C. tomorrow." He went down to Newport Pagnell and made pencil drawings of Mr and Mrs Trevor who ran a cramming establishment for the Army and came home with £10 in his pocket, as well as having a pleasant day. "They are very horsey and sporting, so I was quite happy . . . Tomorrow I am going to make a drawing of Lady Muriel Paget who is in a nursing home near Wigmore Street, and this evening I am to do one of Mr. Witt and stay there to dinner."

Gerald Siordet took Brian to have tea with Mrs William Morris who was living with her daughter at Hammersmith in a house by the river.

> More or less of an invalid, as she has always been, she still retains a great deal of the effect that one sees in Rossetti's pictures of her. Next week I am going there to do a pencil sketch of her, for Siordet; with her gracious permission. She has the strange hands which she poses naturally in the Rossetti manner.

Brian considered the portrait to be a success. He found Mrs Morris an interesting subject, "but as she was unable to talk without moving, she didn't say much!"

In August he went to say with Mr and Mrs Deakin at Hollingbourne Manor in Kent to paint a three-quarter length portrait of their daughter. It is clear that by now he had become an assured portrait painter, for he said;

> I may be down at Hollingbourne about ten days or a fortnight, or I may find the light in their rooms unsuitable and come back at once. In which case I shall do the girl here at end of Sept.

*It now hangs in the Imperial Chemistry School.

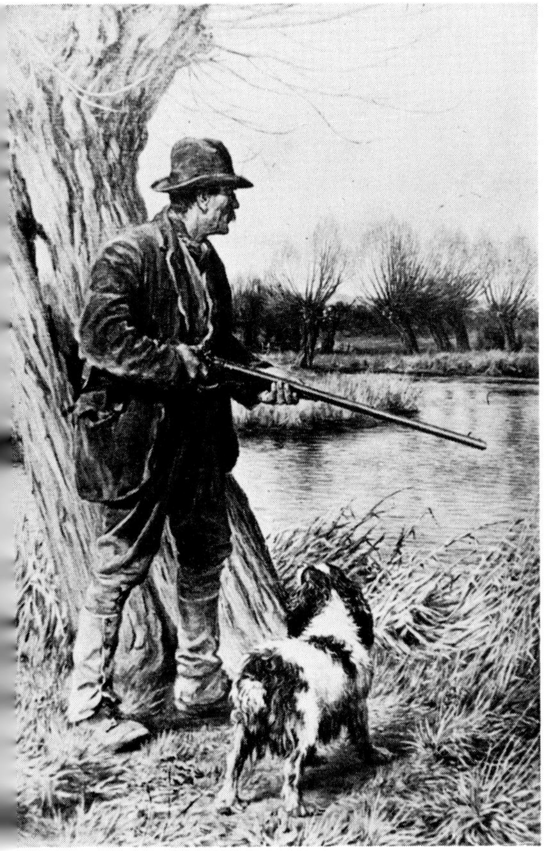

an duck shooting with dog on the Lugg.
, 1910

E. G. F. Davey

It was essential that Brian should establish his position as an artist in London, and the quickest and most certain way of doing so was as a portrait painter. But because of his great understanding of horses and the relationship between the rider and his mount, and his love of all aspects of country life, it seems sad that so much of his time should be taken up with portraiture. However, once his position was assured he would be able to paint what he liked. Not that he disliked painting portraits. His sociable nature and his intense interest in people produced all the necessary incentive. Needless to say, he found time to go to the Derby and the Richmond Horse Show, and he paid visits to the Zoo (once to sketch a little goat for a composition) in the company of Geoffrey Vevers who was ultimately to become superintendent of the Zoo and co-creator (with Chalmers Mitchell) of Whipsnade.

Artists were beginning to be interested in Brian. After seeing some of his drawings Goscombe John was very nice to him and introduced him to George Clausen. Clausen realised what a brilliant illustrator he was and gave him an introduction to the Art Editor of Cassell's Magazine, where Brian hoped he might obtain some work. At the end of the year he went over to Paris to meet his two young sisters, who were returning home from Switzerland, where they had been at a finishing school.

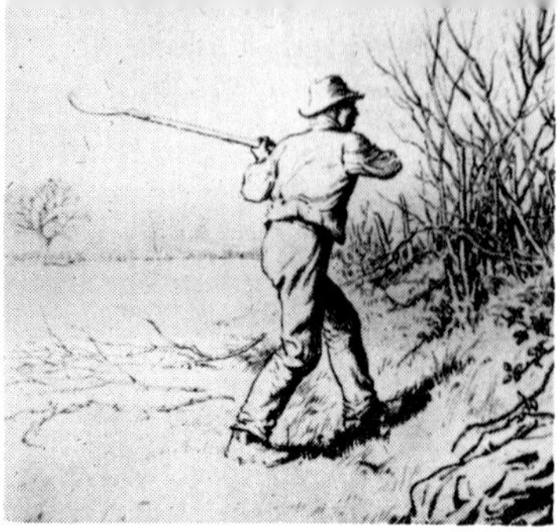

CHAPTER EIGHTEEN

The Struggling Artist

THE YEAR 1913 started well for Brian. Through the auspices of his good friend, Raper, he went to Windsor Castle to make drawings of Princess Alice's children, Prince Rupert and Princess May. Princess Alice, the daughter of Leopold, Duke of Albany, Queen Victoria's youngest son, was at that time known as Her Serene Highness, Princess Alexander of Teck. Her husband, Prince Alexander of Teck, was not given the title of Earl of Athlone until 1917.

Brian, with his romantic nature, got great pleasure out of his visits to Windsor and, as usual, wrote a lively account of the event.

Jan 28th 1913 The Bronze Door
My dear Old Dad,
I expect you would like to know how I got on at Windsor yesterday, so I will endeavour to write a few lines about it, since it doesn't happen to me every day — or at least it hasn't happened so far.
I found Princess Alice very fresh and jolly and I soon got over any feelings of nervousness I may have had when being ushered in to her. The children too were very jolly and just like any others of course. Prince Rupert aged 5 had to be smacked by his old nurse and he smacked her in return! They rode a rocking horse while the Princess read aloud to them, incidentally mispronouncing 'Hesperides'! She also insisted on sitting in one of their little arm chairs and stuck fast in it so I had to pull her up and pull it off her afterwards! Needless to say the children were in great glee and she herself nearly had hysterics! I had lunch with her and a lady of uncertain age, whom I gathered was the Chaplain's or Dean's daughter brought in to chaperone us! I noticed a fact that might interest you, viz that the Princess wore patent leather shoes which squeaked audibly!
The King and Queen were in residence and were to have paid a short call just after I left, so they just missed seeing me! An interesting item of Court news: Prince John's box of bricks which he had lost for several days, was found in the King's sitting-room yesterday.
I finished the drawings of the little prince and princess to their parents satisfaction I think. I also began one of Princess Alice, which I was to have gone back to finish tomorrow, but I have just received a wire asking me to postpone the sitting until Tuesday.
Today I went to Slough and drew a girl of about 15, which I did, and it *was* good . . .
Much love to all of you. It is pouring cats and dogs again tonight.
Your loving
Brian.

A week later Brian said that his second visit to Windsor went off well and that his drawing of the Princess was approved of. He was fascinated by Princess Alice, saying, "She is a delightful little person and very easy to get on with. After the drawing was done she took me to see the Holbein drawings and some of the pictures. Afterwards we had lunch in the same manner as before".

A little later Brian was approached by Lady Helen Lucas-Tooth who said that Princess Alice had shown her the drawings of her children. She was so impressed with them that she wanted Brian to do a drawing of her own granddaughter. One commission generally led to another in this way.

In September he went to stay at Higham Hall, Nuneaton, to paint three large equestrian portraits of the Morris family, who were well known in the hunting field.

Sept. 21st 1913 — Higham Hall,
Nuneaton.

My dear Old Dad
. . . Everyone has gone to church and I am left to do some work on the background of the picture! I have nearly finished the big one of the two children, and yesterday I began the one of Mrs. Morris. I think they are pleased with what I have done.
I have had no cubbing as yet . . . Until two days ago there had been no rain to speak of for a long time and the ground was far too hard to gallop or jump. I have had three or four rides and have sampled most of the horses in the stables.

C. H. Morris on "Meteor". — Oil, 1913. 40″ × 50″

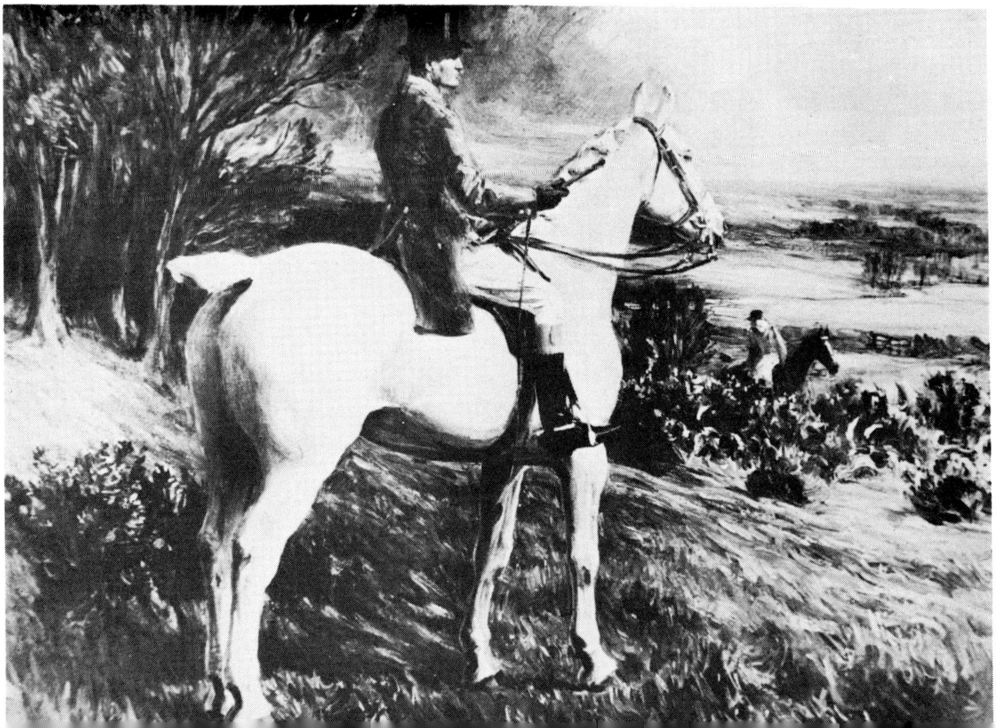

On his return to London, Brian was busy moving house. He had obtained the lease of 33 Nevern Square, Earls Court, and after some repairs and decoration had been carried out, he and Gerald Siordet moved in. More furnishings were sent from home, and from Nuneaton Brian brought "a nice plain old church chest" for which he had paid £2.

Brian kept in touch with Mary Watts and perhaps through her he became acquainted with Arthur Hughes, whom he described as the last of the pre-Raphaelites and "a nice old man aged 83". Hughes took Brian and Siordet to visit the painter, Cadogan Cooper. As well as being very impressed with his work Brian felt sympathetically inclined towards him, on account of his stammer.

> He has the worst stammer I've ever heard. He takes hours and jumps about the room buzzing like a bee! I shall dream about it for weeks. His work is simply wonderful of the pre-Raphaelite sort.

Brian's letters to his family were now becoming much less frequent, and possibly the ties with home were loosening. Another reason may have been that he had made the acquaintance of a Hereford girl, Lydia Bidmead, and a friendship was growing up between them. Lydia, or Biddy as she was called, was well known in dancing circles and was a talented teacher and performer.

In 1914 Brian submitted three pictures to the Royal Academy and one, "Night Piece to Julia", was accepted. However, when Brian went to view it on Varnishing Day, he was far from pleased.

> I felt very sheepish when I saw "Julia" looking like a dirty fried onion rather high up amongst some other frightful stunners. It was the worst picture of the three so I suppose that is why it is hung. I can see no other reason.

A week or two later Brian had cause to feel more cheerful. He had been approached by a member of the Royal Institute of Oil Painters, who asked him if he would like to be proposed for membership of the Society, although the election would not take place until November. With this in mind, Brian sent some of his best work to the R.O.I. summer exhibition. One of the pictures, called "The Outcast", created a lot of interest. Brian had used a model for his subject. She was Beatrice Stewart, a well-built, handsome girl who was lame. He had given her strong features a curious expression of resignation, mingled with defiance and a haunting sadness. It is not surprising that this picture was awarded a "highly commended".

It was during this summer that Brian painted "Sunday Morning in the Park". Not only is this a very evocative picture, giving us a glimpse of a way of life so soon to die; it is also of special interest because unlike any of his previous work, it shows the influence of the Impressionists. One can only speculate as to whether Brian would have continued to paint in this style.

The Outcast. Oil, 1913/14. 35½″ × 27¾″ ⇨

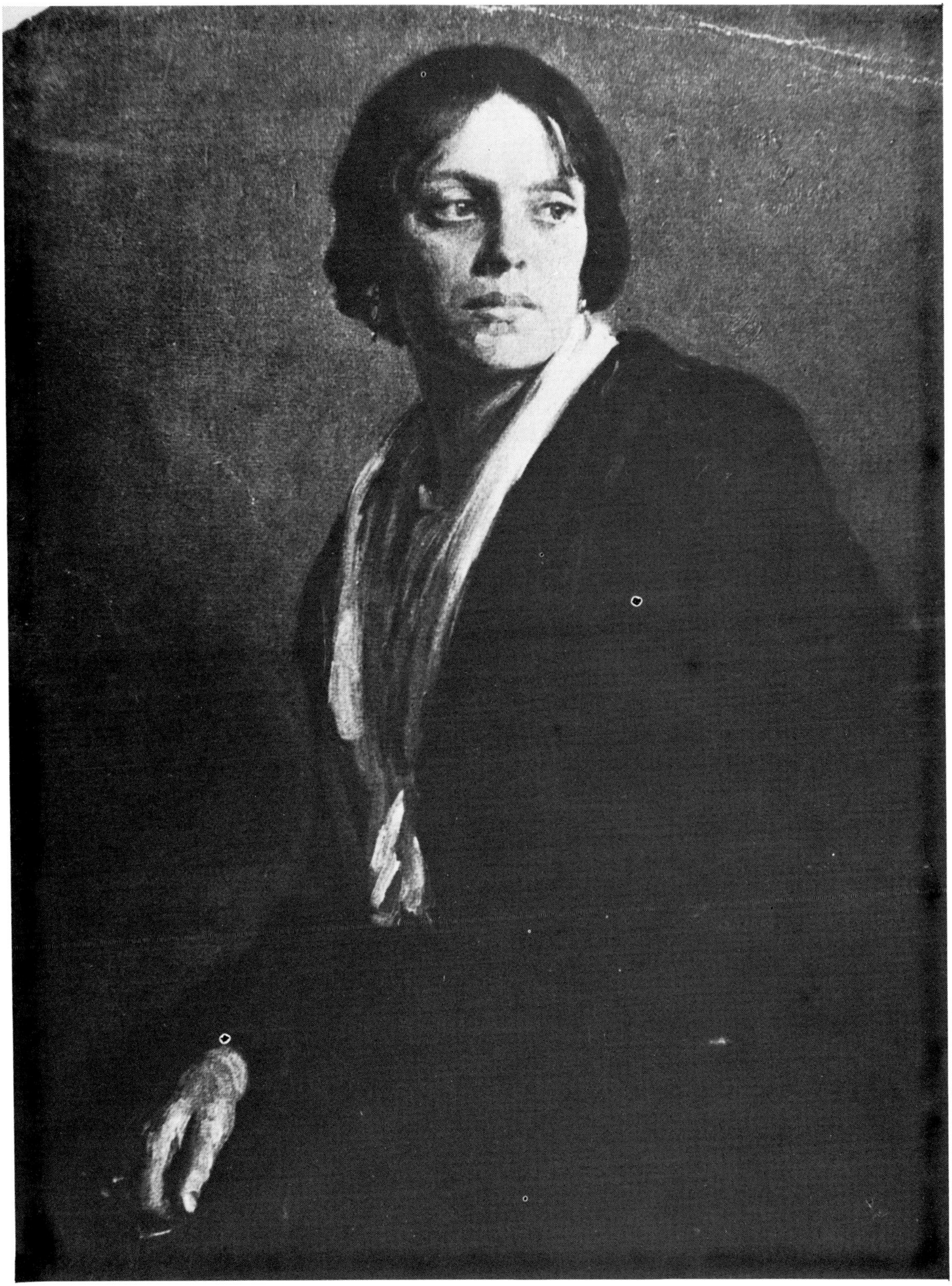

In spite of his apparent success, Brian went through one of those bad patches that most artists experience at some time, wondering where his next commission would come from. He advertised in the *Morning Post* and the *Church Times* with no result, and said "I shall have to do a moonlight flit soon".

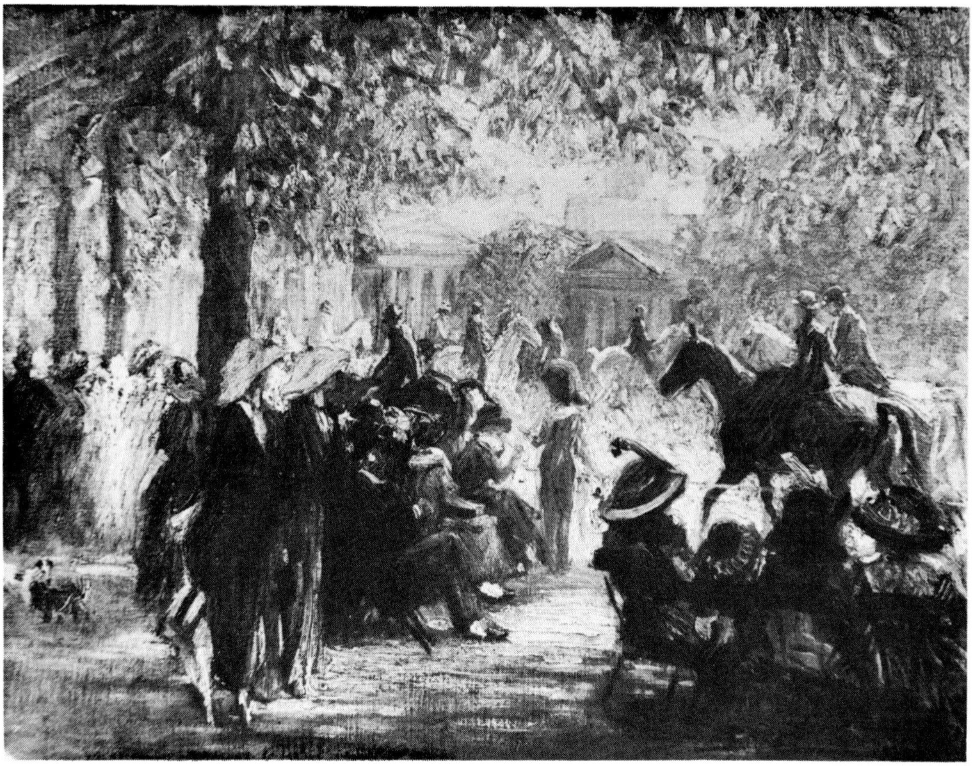

Sunday Morning in the Park. Oil, 1913/14. 10¾″ × 13¾″

Although the situation had improved a little by July, work was still scarce. There was, however, a possibility that he would be commissioned to illustrate John Masefield's "Everlasting Mercy" which had first been published in 1911 in "The English Review". Even though the pay would be "pretty bad", this would give full scope to his imagination and brilliant draughtsmanship, and bring his work before the public eye. In the meantime he decided to accompany Uncle Charles Marr on a trip to Belgium. They set off towards the end of the month, but returned hastily, owing to the imminent threat of war.

Aug. 4th 1914 33 Nevern Square.

My dear Old Dad,

We returned to Dover in the early hours of yesterday (Mon) morning and had to sleep in chairs in the lounge of a hotel as there wasn't a bed to be had anywhere, everyone is coming over. I should have liked to have stayed a little longer in Belgium. Things were just beginning to get interesting, but the trains were uncertain and they were stopping the boats so we thought we had better come back while we could. Money was a great difficulty, no one had enough to change a sovereign . . . and they wouldn't look at paper money. It is not much better here.

Aren't you on the reserve? Have you been called up yet? What will you do? Would you like me to come down to Hereford and look after the business for you?!!! I am going to stay in town for a few days and then will either go to Devonshire with Hyde to his home, or come to you . . . I do not know whether the train services have been very much upset yet. We were four hours getting up from Dover to London yesterday. We had to wait for specials and troops to come through.

Everyone in Belgium was expecting England to send an army over to defend them. We shall have to do it soon. I don't know why we are delaying so long.

I don't think anyone will buy pictures now money is so tight and I don't know how I am going to live. It is damned serious. Can't you make a fortune by supplying boots to the army? . . .

There are only about half the usual number of buses running today and yesterday, owing to lack of petrol, and many having been converted into ambulance waggons.

With much love to you all,
Your loving
Brian.

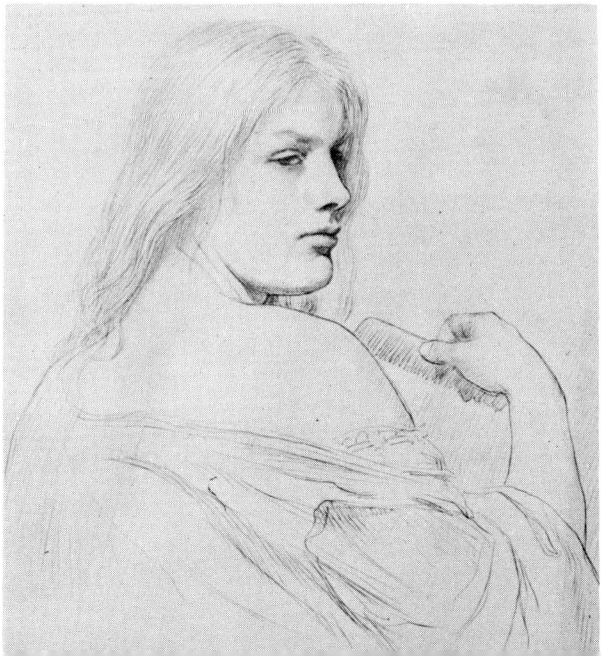

Young Woman Combing Her Hair.
Pencil, 1912. 16″ × 12″

It is obvious that Brian wrote this letter on that fateful 4th August before the news that England had declared war on Germany had been released . . . "I don't know why we are delaying so long". Brian was just about to celebrate his 27th birthday and he saw quite clearly that this would be the end of his career as a professional painter, for the time being, anyway. He had no cash reserves to fall back on and it was indeed "damned serious". On 13th August he wrote to his grandmother to thank her for her good wishes on his birthday.

> I hope my next 'return' will be happier than this one, as I have absolutely no work to do at present. I am going down to Richmond Park tomorrow morning early to see the Territorials do cavalry drill, perhaps I can make a drawing of it for the Graphic or some other paper, i.e. if I am not taken as a spy when they see my sketch book!
> I think I shall stay in London a little longer and will then go home or away with the family to N. Wales unless I can get some work to keep me going. Geoffrey has signed on as a reserve naval surgeon but hasn't been called on yet. I hear that all departments have more volunteers than they need. I would rather like to join the Terriers but I see very little chance of getting a decent horse to ride!

On 20th August Brian said it was practically settled that he should do the illustrations for the "Everlasting Mercy" and although the pay was poor, it would pull him through until the end of the year. He was planning to go and stay with Mabel's sister at Ledbury where he could get local colour for the illustrations. However, the whole thing came to nothing, although he completed seven pastel and pen and ink drawings. The illustration of the fight was a particularly moving and vigorous piece of work. At the end of August Geoffrey was "strutting about in khaki, awaiting orders to go to the front with Red Cross Society".

Brian decided that it was time he went back to Hereford, but just before leaving London he sold a picture. The subject was Siordet wearing a helmet. "But I only got 35 gns for it." Once back in Hereford, Brian hastened to enrol at the Drill Hall and on 4th September he joined the 1/1 Worcestershire Yeomanry as a trooper. It was inconceivable that he should join anything but a cavalry regiment.

Mrs. 'Awkins.
Oil, 1914. 37½" × 22½" *Brian Hatton Gallery, Hereford*

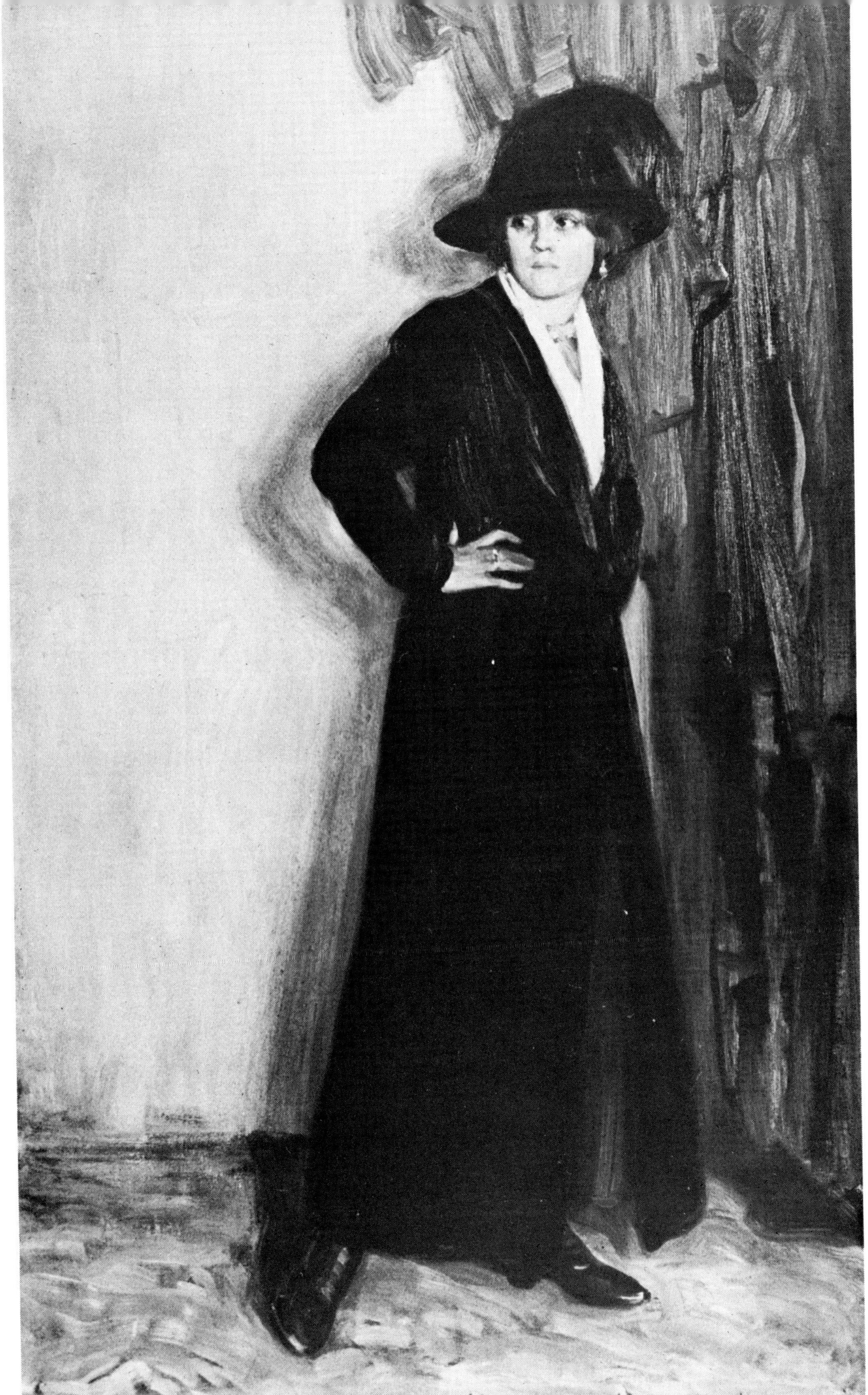

CHAPTER NINETEEN

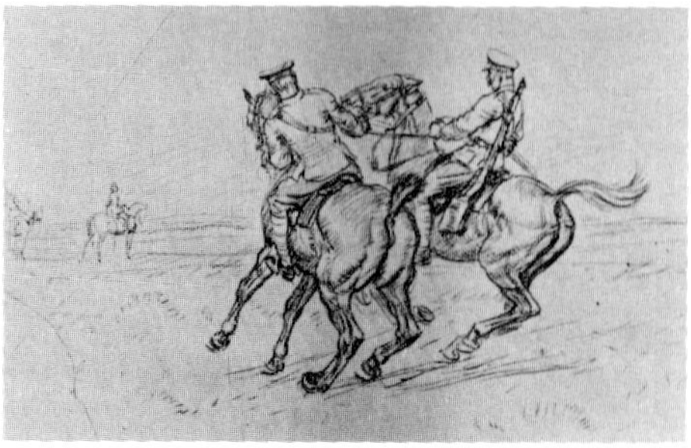

B. Hatton 2441 WOR YEO

AT Worcester, Brian was billeted in the Crown Hotel. On his arrival, he was spotted by Captain Blew, a family friend, who saw to it that Brian had a good billet. He was issued with some uniform; a tunic and puttees, and a cap which was a size too large. Breeches were in short supply and there were none to fit him.

> But of course I have my own to go on with. They also gave me a kit bag, but they will allow me to take my other saddle bag as well, . . . so kindly have the following painted or inked on it.
>
> B. Hatton 2441 WOR YEO

A few days later Brian wrote from Newbury where they were now under canvas on the race course. He had not been there long before he gave a fine (if ill-advised) display of horsemanship.

> I am very fit having slept last night on the ground and got up at five to groom horses and take them to water etc, also shovel dung, and spent nearly all the morning digging holes for the officers' latrines! . . . This afternoon I distinguished myself by jumping on one of my horses that I took to water and they quickly bolted on the way back, having only a strap round their neck with a rope on it and of course no saddle, I hadn't any chance of stopping them. However, after some marvellous jumping over tent ropes and swerving about, we eventually pulled up after about ½ mile gallop near my own lines and got cursed by Major Cheape for riding without a bridle, against regulations. He was very amused all the same . . .
>
> P.S. I am with two gents like myself (!!) and five old stagers in our tent. One of them has very fruity feet!

On 21st September, his father's birthday, Brian wrote to say he had not forgotten it but had lost count of the date, having no time to think or read a paper.

> I've been on the go since 5.15 this morning and now it's 8 o'clock and I'm feeling very fit! . . . We are going into billets shortly I believe. It is getting so cold for the horses at night.
>
> Well you are doing jolly well for 58. I hope I shall look and feel half as fit when I reach your age, if ever I do. If I crock up I think I shall change places with you . . . I'm afraid you'd get a sore ass at riding school though. I've been jogging round without stirrups most of the morning.

Brian took happily to the life of a trooper, and continued to emphasise how fit he was in spite of the hard work.

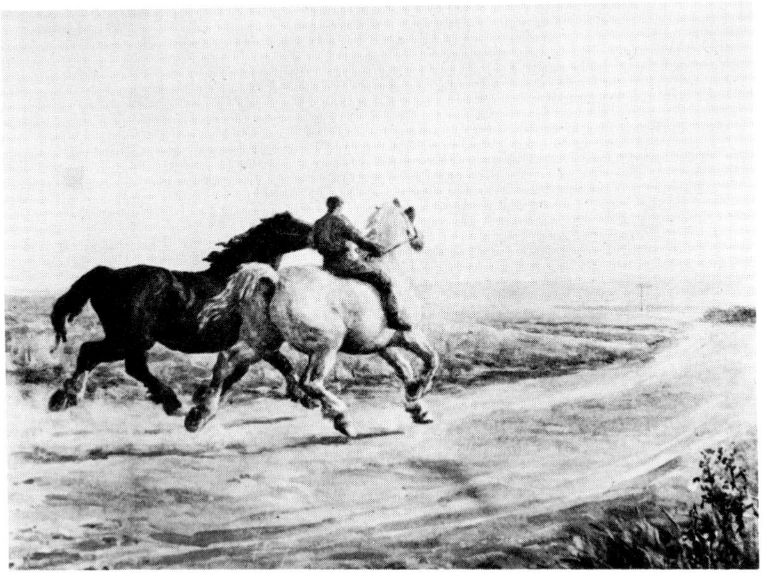

Man with Two Horses.
Pastel, 1905. 14½″ × 17¾″ Brian Hatton Gallery, Hereford

> I realise now that a soldier has to be a groom and muck-shifter and navvy and kitchen maid and horsebreaker besides a fighter. All our best horses are gradually being sent off to the regular army and we are left with the rotters to do our best with, and it is wonderful what we make them do.
> . . . We live in filth and dung and wash six deep in one bucket. It's such a long way to fetch water. I've not had my clothes off for a week and consider myself lucky if I get a wash once in 24 hours . . .
> I had one of my usual escapes last night when I went to fetch some remounts from the station. I collared a nice looking one and scrambled up bareback whereupon she immediately tried to plunge and get me off; however, finding that no use she stood bolt upright and came over on her back while I slipped over her tail and ran out of the way! Luckily it was dark and no officer saw me . . . We've had a longish day in the field rifle firing . . . I never knew 100 rounds were so heavy to carry . . . The old hens have laid an egg in my manger today which I am carefully concealing until I can get it cooked!

At the end of October, the Regiment was under orders to proceed to France and Brian was anxious to settle his affairs. He wrote to the Secretary of the Imperial Arts League who was a personal friend and asked him to look after his house in Nevern Square. To his father, he said;

> I suppose you would like some of your old furniture back. There will be nothing but a few sticks and sketches. However I quite expect to be invalided home in a few weeks to look after it myself! . . . There is a lawyer among us and he is going to make our wills out for us, so I will send you a copy of mine! . . .

We have a new Troop Officer (named Chamberlain, some relation of old Joe), who is quite nice but knows nothing at all yet. We have two or three like him and these are the men we are expected to follow and trust!! We are supposed to be going to a base in France for about six weeks or so and then will be sent up gradually to relieve troops nearer the firing line until we are considered fit to go in the firing line itself, or until the Germans come in our direction and force us to make a firing line willy nilly! . . . The whole of the South Midland division is going with us to France.
. . . The latest official news is that we do not go until Sunday Nov. 8th.

Only ten days after receiving his news, Mr Hatton got another letter from Brian, dated 5th November, in which he boldly stated the fact that he had just got married. This was indeed a great shock to his father.

Nov. 5th 1914 Newbury

My dear Old Dad,
I have just got married to Biddy today by soldier's licence. I only decided to go through with it last night and got Biddy down to talk it over with her. I suppose on the whole it is a very rash thing to have done, especially in my present circumstances. But we were both very keen and I think it is a good thing to give way to sentiment sometimes instead of always calculating the odds. Anyway you can rest assured that my wife has not 'grabbed' me for her own pecuniary or social gain, as she knows what I am worth and what my chances are, and is content to go back to Hereford and slog on with her dancing classes until I come back and am able to support her. I have every hope of surviving! We were told at a review on Wednesday that Kitchener's message was to hold ourselves in readiness to go at any time. He might want us in a few days, week or months! . . . Meanwhile we are not allowed any leave. I have only got one day's honeymoon in Newbury!
I hope when you have got over this little shock that you will give us your blessing. We shall need all that we can get! Yes I know that I'm a silly young fool and all that. But I'm still your

Loving son

Brian.

This must have been a difficult letter for Brian to write. He was usually very considerate about other people's feelings, but now it is obvious that he could think of no way of breaking the news gently to his father, therefore he went boldly into the attack with a plain statement. Up till now he had kept all mention of Biddy out of his letters, but of course he must have been in close communication with her for some time. This was a time for hasty marriages; the present was all important when the future held so little promise. Brian anticipated his father's reaction by saying that he supposed he had done a very rash thing and was a silly young fool, but then asked for his blessing and reminded him that he is still his "loving son". The family ties were still of great importance to him.

Colonel Lutley's Charger on Picket.
Pencil and wash, 1915. 14″ × 20″ *Brian Hatton Gallery, Hereford*

The marriage between Brian and Lydia May Bidmead took place in Newbury church. It is rather remarkable that Brian found time to write to his father during his brief, one day honeymoon, but any form of deception was against his nature. The move to France was postponed and in December the Regiment was stationed at King's Lynn. All Christmas leave was stopped and "there are rumours that we are going to all sorts of places, but nothing official as yet".

On 10th January Brian experienced one of the very early Zeppelin raids. It was a very dark night and at 11 o'clock, just as he was getting into bed, he heard what he thought was an aeroplane overhead. Then there were bangs and crashes which rocked the house and a terrific buzz overhead. Lights were switched off and "there was an awful scramble for boots and rifles and ammunition". Out in the street it was disappointing that they could not see anything to shoot at, although they could "hear the damned thing overhead". Seven or eight bombs were dropped, damaging several houses and blowing windows and doors out of many more, but no one was killed. The rest of the night was spent guarding shops to prevent looting.

Brian had a great admiration for some of his officers. "Major Gray Cheape hunts a pack of hounds. His brother, Captain Leslie Cheape, the Adjutant of the Regiment, is the polo man." It was inevitable that Brian should find time to make drawings of camp life and before long he was doing pencil portraits of some of the officers. He also drew a portrait of Colonel Lutley (of Brockhampton Court, Herefordshire) and a line and wash of his charger on picket. Unfortunately an accident held up his work for a time.

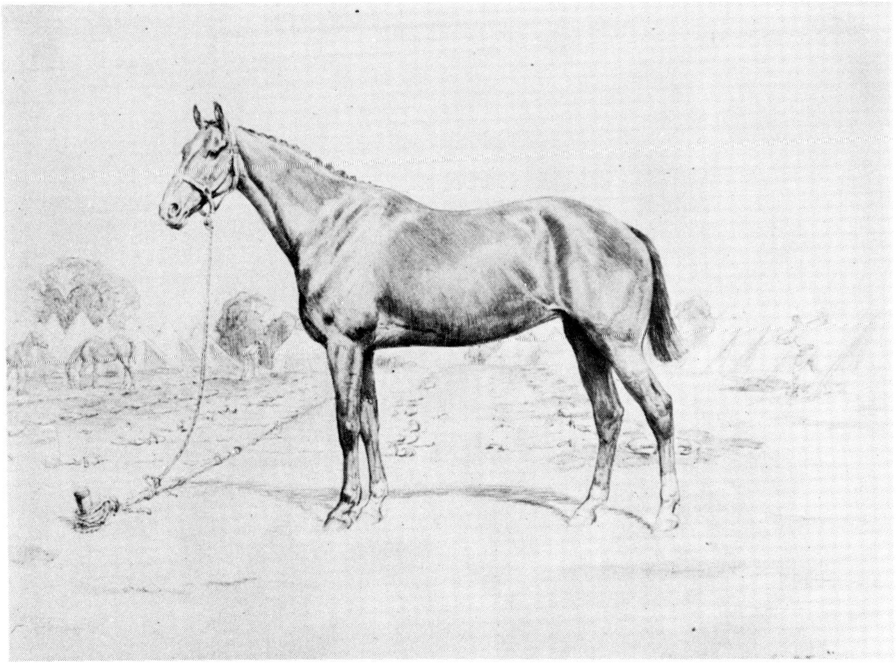

> I am rather sick that I cannot fulfil my commissions just now as the horse I was riding turned a somersault over a jump the other day (nearly breaking it's neck and only just missed rolling on me). However I only got a few thorns in my hand, some of which have festered a little and make it difficult for me to write, much less draw.

At the end of January, Brian was offered a commission in the Denbighshire Yeomanry, having been recommended by his old friend, Raper. "He is a good old sort," was Brian's comment. It was not surprising, however, that Brian's Colonel did not want him to leave the Regiment.

> He didn't seem keen on my leaving (I'm too good of course) and offered me a commission in the 1st reserve regiment at Worcester, which, after consideration, I accepted.

Several other men in Brian's troop were given commissions about this time, but he was the only man to receive one without first applying for it. He noted that a Second Lieutenant got 8/6 per day, plus a messing allowance of 12/6 and a kit allowance of £50. "I can draw horses and saddlery etc from the army stores for nix. They would be good enough for me."

Back in Worcester once more, Brian was unable to find digs, so he stayed with a cousin by marriage, Tom Wyatt.

> 13th March 1915 — 4 Park Avenue, Barbourne, Worcester
>
> My dear Dad,
> We are kept on duty pretty long hours. From 6.30 a.m. to 5.30 p.m. and then a lecture at 6 p.m. I am now attached to No. 4 troop A Squadron as they need bucking up a bit. I suppose one day they will give me a troop. I should probably have had one the first day if I had had my uniform but the others got in first . . . We are very short of horses as we have sent so many drafts away . . . Therefore I shall have to buy one and re-sell it to the government . . . Will you please tell George Bull or any other horsey pals to look for a sound animal about 15.2 or 3 capable of carrying me . . . Price about £50 or £60 . . . Must have a fairly good mouth and be a hardy animal that I can lead a troop on. A kicker is useless . . . Ask Mabel if she would like some hat pins made out of regimental buttons.

Soon they were moved to Cirencester, "a very good place", and in June they were back in King's Lynn.

> This place is as bad in summer as it was in winter. All that was mud before is filthy brown dust now and the whole place chock-a-block with soldiers who have nowhere to drill!

A few weeks later they were moved to Holkham and were under canvas again. On 19th July Brian wrote:

> I am awfully sorry about poor old Raper. I saw his death and a little account of him in the Times too. I am glad I did that sketch of him.
> We have had several rough days and nights since we came here, some tents blown down, but the ground is sandy and soaks up the rain!
> I am jolly sick of this life . . .
> I am seriously thinking of putting in for a transfer to R.F.A. If I was a good walker I would try infantry (nice and cheap) but artillery would give me a chance of riding a horse . . . I don't think this regiment will ever see active service in its present form.
> If I were abroad on active service I would be saving my pay instead of spending it and more on expensive messes, to no useful purpose. Then there is the cheerful prospect of having to tell people that I marked time on the east coast during the Great War!

Some officers were drafted out to Alexandria from where two squadrons had been sent to the Dardanelles and Brian remarked that he expected his turn would come in due course. In the meantime life was enlivened by the fact that they were getting up a gymkhana . . . " jumping, tug-of-war, night shirt race etc etc". Brian didn't win anything but because of the antics of his horse, his performance in the jumping ring was the show piece of the afternoon!

> In spite of refusals and various kind of tangos on two legs I got all the way round with only two mistakes, which was generally conceded to be a very creditable performance in the face of such odds.

On 31st August Marjorie, who was working as a V.A.D., received a brotherly letter from Brian.

> Can it be that you are 20? Have you 'got off' with any of the soldiers at the Convalescent Home? Why were you warned off by the matron? Is she the same darned old bitch who wouldn't allow me to go up one morning? She ought to be pegged out in the rain for a few nights; it would take the stuffing out of her . . .
> Will you send me a dozen sheets of the pencil paper that I pointed out to either you or Ailsa? It is white with a faint rubbed line in it and a large watermark 'Aldwych'. Send it in a cardboard tube.

Although Brian had adapted easily to the routine of Army life and managed to find plenty of amusement in day to day events, he was yet fully aware of the horrors of war and its far reaching consequences. It was during this year (1915) that he made a drawing called "Civilisation" which was quite out of keeping with anything he had ever done before. He may have intended to sell it to an illustrated paper but the stark horror of the picture probably prohibited its publication.

Time was running out and Brian was busy choosing strong boots which would stand up to hard wear. Then, on 21st September, his father's birthday, Biddy gave birth to a daughter.

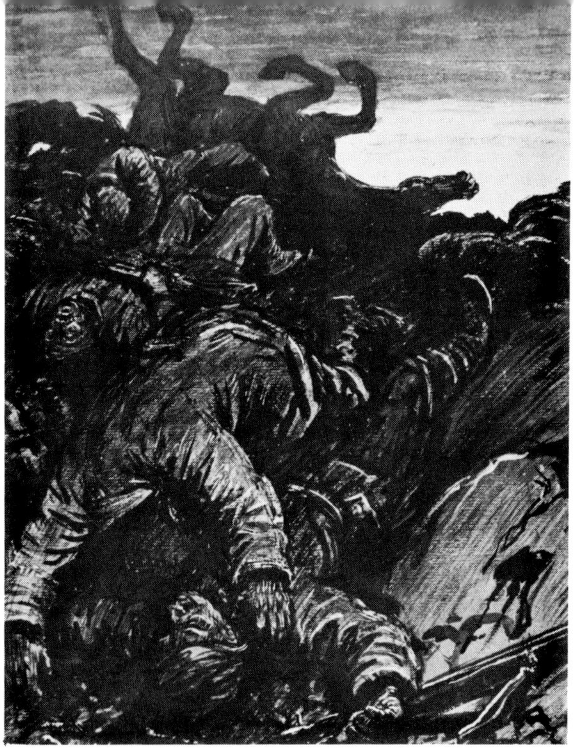

Civilisation.
Charcoal and wash, 1915.
23¾″ × 18″
Brian Hatton Gallery, Hereford

Brian went post haste to Hereford and then wrote to his grandmother to tell her the good news. He described his daughter, who was to be called Mary Amelia, as "the usual funny little reddish object (rather a long upper lip!) but otherwise quite nicely made. Biddy is as pleased with it as if it had been a pocket edition of Venus". He added that his father seemed pleased, "although he would probably have preferred a son".

Soon after Brian returned to Norfolk, he was informed that he was to join a draft of officers going overseas and that he was to embark at Devonport on 12th October. There was just time for him to go back to Hereford to do his final packing and bid farewell to his family. He wrote one more letter to his grandmother when he was in the train on his way to Devonport.

> I left Hereford at 3.37 a.m. this morning! having spent most of my scant leave in unpacking and packing again. I am allowed to take a good deal of stuff so no doubt we are going to Alexandria at any rate for a time . . .
> I am thankful to be leaving my little wife and baby well and both making good progress, and all well at Mount Craig. Dad came down to see me off this morning like a good angel at that uncivilised hour. I shall not be able to see my wee mite being christened unfortunately. Mrs. Lancaster is the godmother and has good-heartedly offered to look after her if I should get knocked out. Somehow I haven't much fear of that. Nor do a V.C. or D.S.O. come into my calculations! I shall be thankful to return with a sound right hand and eyesight.

How significant was that last remark!

CHAPTER TWENTY

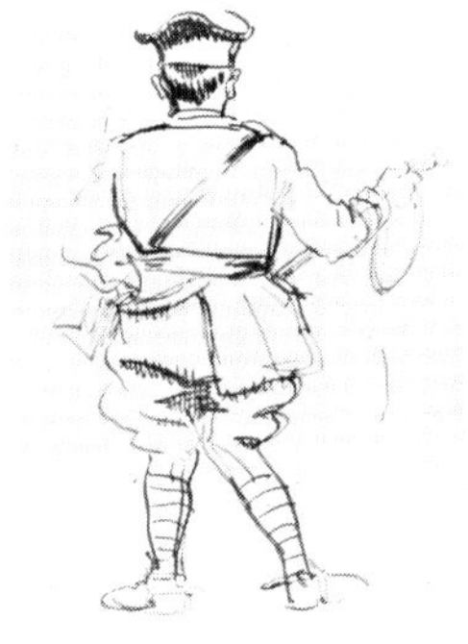

Off To The War

OCT. 12th 1915 R.M.S. "Scotia"
2 p.m.

My dear Old Dad,

Just a line to say I am on board this old tramp of a transport. It is full of various drafts, both men and officers; amongst the latter an artist friend of mine, a member of the Chelsea Arts Club. We are supposed to sail tonight. Our cabins have absolutely no ventilation, and as we are four in each, we shall keep warm.

In great haste — much love to you all — Au voir.

Your loving
Brian.

At last Brian was on his way to the Middle East. He got over the unpleasantness of a stuffy cabin by sleeping on deck in his valise. No longer was he troubled by seasickness; he said that he had never felt better, in spite of the rolling ship and the heavy Atlantic swell. There was a draft of Hereford officers on board, some of whom were old friends. Before reaching Malta they passed a hospital ship on its way to England.

> I wish I had been in it coming back to all that I have left behind, including poverty (the latter accompanies me everywhere!) By the way, Major Lutley said he would do his best to find out any information about me for you if I ever get into the thick of it and don't send you any news. His home address is Brockhampton, Herefordshire . . . I hope the need won't occur. I don't suppose so. There are 4 or 5 Hereford officers on board — Tommy Ragg,* Trumper Llewelyn, also Dunkerly of the R. West Kents.

Brian with his sensitive nature, was fully aware of the agonies his family would suffer, should he be reported "missing".

On 24th October *Scotia* docked at Mudros, on the Island of Lemnos, one of the bases used for the fighting in Gallipoli. Brian had been uncertain as to whether their ultimate destination would be Alexandria or Gallipoli. He said "We may be sent anywhere . . . I hope we get sent to Servia *with* our horses". He described Lemnos as,

> a bleak little island without a tree apparently. Plenty of warships and transports in the harbour and canvas camps on the shore — miles of them. Lord Dudley is Governor here I believe so we ought to get well looked after . . .

*Son of the headmaster of Hereford Cathedral School.

> We are moving into another camp a few miles off soon where there is a good water supply, but food will be just as scarce. I should be glad of small packets sent out separately so that some of them may reach me. Plain chocolate, candles, Horlicks malted milk tabloids and meat or soup tabloids. Also Quaker oats . . . Don't send me much at a time, small dribbles, so that if some of it gets lost, I shall get a little of it.

No doubt the indomitable Mabel got busy, dispatching the parcels. Brian said that the rations on the island were in short supply, and that they seemed "to shrivel in the cooking".

Life on the island was rather boring and as the ratio of officers to men was about one to ten, there was not much work to be done.

> We are just dumped here waiting until we are taken away to be dumped somewhere else. If it wasn't for the censor I could tell you one or two things that you will never read of in the papers! . . .
>
> I'm all right and haven't been attacked by dysentry yet which is rife everywhere on this island . . . The poor beggers back from Gallipoli for a rest look like haggard scarecrows. They say most of the men couldn't charge if they were told to, and I can quite believe it.

Lord Kitchener paid a surprise visit to the island, and for Brian this was an opportunity too good to miss. He made two drawings; one of Lord Kitchener inspecting the troops and another of the men, "the poor beggers", returning from the trenches, wounded and weary. Brian sent the drawings to *The Graphic* and they were both published in the issue of 11th December, 1915. It's not difficult to imagine what a first class war artist Brian would have made. How much more worth while it would have been if his talent had been used in this way!

> Nov. 17th 1915
>
> We are still in Mudros though we have moved camp and joined the old regiment and the division back from Gallipoli or rather the remnants of it.
>
> It was blowing great guns yesterday and everyone was smothered in dust and dirt. Last night there was a frost! It is a lovely clear pristine sort of day and I am proposing to walk up to the top of a mountain not far off and see the view.
>
> I've had no letters as yet. Either they have not been forwarded from Alexandria or else have gone down on a ship that was torpedoed just outside here with 2,000 mail bags on board, a few days ago. It is sickening, I haven't heard a word since I left Hereford over five weeks ago.
>
> Do you see anything of Biddy and the babe? I wish I knew how they were getting on.

The soldier's universal hunger for news from home was acutely felt by Brian, increased by the fact that he now had a wife and child of his own. He had to wait until December, when the regiment had moved to Egypt, before he got his first mail.

Dec. 4th 1915

2nd Mounted Div. Base
Egypt B.M.E.F.

My dear Old Dad,

We came here last Tuesday having had a pretty rough passage in a rotten little boat* which was filthy, and filthy food and with a lot of filthy sick Egyptians on board, several of whom died on the way. However everything has an end and I was only a bit seedy for one day.

After various adventures we have all arrived in a camp close to the Pyramids (The Mena Camp). It is a fine situation and a well arranged camp but the desert is very soft and heavy going. We are about eight miles from Cairo. Everything is at sixes and sevens at present; no grooming kits to groom the horses and not enough saddles etc to mention only a few of the little inconveniences. I have been put down as regimental signalling officer (knowing nothing about it). My little smattering of Arabic, which I have been rubbing up, is quite useful in dealing with them . . .

I was very glad to get the kids letters which I found when I got here. Also your's and Mabel's . . . The weather is just the right English summer temperature though it gets cold as soon as the sun goes down.

From what Kitchener is reported to have said the War will last another two and a half years. I hope he is wrong. Our staff arrangements are appalling. The waste of time and material is disgraceful. Troops and materials are left for weeks on ships apparently forgotten (though they are badly wanted somewhere) and finally sent back to the place they started from without having disembarked at all.

I've no news. Life here is settling down to the monotonous. It is too expensive to go to Cairo often.

With lots of love to you all

Your loving son Brian.

It was strange that Brian should find himself back in the dusty places he had known with the Flinders Petrie Expedition. No longer did he write descriptions of the beauty of the sunsets, but rather about the frustrations of day to day events. He did not enjoy the signalling course and having no previous knowledge of semaphore and morse code he found it almost impossible to learn in two and a half weeks, what usually took three to four months to assimilate. He thought that the next course on cable laying and telephones would be of more use to him. In the meantime he was planning to spend two days in Cairo over Christmas, where he could get some decent meals.

. . . The Mess here is the worst in Egypt I should think, perfectly disgusting. I've already shown my wholehearted disapproval to the seniors . . . they woke up yesterday when they found kerosene in the whisky! . . .

Thank God I am not in the Peninsular now. The weather is killing them off like flies — I met Trumper in Cairo a few days ago. He is in the Herefords. They had a thunderstorm about a month ago which filled their trench with about five

*The ancient battleship *Hannibal.*

feet of water and then it froze towards morning. Three quarters of their rifles were washed away and most of their baggage. He stuck it for four or five days and then was brought away in a hospital ship . . .

Marjorie seems very keen on nursing, I should think she would make a comfy looking sort of nurse! . . .

I hope this war isn't going to run on for many more years . . . I don't think the Turks are ready to attack us there [The Canal] for some time yet. Our people have come back safely from The Senussi scrap. They were badly outnumbered and had to retire. It is hellish country for horses. Sudden caves and precipices which can't be seen until one is right on top of them. Several Yeomen broke their necks in this way . . . The Berks Yeo charged gallantly through the enemy and back again (led by one of our officers) and an Australian regiment refused to take part against such large numbers. The bloody quitters.

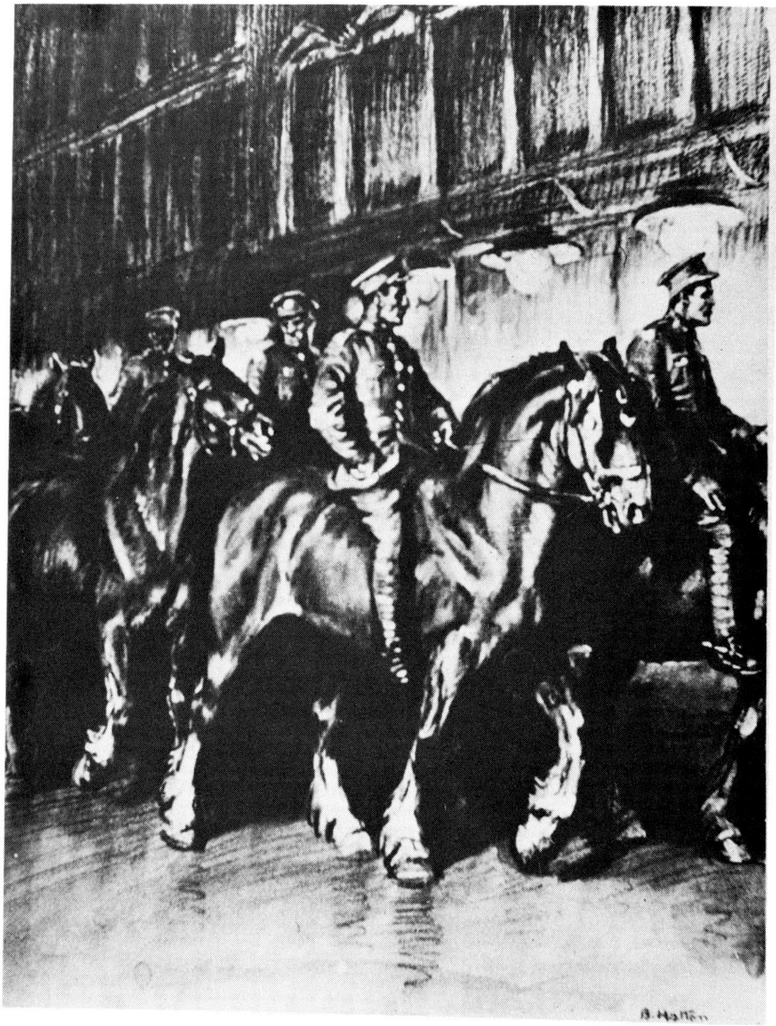

In the new year Brian was at Zeitoun, where he was making progress on the telephone and cable course.

> I am really getting hold of it at last and don't feel quite so panic stricken when I hear the buzzer tapping away . . .
>
> I have got my horses here, at least one of them and an old plug for the groom to ride. Mine is a very fast pony; no German or Turk will ever catch me! . . . I have enjoyed this slack week and have been riding every day.
>
> I am damned glad to see that conscription is being enforced under the title of 'scheme' — that is what I always thought would happen. It is the name 'conscription' that frightens the plebs.

Letters from home continued to go astray and Brian, who longed for news of his little daughter, was very disconsolate. However, on 14th February he wrote saying that he had heard from Biddy and from Mrs Lancaster, who gave him a full account of his daughter's christening. He said he had rejoined his regiment and that they had trekked 20 miles over the sand to a place called Kantara. Here the surrounding country was nothing but desert, covered with fine, deep sand, formidable for horses and infantry alike. Eventually wheeled transport had to be discarded and everything was carried on camels or pack horses, and owing to the lack of distinguishing land marks, marches were made by compass.

> We have to patrol the desert on the far side of the Canal. It is a change from everlasting drill, but it means a long ride out and back (ten miles each way) and an early start in the dark, about 4.30 a.m. . . .
>
> I have got to train signallers now; it is a bloody nuisance! I wish I had never taken the course. Signalling is a very important part of our work here. There doesn't seem to be much danger about our part of the job.

> March 24th 1916
>
> We are now back with the rest of the Brigade on the western side of the Canal. It is a large camp without a scrap of shade, and an awful glare off the white sand. Luckily we have got an issue of tinted spectacles. I wish we had double tents too. The ordinary single bell tents are stifling in the middle of the day . . . We seem fated to be left here for ever to melt away and die . . .
>
> I enjoyed our three weeks patrolling that we have just finished. We pushed out some distance but never saw a sign of an enemy the whole time. It is quite obvious that there's no chance of an attack on the Canal now.
>
> I wish I had been on the Senussi frontier. The Dorset Yeo had a proper Charge and did damn well. Every man who was unhorsed was slashed to bits, owing to our having no support to get the wounded away . . . I see no chance of our ever doing anything again. We are all very down in the mouth. There is too much sand and not enough ice in our drinks.
>
> Have you had any more Zepp raids lately? I hear King's Lynn had a raid in the daytime not long ago. I call that infernal cheek. I think Egypt is the safest place to be in after all.

⇦ Troops Returning on Horseback.
Charcoal and white paint on brown paper, 1915. 22″ × 16½″

I have sent two sketches to the *Graphic* since those they published first. They ought to be in print by now, if they have accepted them. One sees very little on this front nowadays. There is no fighting therefore it probably does not appeal much to the public at home . . .

Cheero. Your loving son
Brian.

But the fighting was soon to come. In two weeks time three troops out on reconnaissance became involved in a lively skirmish with Turks and conscripted Bedouins. In a letter to his wife, Brian gave a graphic account of the incident which clearly describes his delight at being involved in active warfare at last, and a cavalry battle at that.

April 10th 1916

Now I must tell you that we have had a *Hell* of a battle against the Arabs and Turks. We fought like lions for an hour and a half and our casualties were one flag pole broken and a horse with a bullet in his stomach (which was not discovered until after we had come home)! So you can guess it was a top hole fight. A certain number of us (I mustn't give the exact number because of the censor, but the Turks know exactly how many we were, as every damned Bedouin woman and child who hangs about the camp is a Turkish spy . . .)

Well . . . a certain number of us started out on Saturday night to go to a place 'somewhere' in the desert. We halted for a rest and to feed the horses and some of us tried to sleep, but it was too damned cold and we had no overcoats. Then before it got light we started again. We arrived at a place which was our objective about sunrise, having galloped the last two or three miles in the hope of catching a few fleeing Arabs and perhaps getting a little loot. Of course they knew of our approach through their Bedouin friends an hour or two beforehand, owing to our having had to halt on the way.

However, as we galloped into this place, we caught sight of a few Arabs running like hares and some on camels. The light was bad as the sun was rising in our eyes and there was a good deal of mist in the hollows. So we spurred on our horses and 'tallyhoed' in the approved Yeomanry style, when to our surprise our advanced guard was fired on and then we could see a large group of camels and Arabs and Turks on the ridge about threequarters mile away. We went on a little further and dismounted for action in a convenient place and sent a party out on each flank to try and outflank the enemy. All went well for a time and altho' they loosed off a hell of a lot of ammunition it seemed to be all over our heads except a few that kicked up the sand just in front.

We pushed on a bit nearer and the Turks retired to a further, higher ridge where they seemed to be quite content to stay for ever. Very unlike the Arabs usual procedure. From their confidence we conjectured that they must have some strong supports. Presently we found that our conjecture was right and that our outflanking parties were being themselves outflanked. So having tasted the strength of the enemy we retired gracefully and sedately.

> We could get no news of the one outflanking party and the C.O. thought they were in considerable danger of being cut off so I volunteered to go and find them and rode off thinking myself no end of a hero, only to find when I got to them that another messenger had got to them a few minutes before! Personally I don't think there was much danger as the Arabs were very content to stay where they were and fire at about 1,200 to 1,500 yards, which is pretty safe. Many of them danced about and yelled and fired their rifles off in the air! I suppose that was to keep things cheerful. I don't know whether we hit any of them. I don't suppose so, but I saw a few camels topple over.

Brian added a postscript to his letter, written a little later, in which he said that from their intelligence reports they learned that two Arabs, one a man of some importance, had been hit and probably killed. Being the signalling officer, Brian had had a busy time, but he was able to enjoy the situation to the full.

> I thoroughly enjoyed myself and hopped about to different points of view and tried to send messages back to camp and to our supports but it took some time as the ground was unfavourable for getting into touch with our helio stations. We had a long hot ride home. Our horses were done to a turn and could scarcely be kicked along through the heavy sand. It seemed never ending and we were tormented by myriads of sandflies.
>
> However, we are very pleased with ourselves now. To me, at the time, it all seemed ridiculous — like a comic opera. The men were all smoking and joking and nobody seemed in the least danger. One only has to take reasonable precautions and lie down behind a few inches of sand hill to be quite safe from any bullet.

There is no doubt that Brian enjoyed his first battle.

CHAPTER TWENTY-ONE

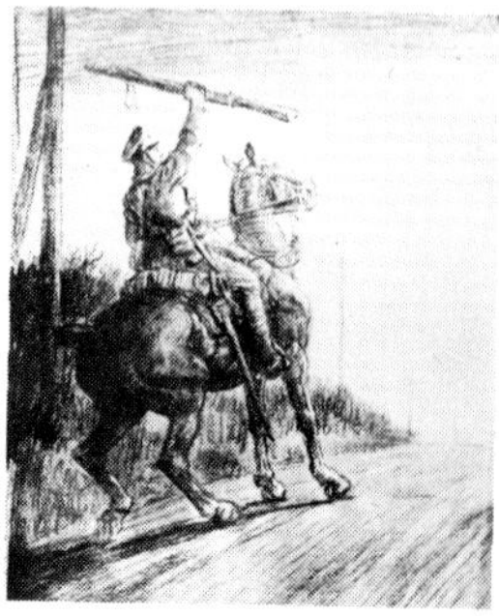

The Last Battle

THE BATTLE of Katia was the first serious action of the Egyptian campaign.

The Worcestershire Yeomanry, who formed part of the 5th Mounted Brigade, under the command of General Wiggin, were at Katia (Qatia), some 25 miles to the east of the Suez Canal where they were protecting the newly constructed railway. On 21st April, a party of 50 Sappers were sent to sink wells at Oghratina, some five miles to the north-east in the Sinai Desert, where a grove of palm trees lay at the foot of a steep, horse-shoe shaped hill. This was a very isolated position and a detachment of Worcester Yeomanry some 180 strong, which included A Squadron to which Brian was attached, were sent to protect them. Major Williams-Thomas, in command of the garrison, was fully alive to the possibility of attack and strongly urged that the engineers should be mounted, in order that the mobility of the cavalry should not be compromised in such an event. He was over-ruled and told that there was no such danger. This was strange, in the light of the fact that a secret agent had already reported that a Turkish regiment, with some guns and some German Officers, was in the vicinity.

The morning of Sunday, 23rd April, opened with thick fog which obscured the whole countryside and visibility was not more than twenty yards. At 4.15 a.m. camels were heard moving and all ranks stood to their posts. Soon indistinct figures were seen through the mist and at the foot of the hill the enemy could be heard pumping water, apparently for their men and animals. Rifle fire, augmented by machine gun fire, was directed on them and they withdrew. The sound of firing was probably the first intimation the enemy had that the post at Oghratina was being held by the British.

It so happened that a large body of Turkish infantry, estimated at between two and three thousand men, was passing to the north of Oghratina towards Katia and the Canal. Once alerted, they began to attack the hill, up the steep north slope, but were repulsed. They made a second attack from the south-east, covering it with heavy machine-gun fire from a small ridge some three hundred yards away. The Yeomanry were pressed back by the weight of the onslaught, their ranks being thinned so quickly that they had to contract into a circle of defence on the crest of the hill. By 7.30 not more than thirty rifles were still in action when they were rushed from all sides and the survivors were made prisoners.

Only sixty-five unwounded officers and men of the Worcestershire Yeomanry survived the battle at Oghratina. Brian was not among them. In the heat of the battle, the commanding officer had asked for volunteers to fetch help from the Gloucesters, who were a few miles away. It was characteristic that Brian, who was such a fine horseman, should volunteer. He rode off and was not seen again.

Brian was posted missing, but a few months later, his family had definite confirmation of his death. His wife received a letter posted from Egypt on 1st July and written by a Corporal in the 1st Australian Signal Squadron. He informed her that he had found "the body of an English Yeomanryman" in the desert, which had been identified as Brian Hatton. In a wallet was a tiny photograph of Biddy stuck on a postcard addressed to her.

Gerald Siordet, who was perhaps Brian's closest friend, was on active service in France with the 13th Rifle Brigade when he heard the news of Brian's death. Anxious for more details he wrote to his cousin (Captain) Val Burkhardt who was serving in Egypt. In the course of time he received the following letter from his cousin.

My dear 'J' 27th Sept: 1916

I have been over several times to the place where Brian Hatton was killed.

They made a first class fight of it, hopelessly outnumbered and when they had all their horses shot and were taken in the flank they died fighting.

There is a sad little monument put up to them, consisting of a couple of sticks in the form of a cross, and the bottom of a biscuit tin with an illegible inscription. I worried it out by the rubbing process and it read 'To the memory of many officers and men of the Worcester Yeo. and the Royal Engineers who gave their lives for their country 23rd April 1916.

I am having something better put up to them and a separate one to Brian as he was your friend. I haven't the means of knowing what you would like and I may not be here long enough to ascertain your wishes.

They are putting simply.

2 Lieut Brian Hatton Worcester Yeo.
A fine artist and a gallant soldier.
23rd April 1916
R.I.P.

They must have put up a great scrap and some were found absolutely surrounded by dead.

This is where the horses were killed and the little cross on the hill commemorates the last stand by the regiment. There is a palm grove in the hollow and the road runs up so steeply to the hill as to be impossible to ride up. I sat down on the ground last night and made a sketch of the existing cross, a copy of which is on the back side of this.*

Glad to hear you are all right again. I hope you are not for Mespot.

Yours ever,
Val.

*After the war was over the Yeomen were reburied in the Great War Cemetery at Kantara on the Suez Canal.

Brian's one hope had been that he would return home with "a sound right hand and eyesight". If his wish was not to be granted, I think that he would have chosen no better way to die than in the heat of battle, mounted on his horse. He was killed on Easter Sunday, 23rd April, 1916. He was twenty-eight years old.

Brian's widow and daughter lived on in Hereford. Biddy continued to teach dancing and in the early 1930s she remarried. Her new husband Angus Wilson, was a Hereford man and they continued to live in the town. Mary was trained as a dancer by her mother. For a time she danced with the La Scala Ballet and then with the Ballet Rambert. In 1945 she went to America and married Cecil Shaler of Crystal Lake, Illinois, by whom she had two children, a daughter, Gail, and a son, George Brian.

An Advance Guard Patrolling A Road.
Pencil, 1915. 15″ × 13″ *Brian Hatton Gallery, Hereford*

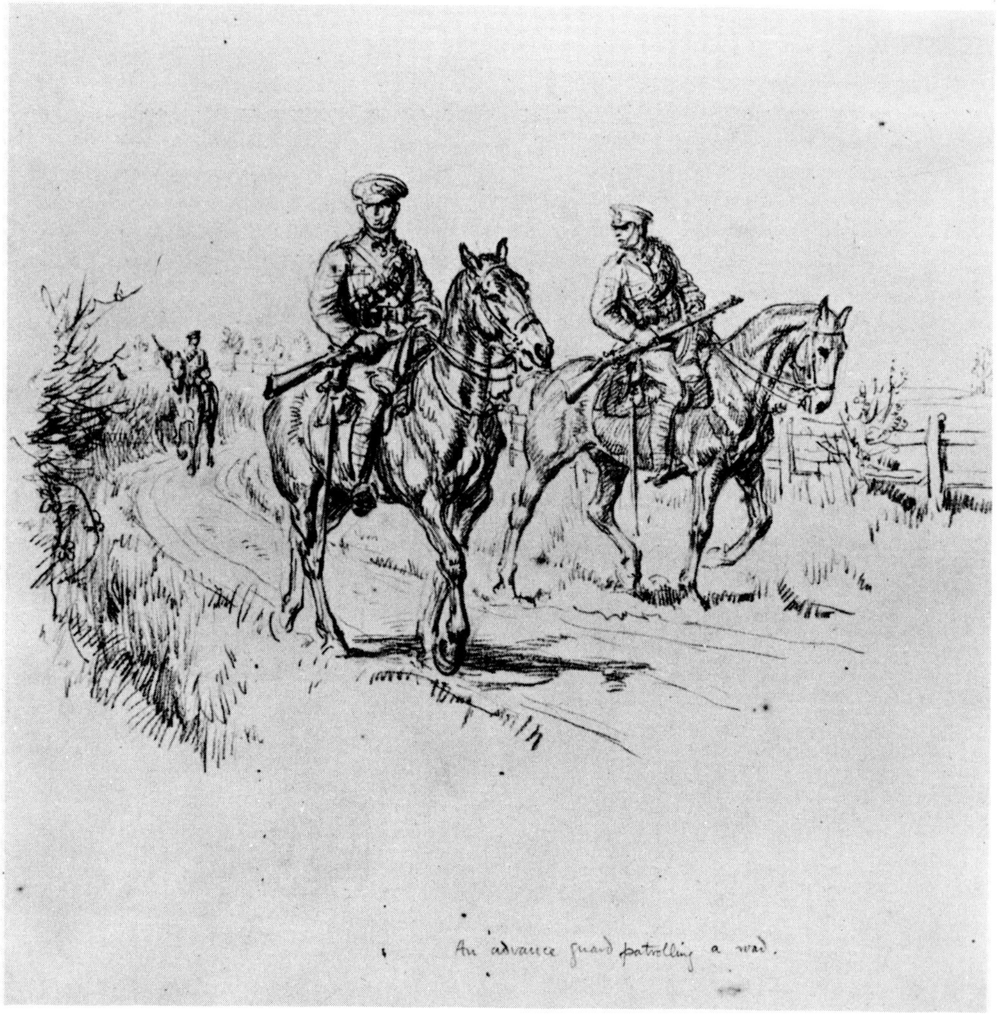

It is now 62 years since Brian Hatton was killed. What has become of his work, and how is it rated today?

One of the reasons why his name is not more widely known is that so little of his work is in circulation; as yet only two of his pictures have come under the hammer at Christies. A large number of portraits and drawings and equestrian works are in private collections but the bulk of his work is housed in the Brian Hatton Gallery at Churchill Gardens, Hereford.

Marjorie Hatton has devoted her life to the care and preservation of her brother's artistic output, and in taking an active part in the showing of his work. In 1925 the first exhibition was arranged by Mr F. C. Morgan, then Librarian and Curator at Hereford Art Gallery. This was followed by a Memorial Exhibition at Walker's Gallery, Bond Street, through the generosity of relations and a friend, when the British Museum and the Victoria and Albert Museum accepted examples of Brian's work. Several exhibitions have been held in Hereford and London and a selection of Hatton's war drawings was shown at the "Fifty Years Ago" Exhibition at the R.W.S. Galleries, London, in 1965, and two arranged by Clarges Gallery when the public were able to purchase works. The W.H. Library at the Courtauld Institute, Portman Square, possesses a large number of photographs. Perhaps Marjorie's biggest achievement is her part in the building and endowment of the Brian Hatton Gallery in Hereford.

Walter Shaw Sparrow, writer and art critic, wrote a small volume entitled "Brian Hatton, Painter of Genius, Killed in the War". It was published by Walker's Gallery as "Walker's Quarterly" in 1926 and sold at the exhibition. He stated simply that Brian had "the rarest of all things — true genius". He described him as "a boy endowed with gifts of the spirit so extraordinary that the first period of work from the age of ten, 1897, to that of nineteen, 1906, was a period not of rare promise only but also of wonderful achievement, showing not only maturity of Design, but maturity of Poetic Feeling, and a charm brimming with country life and English humour".

Adrian Bury, R.W.S., writer and art critic, has described Hatton as "a genius unique in the history of British art". He went on to stress the point that Brian was "mainly self taught, his powers of observation and felicity of hand being quite phenomenal". Another admirer stated simply, "He was not, as some artists are, a *spectator;* he is *part* of the countryside and country life, people, horses, animals; you *feel* the wind".

Work of such sincerity, in no way influenced by passing fashion, must surely be timeless in its appeal. Brian's philosophy can be summed up in the words of François Millet, "To see is to draw".

INDEX